NEWSGATHERING
IN
WASHINGTON

Co-Winner of the 1962 Atherton
Press Political Science Prize

Prize Committee

CLINTON ROSSITER, CHAIRMAN
CURRIN V. SHIELDS
RICHARD C. SNYDER

Published simultaneously in Great Britain
by Prentice-Hall International, London

NEWSGATHERING
IN
WASHINGTON

A Study in Political Communication

Dan D. Nimmo

ATHERTON PRESS
A Division of Prentice-Hall, Inc.
70 Fifth Avenue, New York, N.Y., 10011

NEWSGATHERING IN WASHINGTON
A Study in Political Communication

Dan D. Nimmo

Copyright © 1964 by Prentice-Hall, Inc.
Atherton Press, New York, New York

Published simultaneously in Great Britain by
Prentice-Hall International, Inc.
28 Welbeck Street, London W.1, England

Copyright under International, Pan American,
and Universal Copyright Conventions

Atherton Press, A Division of Prentice-Hall, Inc.
70 Fifth Avenue, New York, New York, 10011

Library of Congress Catalog Card Number 64-10459
Printed in the United States of America 61598

The American Political Science Association Series

NEWSGATHERING IN WASHINGTON
Dan D. Nimmo

NATION-BUILDING
*Karl W. Deutsch and
William J. Foltz, editors*

PARTY AND REPRESENTATION
Frank J. Sorauf

THE FUTURE
OF POLITICAL SCIENCE
Harold D. Lasswell

PREFACE

In 1919, Walter Lippmann enunciated his belief that the presentation of truthful news lies at the heart of democracy. But, he said, there are difficulties: "They are that there *is* a problem of the news which is of absolutely basic importance to the survival of popular government, and that the importance of that problem is not vividly realized nor sufficiently considered."[1]

Although more than four decades have passed since Mr. Lippmann penned this appraisal, the problems of news communication in a democratic society are still with us. The following study stems from the author's conviction that opinion- and policy-making remain significant, interrelated processes within any political system. A democracy, based on criteria of popular control and consultation, poses its particular ticklish questions of the manner and means by which political ideas, opinions, and issues are transmitted throughout the body politic.

[1] Walter Lippmann, *Liberty and the News* (New York: Harcourt, Brace & Howe, 1920), p. 14.

In the United States, such communication is carried on primarily through the news media. Newsmen and their sources of news interact to form a set of relationships crucial in the linkage of citizen and official. This book focuses on such interaction between news channels and news sources. It is based upon evidence collected in the form of personal interviews with selected samples of Washington correspondents and their official news sources, the public information officers of executive agencies. Although it is primarily a report of research, it also purports to draw modest conclusions in two areas: (1) the statement of significant hypotheses explaining the officer-reporter relationship, and (2) the assessment of the consequences of that relationship for the opinion-making processes of American democracy.

Several acknowledgments are in order. I am thankful to Vanderbilt University and the Ford Foundation for funds made available under the program for Small Grants for Research in Public Affairs. Such financial aid made it possible to spend the period between February and May, 1961, in Washington, D.C., conducting the field phase of this research.

I am also grateful to Professors Avery Leiserson and John C. Wahlke for assistance in the planning stages of this research project and to Professor Wilder Crane for critical commentary on the initial draft of the manuscript.

CONTENTS

LIST OF TABLES

CHAPTER I
NEWS SOURCES
& NEWSMEN:
INTRODUCTION

Times of crisis have a way of bringing into sharp focus certain activities which, in more placid periods, are generally taken for granted. Few Americans, for example, are normally sensitive to the function served by the reporter in the politics of their democracy. Although we may accept in principle Jefferson's maxim that "No government ought to be without censors; and where the press is free, no one ever will," [1] we seldom concern ourselves with whether the press can and does perform this critical role. We ask little more of newsmen than that they provide a written supplement to morning coffee or a televised nightcap to "wrap up the day's events." But, in a period of grave concern, one of so-called national peril, we seek out the aid of the reporter, the columnist, and the commentator by reading beyond the headlines and eagerly twisting the dial.

[1] "Thomas Jefferson to the President of the United States, September 9, 1792," *The Works of Thomas Jefferson*, ed. Paul Leicester Ford (New York: G.P. Putnam's Sons, 1904–1905), VII, 146.

The significant information on which a citizen in a democracy must base his political actions is most often channeled, in some form, through the written or spoken press. A crisis situation simply makes this ever-present fact more apparent. But what the citizen is only passingly aware of, the politician, the public official, and the reporter emphasize repeatedly through their actions and their utterances. The actions of our presidents are illustrative. Harry S. Truman, for example, enjoyed the working reporter and likened his meetings with the press to the question periods faced by cabinet ministers in the British House of Commons. Dwight D. Eisenhower, perhaps less eagerly, retained the news conference as a form of public communication. And, finally, the value of the press to administration policy was clearly evidenced in the opening days of the New Frontier when Pres. John F. Kennedy emphasized the need for more numerous, larger, and televised confrontations with the Washington press corps. In fact, no previous American president used such a great variety of tactics in dealing with the news media—exclusive background sessions with newsmen, regularized television performances in news conferences, and television "chats" with reporters. And few lectured the members of the press themselves so frequently on their relation to the "national interest" and the "public interest" as did President Kennedy with regard to Cold War responsibilities and the Cuban crisis.

It is not only the relation of president and press which supports public officials' recognition of the crucial nature of the reporter's performance in politics. The growing popularity and utilization of the press secretary is also testimony to official desires to regularize relations with the news media. The names of Stephen Early and Charles Ross became known after World War II, but nowhere near the extent to which more recent "official spokesmen"—Pierre Salinger, Lincoln White, and Arthur Sylvester—have gained public notice. President Eisenhower, on his sickbed in 1955, was reported to have said to Press Secretary James Hagerty, "Take care of things while I'm gone." Whether the report is verifiable is not relevant. Rather the mere existence of the story illustrates the increased focus on public relations men who are to "meet the press."

Certainly, the practicing politician is quick enough to estimate the value of recognition by the working press in elevating him to the office which he seeks. Wisely, he courts the press accordingly. And the administrative bureaucracy realizes the necessity of assigning specific people the lion's share of responsibility in dealing with the press; hence the rise of the public information officer, the press secretary, and the secretary for public affairs. As a person, the reporter may or may not always command deference from public officials, but as the performer of a critical function in the politics of democracy, the reporter is either respected as a positive good or tolerated as a necessary evil.

Newsmen are in politics; officials recognize it and so do the correspondents themselves. But what is particularly bewildering to the professional journalist is that his reportorial efforts within the political environment go seemingly unnoticed, not by the practitioner of politics, but by the student of politics. Recognition by presidents, congressmen, and cabinet officers has thus not been sufficient to offset the scholar's failure to recognize the importance of the press in the political realm. The magnitude of this "slight" prompted Walter Lippmann to declare:

> So deep is the tradition, that until quite recently, for example, political science was taught in our colleges as if newspapers did not exist. I am not referring to schools of journalism, for they are trade schools, intended to prepare men and women for a career. I am referring to political science as expounded to future business men, lawyers, public officials, and citizens at large. In that science a study of the press and the sources of popular information found no place. It is a curious fact. To anyone not immersed in the routine interests of political science, it is almost inexplicable that no American student of government, no American sociologist, has ever written a book on news-gathering.[2]

It is not relevant here whether the condition of the discipline in the 1920's warranted such an observation. It is sufficient to note that changes take place in approaches to the study of politics as well as in political activity itself. In recent years, added

[2] Walter Lippmann, *Public Opinion* (New York: Harcourt, Brace & Co., 1922), p. 320.

emphasis has been placed on the function of the mass media in the political process. Students of politics have become sensitive to the fact that the press possesses a political function—one with which the political scientist may legitimately concern himself without incurring the wrath of the professional journalist or feeling guilty at having concerned himself with matters formerly regarded in his discipline as beyond the scope of his professional investigations. Yet the tardiness of this recognition has permitted another concerned and self-styled reporter to twit the student of politics:

> Increasingly of late those of us who report from Washington find ourselves the object of curious scrutiny by the political scientists. The press, it has been recognized belatedly, plays an important role in our nation's capital, though nobody seems exactly sure what it is.[3]

These chidings of political scientists by professional journalists are cited neither to start an argument nor to settle one. More important is the premise that underlies the journalists' feelings —that the news media performs a significant political service in making available that intelligence on which government in a democratic society rests. Certainly, the political performance of the press does not take place in isolation. Newsgathering is not an independent process. Any reporter must have his sources; these sources give him information on problems, personalities, and issues—information which he needs to produce stories commanding reader attention. Both newsgathering and information-dispensing form a continuous process involving the activities of newsmen and news sources. Those activities are so tightly intertwined that they lend validity to Lippmann's assertion that a book on newsgathering involves both a study of the press and the sources of public information.[4] Government-press relations in any political system take their character from the interactions of newsmen and their news sources.

This is a study of government-press relations. Its focus is on exploration of the information-dispensing processes involving

---

[3] Douglass Cater, *The Fourth Branch of Government* (Boston: Houghton Mifflin Co., 1959), p. vii.
[4] Lippmann, *Public Opinion*, p. 320.

governmental officials and the newsgathering processes in which members of the news media take part. Its purposes are threefold: (1) to specify the relationships that develop between news sources and newsmen as each engages in processes of political communication, (2) to indicate the factors most influential in determining such relationships, and (3) to suggest the implications that such findings have for interpreting the tension that characterizes government-press relations in a democracy such as the United States.

Underlying the research effort devoted to these purposes is a series of assumptions which should be made explicit regarding public opinion, information, and political communication. Taken collectively, these premises form a framework of political opinion and communication within which research findings should be interpreted. Public opinion appears to be pluralistic. It is not here regarded as consisting of an unchanging set of values existing apart from political controversy; it is not treated as a constant that can be used to judge right and wrong sides of political issues. Rather, we speak of public opinion developing when persons are prompted to express opinions on issues around which the public forms. These issues of community-wide concern are generated at several points within a political community. One such source of issues is the formal governmental structure of the community itself. Governmental officials, through advocating, adopting, and pursuing certain policies, are constantly communicating facts, issues, and ideas to the citizen in the hope of making the tasks of governing easier and more responsible. Citizens of the political community are seldom involved in the opinion process until their individual or group behavior is oriented toward particular issues. This becomes the essential feature of that process of public opinion described by Davison as the formation of personal opinions on public issues.[5]

The number of governmental officials who wish to influence

[5] W. Phillips Davison, "The Public Opinion Process," *The Public Opinion Quarterly*, XXII (1958), 91–106. See also the definition of the "public opinion situation" in Floyd H. Allport, "Toward a Science of Public Opinion," *The Public Opinion Quarterly*, I (1937), 7–23; the conception of a "public opinion system" in Robert M. MacIver, *Academic Freedom in Our Time* (New York: Columbia University Press, 1955), pp. 21–33; and James N. Rosenau, *Public Opinion and Foreign Policy* (New York: Random House, 1961), *passim.*

public opinion by distributing information is quite remarkable. They may be legislators, bureaucrats, diplomats, or judges; their variety and purposes are endless. Increasingly on the national level, the citizen encounters these officials not as individuals, but as parts of that ubiquitous image of "official Washington" appearing in the news media. When some attempt is made to analyze this strange eminence that touches the lives of all in the United States, we find that "official Washington" is primarily composed of those public officials whose reason for existence is ostensibly to tell the citizen what government is doing. This is the function of the public information officer (PIO). These people serving in publicity offices of administrative agencies make up one set of political communicators—the communicators of messages which have political consequences in the activation, shaping, and articulating of public opinion. Messages of governmental publicity serve both as information and justification; they fulfill information requirements of the citizen and compete with rival explanations for the support of public opinion in defining the limits of agency authority. A primary channel for conveying these messages is that of the press or news media—terms referring to all news outlets and news channels of mass communications. From the standpoint of the governmental body interested in publicity, its relationship to the news media is critical in influencing or soliciting citizen support for programs.

> In no area is public relations more important to the American democracy than national government. This is literally the field of "public information." Modern administration would come to a standstill if government could not constantly speak to the people as individuals and in and through the different groups to which they belong. It must do so mainly through the mass media.[6]

Although the press affords the bureaucracy ready access for communication to the citizen, it also operates in another capacity. Messages of governmental publicity do not necessarily fulfill all the informational requirements of the citizen participating in

---

[6] J.A.R. Pimlott, *Public Relations and American Democracy* (Princeton, New Jersey: Princeton University Press, 1951), pp. 64–65.

the opinion process. It is a primary function of the news media to obtain such additional information as is required to fulfill these needs. It performs this function through the process of selection and transmission of information not necessarily originating with bureaucratic publicity. For the news media, this process is that of defining news; for members of the news media, the relationship to the government is a vital one in determining access to the source of news.

This is a model of the explanatory and news defining processes closely akin to that used in opinion and mass communications research. A governmental body acts to formulate, select, and transmit promotional messages to explain and justify its policies. These messages are directed to the citizen, either as an individual or a group participant, who requires information about his political environment in order to satisfy the needs and problems encountered in adjusting to it. The news media serve both as the channel through which the promotional message is conveyed and as an agent in obtaining information outside the citizen's immediate experience which is non-promotional in nature but also required for adjusting to the political environment. A critical point in the opinion process is the government-news media relation; it determines the official's access to the public as a source of support and the reporter's access to the bureaucracy as a source of news. This is not to say that this is the only process through which the citizen adjusts to his political environment. Others include those involving political parties, interest groups, bureaucracies, mass movements, and so on. It is to say that this connective link between government, news media, and citizen shares significance with such alternatives and merits independent consideration.

In this process of political communication, the official and the newsman play specific roles in the fulfillment of the citizen's information requirements. Ultimately the pictures of political reality perceived by the citizen are traceable to actions and utterances of public officials. However, the official source of information transmitted to the citizen is often the information specialist of the department or agency concerned and not the policy-maker himself. He may be designated in the news column as "a high spokesman" or an "unimpeachable source." In those instances, the source role is played not by the policy-maker but by the information officer titled, perhaps, "Information Specialist," "Director of Information," "Public Information Officer," "Public Relations Officer," or "Special Assistant for Public Affairs." The manner in which he performs in that role and the informational requests he fills for the citizen depend upon the view he holds of his own function—advocate of agency policy, informer of the "public," or link for the reporter, and so on. Although such officers are not the sole source of public intelligence—perhaps, in some instances, they prove to be a minor source—they do comprise a group of officials (information officers) acting in source roles who interact with a group of newsmen in channel roles. This interaction can be examined, explored, and analyzed in order to obtain greater understanding of the process of political communication. We may concur with Herring:

> This relationship between the government and the public in actual practice is narrowed down to contacts between a small group of officials and a small group of newspaper correspondents. . . . In the main the view of government presented to the public is the product of official publicity men within the government and the newspapermen stationed in the capital.[7]

INFORMATION-DISPENSING AND NEWSGATHERING IN THE NATION'S CAPITAL

At no better place can the relationship between information officer and newsman be observed than in the nation's capital, Washington, D.C., which serves as the geographic source center of political news available to the citizen.[8] Here are located by far the largest number of public information personnel assigned the task of dispensing information to the newsman. The exact number has never been exactly determined; the total varies with the definition of those designated as information officers, those who

[7] Pendleton Herring, "Publicizing Administrative Activities," in *The Press and Society*, ed. George L. Bird and Frederic E. Merwin (New York: Prentice-Hall, Inc., 1951), p. 229.

[8] Leo C. Rosten, *The Washington Correspondents* (New York: Harcourt, Brace & Co., 1937), pp. 10–11.

do the counting, and the counters' attitude toward public information activities. One estimate places the number of information personnel at twice the number of the Washington press corps, or approximately 3,000. A more conservative estimate places the number considerably lower.[9]

The growth of public information activities in the federal government has been a phenomenon piquing the interest of both the student of politics and the practical politician. It has been asserted that "modern administration would come to a standstill if government could not constantly speak to the people as individuals and in and through the different groups to which they belong." [10] The expansion of publicity has taken place largely within federal departments and agencies which designate personnel to make available, usually through the communications media, information regarding programs and policies.

Publicity also is important to legislators and other elective or appointive officials desirous of taking their cases "to the people" or of expanding the "scope of conflict." [11] There is doubtless validity in the assertion that "the United States is an arena of competitive publicity," one in which the publicity of federal departments and agencies must vie with that of interests both inside and outside the formal structure of authority.[12] Recognition of the significance of reportorial influence on the legislator has been indicated by both the political scientist and the journalist.[13] Insights into the importance of the relationships between the campaigning politician and the communications media also abound.[14]

The public information activities of federal departments and

[9] Cater, *The Fourth Branch of Government*, p. 5. One information officer in a confidential interview estimated the number who "meet the press" at 120.

[10] Pimlott, *Public Relations and American Democracy*, p. 65.

[11] E.E. Schattschneider, *The Semisovereign People* (New York: Holt, Rinehart & Winston, 1960), pp. 1–18.

[12] Pimlott, *Public Relations and American Democracy*, pp. 98–101. James L. McCamy, "Discussion: Measuring Federal Publicity," *The Public Opinion Quarterly*, III (1939), 473–475.

[13] Cater, *The Fourth Branch of Government*, pp. 47–74.

[14] Stanley Kelley, Jr., *Professional Public Relations and Political Power* (Baltimore: The Johns Hopkins Press, 1956), *passim*.

agencies, then, are but one manifestation of what has been characterized as "government by publicity." A realistic picture of public information in the political system must, of course, include those activities carried on by all individual and group interests, official and extra-legal, which exert influence in the formulation of public policy by means of persuasion. Within that total picture, we can select those activities of officials of Washington-based departments and agencies who are formally charged with the duties and responsibilities of public explanation. Those activities are so significantly oriented toward the employment of the mass media as a channel for such public explanation that the resulting relationships between Washington officials and newsmen are critical for the understanding of political communication in the United States.

Observers of the origins and growth of informational activities have not been united in their assessment of the causes of this phenomenon in federal departments and agencies. Three lines of thought have been reflected in writings on the subject. There is first the explanation which ties increased informational activities in with the rise of the service state. As a larger responsibility for political action has become associated with federal departments and agencies, there has been a concurrent increase in the necessity for explanations to fill the gulf between policy application by the administrator and policy acceptance by the citizen.[15] The concept is one of official recognition and fulfillment of responsibility. That responsibility was succinctly defined in the formative period of one of the more elaborate present-day informational services, that of the Department of Agriculture:

> The Office of Information is in no wise a publicity agency in the usual sense of that term. Its purpose is not to acquire prestige for itself or for the Department as a whole, not to "sell" the Department to the public or to advertise achievements of Departmental workers, but to make public the results of the Department's manifold activities.[16]

[15] Frederic E. Merwin, "The Reporting of Public Affairs," *The Annals of the American Academy of Political and Social Science*, CCXIX (1942), 120.

[16] Milton Eisenhower as quoted by T. Swann Harding, "Genesis of One 'Government Propaganda Mill,'" *The Public Opinion Quarterly*, XI (1947), 232.

A second view, and one perhaps not as completely incompatible with the first as critics of public information services have indicated, is that informational activities arise from efforts to promote departmental or agency interests. One form of this view stresses the universality of publicity as a social phenomenon, cites the necessity for governmental officials to choose informational messages that promote an effective framework of truth, and argues that such public relations are so specialized as to require separate organizational arrangements to conduct them. Informational activities, therefore, are viewed as inherent in a "natural" relationship between functions performed and the necessity for their support. Or, in more stark terms, "Democracy has proclaimed the dictatorship of palaver, and the technique of dictating to the dictator is named propaganda." [17]

The implications of promotion, propaganda, and the employment of public relations techniques connected with this view are those stressed by critics of public information programs. Such criticism is extensively documented in periodic investigations conducted for three decades by Congressional groups into activities of information offices.[18] It is not an aim of this book to substantiate or invalidate their criticism. We shall, however, note that it has existed and attempt to indicate how an environment of potential criticism serves to establish certain boundaries for any relationship between a public information official and a newsman.

A final view on the origins and growth of informational activities of federal departments and agencies is closely connected with those previously mentioned but deserves separate treatment. Here the public information office is seen as a connective link between the administrator and the channel of mass communication, the news media. It is argued that the combined complexities of mastering techniques of public relations are such that the administrator must have a specialist to perform such a function— the public information officer. Likewise, the difficulties for a re-

[17] Harold D. Lasswell, "The Theory of Political Propaganda," *The American Political Science Review*, XXI (1927), 631.

[18] See, for example, House Committee on Expenditures in the Executive Departments, Publicity and Propaganda Subcommittee, *Investigation of Part of Federal Officials of the War Department in Publicity and Propaganda As It Relates to UMT*, H.R. Rep. No. 1073, 80th Cong., 2d Sess. (1947).

porter in covering ever more highly technical departments and agencies are such that he needs aid from one "on the inside" who speaks the languages of both the technocrat and the newsman—again, the information officer. Recognition of public responsibility, of agency interest, of technical complexities in communication—perhaps all have contributed to the growth of informational services in federal departments and agencies. The pertinent fact is the existence of information units in official Washington and the implications of that fact for processes of political communication through the news media.

The organizational arrangements for official information-dispensing are relatively simple in federal departments and agencies. The most recent systematic survey of such arrangements in the United States was that of the House of Representatives Subcommittee of the Committee on Government Operations appointed to investigate the "availability of information from federal departments and agencies"—popularly called the Moss Committee after its chairman, Rep. John Moss (Dem., Calif.).[19] By use of replies to an extensive questionnaire prepared by the Legislative Reference Service, a compilation of the organizational units for public information at the federal level was developed. Without rehashing the many descriptions which have been based on findings from this compilation, the broad outlines of the report may be cited.

Of sixty departmental and agency level organizations surveyed (this includes the ten cabinet rank departments, the regulatory commissions, and all administrative agencies under direct presidential authority), fifty-seven reported having organizations performing public information functions. Of these, thirty-seven possessed specific information units informing the public of agency programs. The remaining twenty agencies assigned information duties to "responsible agency officials" not having titles specifically pertaining to information functions. The basic pattern for Washington agencies having information personnel was as fol-

---

[19] House Committee on Government Operations, Special Subcommittee on Government Information, *Replies from Federal Agencies to Questionnaire Submitted by the Special Subcommittee on Government Information*, Committee Print, 84th Cong., 1st Sess. (1955).

lows: a legally prescribed information unit staffed with personnel charged with responsibility for explanation of the agency program and, usually, with officers who contact the news media on a regular or semi-regular basis either on their own or the newsman's initiative. These officers are sources for the newsmen and the consequent interaction of public information officer and newsman is that of source and channel.

The intricate pattern of information-dispensing in Washington, however, appears comparatively simple when contrasted with the organizational arrangements of the news media for gathering that information. The communications industry is, as it has been described by one of its members, like "most big business" and "has become specialized, compartmentalized, channelized, even routinized." [20] Although the number and variety of news organizations is remarkable, a few descriptive generalizations are ventured. Essentially, the news media may be categorized on the basis of the type of news organizations involved. To simplify the variety, one can think of organizations formed to transmit *all* varieties of news to a nation-wide audience possessing numerous interests. Such organizations are designated as "general news organizations" and include the wire services, the national radio and television news networks, the several news weeklies which attempt to provide an organizing framework for the "significant news features" on a seven-day basis, and those few newspapers which become "journals of record" and have virtually a national circulation.

A second category is set aside for branches of the news media designated as specialized news organizations. In this classification one finds the following: (1) news services and syndicates that pursue stories of specialized interest to be transmitted to a local audience; (2) newspaper chains preparing articles and features of interest limited to papers in the chain (Hearst, Scripps-Howard, Knight, Gannett Publications, and so on); (3) the increasing array of opinion journals which appear on a monthly, fortnightly, or weekly basis devoted to what is termed in the trade as "background and interpretation"; (4) magazines, newsletters, and fliers communicating topics of specialized interests to restricted au-

[20] Cater, *The Fourth Branch of Government,* pp. 2–3.

diences—trade papers, the ethnic press, and so on; (5) metropolitan dailies with a restricted local or regional circulation transmitting information for an audience often geographically defined
(even to the inclusion of the foreign press); (6) smaller independent radio and television stations relying on their own news seeking efforts in addition to purchase of wire-service facilities.

All types of news organizations have an interest in the transmission of information of a political nature from official sources
to the citizen. Furthermore, all employ personnel who obtain that
information from official news sources. The daily lives of members of the Washington press corps have been chronicled in other
studies, some based on experienced participation and others on
systematic observation. All indicate that the public information
officer plays a part in the newsman's efforts at obtaining information—he may be the source itself, he may control access to the
source, or he may simply be a formalized contact point.

NATURE OF RESEARCH AND ANALYSIS

Within the general theoretical and institutional framework
described in the preceding sections, research into the interrelations of Washington information officers and correspondents was
undertaken in the opening months of the Kennedy Administration, January to May, 1961. A detailed account of research procedures may be found in Appendix I along with a consideration
of parallel studies in government-press relations. Briefly, field
research was conducted through unstructured interviews with two
selected samples—information officers chosen from federal departments and agencies and Washington correspondents representing the structure of the news establishment already outlined.
Samples were chosen in order to represent a wide variety of experience in Washington public relations and reporting; no attempt was made at precise statistical representation of all Washington information officers and newsmen. The period chosen for
observation, the exploratory type of research, and the method of
selecting respondents lend a case study character to generalizations based upon findings. The interpretations contained in this
study should be viewed in that light.

The strategy employed in analysis views information officers and newsmen as occupying specific roles in an interactive communication process—those of information source and information channel. A working hypothesis of this study is that there are differing expectations between these two groups regarding roles in political communication and the manner in which these roles are played. If information officers occupy a specific role in political communication, one expects to find a pattern of expectations among such officers defining that role as common to all; if newsmen occupy a specifically defined role in political communication, one expects a consensus defining that role. Such assertions are implied by the broad outlines of role theory, which suggests that the view one holds of his role in a process of interaction, his role concept, is a significant factor governing his behavior in that process. The general theory and tactics of role analysis have been discussed extensively in other places; [21] although its use here is neither as explicit nor as elaborate as in other studies, a few remarks are in order regarding it.

Research into governmental publicity and newsgathering has suggested that these two activities have become highly institutionalized in the United States. If "the construction of productive external relations" [22] by an agency or the "merchandising of government" [23] does exist as a patterned process in administration, then it should be possible to analyze the components of that pattern. Furthermore, such phrases as "the fourth estate," "the fourth branch of government," [24] "the reporter's trade," [25] or *"the* Washington Correspondent," [26] are indicative of the assumption that there is sufficient pattern in the political behavior of newsmen to lend an institutional character to that activity.

[21] See Appendix I.

[22] John M. Pfiffner and R. Vance Presthus, *Public Administration* (3d ed.; New York: The Ronald Press, 1953), p. 130. Herbert A. Simon, Donald W. Smithburg, and Victor A. Thompson, *Public Administration* (New York: Alfred A. Knopf, 1959), pp. 415–416.

[23] William Lee Miller, "Can Government Be 'Merchandised'?" *The Reporter,* IX (1953), 11–16.

[24] Cater, *The Fourth Branch of Government.*

[25] Joseph Alsop and Stewart Alsop, *The Reporter's Trade* (New York: Reynal & Co., 1958).

[26] Rosten, *The Washington Correspondents.* For the hypothesis that the press corps is becoming professionalized see William L. Rivers, "The correspondents after 25 years," *Columbia Journalism Review,* I (1962), 4–10.

An essential characteristic of institutional behavior is a common set of expectations held by those individuals engaging in the interaction and presumably held by all those so occupied. Or, more simply, consensus on the norms of the institution serves to establish the institutional character of the activity. If empirical investigation produces evidence that consensus is absent, then the institutional nature itself is problematic. Furthermore, questions of the responsibilities of government in informing the citizen or of the press in representing the public's interest must be based on a realistic understanding of the consensus of actors regarding their functions, procedures, orientations, and responsibilities. It is in these areas that the present study seeks to supply clarification.

Four questions are of importance and each supplies a thread running through this study. First, using role analysis as an aid, what is the institutional nature, if any, of information-dispensing by official sources? Second, what is the institutional nature, if any, of newsgathering by channel actors? And, thirdly, is consensus between sources and channels regarding roles sufficient to indicate that the processes of information-dispensing and newsgathering are institutional in character; or is the variation sufficient to suggest that there are two separate processes involved—not interdependent and not complementary? Finally, what are the consequences for the larger issues: popular control and public responsibility of information and news establishments in the United States?

In undertaking an exploration of attitudinal consensus and variation among actors in information-dispensing and newsgathering, a survey of related literature suggests several dimensions of the research problem. Five of these appear significant for definition, investigation, and analysis. Since an effort is made to assess the role concepts of information officers as sources and of newsmen as channels, one aspect of the investigation focuses on asking respondents to appraise the functions of explanation and newsgathering, to define their relation to those functions, and to give their opinions of significant concepts with which they deal in their work—information, news, objectivity, and interpretation. This discussion is detailed in Chapters II and III. A second area of significance consists of orientations of officers and newsmen toward superiors, audiences, friends, and professional contacts who influence their behavior in selecting and transmitting messages with political content. Chapter IV deals with these matters and assesses the consequences for political communication. Since both samples of respondents were chosen partly on the basis of their interaction, the hypothesis is posed that a significant influence on the information officer's relations with the newsman is his perceptions of the latter and vice versa. Both groups were questioned regarding assessments of "good" news sources, "good" newsmen, story values, and professional values. These variables are discussed in Chapter V. Specific techniques have been developed for the release and gathering of information in Washington. News sources and newsmen have opinions regarding the functions of such techniques, their utility, and the consequences of their use. These matters are discussed in Chapter VI. Chapter VII deals with the perceptions of news sources and newsmen of the "great issues" of government-press relations which occupy the attention of officials and journalists on a continuing basis—the problems posed by governmental secrecy, governmental publicity, political reporting, and public opinion in a democracy. After describing such patterns and drawing certain inferences, a final chapter is directed toward evaluating the questions of leadership and responsibility in political communication in the light of research findings.

CHAPTER II
INFORMATION OFFICERS & NEWSMEN: POLITICAL COMMUNICATORS

Although research into the interrelationships of public information officers and newsmen has not been extensive, there has been discussion concerning the appropriate function of the official news source and the newsman in the communication process. The factual basis of such speculation has been the observed activities of the officer and the correspondent, the statutory definitions establishing information units, and the convictions of those concerned with the proper methods by which citizens should be informed of governmental action. Regardless of basis, however, there has been a tendency to specify the functions of information officers and newsmen as though the strictly "political" activities of each are neatly separable from strictly "service" tasks of the former and "truth defining" efforts of the latter. This has produced the implication that the role of officer or newsman is not as political communicator primarily, but as virtually a nonpolitical public servant—objective, noncontroversial, and oblivious to the political environment in which he acts. The purpose of this chapter is to examine this contention in light of research evidence.

THE INFORMATION OFFICER AND
POLITICAL COMMUNICATION

In current literature, the function of the information officer is examined from several points of view.[1] Some writers emphasize the activities of the information officer as a specialist within an organizational structure performing tasks of a service nature— service to the public, service to the communications media, service to the administrator. Others stress the promotional aspects of the officer's duties and view him as a propagandist, publicist, or public relations man. Still others argue that service and promotional qualities imply that the information officer is a policy-maker, prone to decision-making, and legitimately responsible to popular controls over all policy-makers. These interpretations merit treatment for they parallel the views that officers hold of themselves in the governmental process.

It can be conjectured that the service function of public information officers stems naturally from the responsibility of governmental officials in a democracy to report to the people. Simple reporting, not promotion, is then the task of the information officer. He is to (1) fulfill all informational requests of the public, (2) supply information to the news media when requested—regardless of its nature, and (3) tell everything without attempting to propagandize. Advocates of this point of view quickly recognize that this service function must often be performed through the press; indeed, it is but a small jump to the conclusion that the information officer's very reason for being is to be of service to the news media. From the newsman's viewpoint, such service should be provided without any effort to influence what the reporter shall write. Above all, the officer's job is to open the reporter's access to news sources, never to limit it.

Or, we may take the view that the officer is less a servant to public or press than to his own organization. His function is not promotion explicitly but is built on the assumption that if gov-

---

[1] Pimlott, *Public Relations and American Democracy*, *passim.* James L. McCamy, *Government Publicity* (Chicago: The University of Chicago Press, 1939), *passim.* Dick Fitzpatrick, "Public Information Activities of Government Agencies," *The Public Opinion Quarterly*, XI (1947–1948), 530–539.

ernment explains itself greater cooperation is achieved. The information officer is an administrative specialist, skilled in the employment and manipulation of symbols. His expertise lies in mastery of the means of distribution which will make his audience aware of his agency's information policies and which will give a rationale for binding the citizen to the program in a spirit of sympathetic loyalty.[2]

These views illustrate the tendency to focus on a single aspect of the information function. Whether the master be public, press, or agency, the information officer is viewed as serving the wishes of others with a minimum of discretion on his own part. Service, however, is not carried on in a vacuum, and observers hasten to point out that the activities of the information officer are by their very nature political in scope. Information, whether sought on the initiative of public or press or used as official explanation, is a tool of *policy*. Public explanation of policy with or without propagandistic intent competes with other explanations publicizing conflicting policies. Within an environment of competitive explanation, information-dispensing thus serves a political purpose.

Once we emphasize the inherently political nature of information policies, the function of the information officer is revealed as that of a publicist. Information-dispensing is simply a process for adjustment and resolution of conflicting interests, attitudes, and ideas. If handled adroitly, the official explanation of policy overcomes the competition of opposing publicity and even diminishes the necessity for added legislation. Douglass Cater, for example, has pointed out that it is through the use of publicity that officials are able to appeal to public opinion as an arbitrator of dispute.[3] David B. Truman stresses the manner by which publicity, in effect, can control access to administrative and legislative decision-making by "enlarging the public for the policies favored by the agency and consolidating the segments of the public that will support those policies." [4]

The position of the information officer in such a political

[2] McCamy, *Government Publicity*, p. 121.
[3] Cater, *The Fourth Branch of Government*, pp. 10–13.
[4] David B. Truman, *The Governmental Process* (New York: Alfred A. Knopf, 1958), p. 463.

process can no longer be defined as that of mere servant. As a specialist in the selection of messages designed to attract reader attention, the officer is in a position of decision-making vital to the success or failure of policy; to the extent that he is successful through the manipulation of messages in harmonizing interests and adjusting controversy, he is clearly acting in a political capacity.

This view of the information officer as a publicist stresses the implicit nature of his function as policy-maker as well. One observer has pointed out that any public relations man rises quite naturally to the level of explicit policy-making by engaging in consultation prior to decision, in the articulation of policy alternatives, and in the shaping of a final choice. Simply because policy-making is a continuing process of which information-dispensing is an integral portion, the skills of the information officers are policy skills.[5]

Distinguishing the various levels of information activity in order to sort the "political" from the "non-political" tasks of the information officer is a frustrating job. Inevitably one generalization recurs—the information officer's job is a political one which immerses him in one portion of a total process of policy formulation. In the most explicit statement of that role, the information officer makes policy decisions himself; at the other extreme, he is regarded as passive, almost automatic, in his responses to information requests. Between these two poles lies a variety of activity—including selection, manipulation, and distribution of information messages—which defines the role of the information officer as a political communicator.

From a survey of writings on the matter, we conclude the information officer is a political servant. This conclusion is convincingly reinforced when we examine how it agrees with that view held by officers themselves. Respondents too stressed the service nature of information activity; each viewed the officer as in his position to serve the needs of others, either by meeting the information requirements of the citizen or the explanatory requirements of his organization:

[5] Kelley, *Professional Public Relations and Political Power*, p. 212. Pimlott, *Public Relations and American Democracy*, pp. 54–55.

Well, the function of the press officer of any governmental
department is through the press to keep the public aware
and acquainted with the operations of the department, and
its programs, and its development of new programs, and the
development within existing programs.

I think our general function is to acquaint the American
people—the farmers, the consumers, the trade organizations,
and the agricultural trade and business—with what is being
done in the department to serve them, the whole economic
segment, and its relationships with all other parts of the
economy.[6]

Such interview responses provide us with a handy tool for
assessing what officers themselves consider to be the basic criteria
for judging their own performance. In examining the pattern of
typical responses in our sample $(N = 38)$, we find officers accepting their tasks as those of service and then defining the clienteles
served in three categories: 37 per cent insisted that they served
the governed either as the "public" directly or through the press;
an equal percentage of officers viewed their service as directed
toward governing powers, either "the organization" or their direct superiors; and, the remaining 26 per cent viewed themselves
as servants of both governing and governed groups. This distribution indicates both (1) the extent to which officers adopt "service"
as descriptive of their tasks in information-dispensing, and (2) the
variety of generalized interests which operate as the stimulus for
that service.

In the agent-of-the-public view, the officer performs a distinctive service when he distributes information the public may explicitly request or even information it may not care about at all.
The information officer thinks he is performing a requirement of
democratic activity, an open accounting to the ultimate rulers.
One officer stated:

Well, of course, basically a public information officer's
function is to tell the people how their tax money is being
spent. I think ideally it is an educational process. Our pro-

---

[6] Responses quoted come either from interviews with correspondents or
from interviews with officers; the context in each instance will make clear
which sort of interview is being quoted.

grams are approved by Congress; the law says we should carry out certain programs; and it seems to me the government agents have to account to the public from time to time as to what progress they are making, how they have succeeded in carrying out the functions which are laid down by law. Our primary duty is to educate the public as to what we are doing. It is a matter of communicating to the guy who foots the bill, if you will, how well we are doing the job.

That is an idealization and a simplification actually because the public largely doesn't give a damn; very often they are not out there begging to be told. But it seems to me in a democracy you owe it to the constituency; obviously an ill-informed constituency is a weakness, it seems to me, to the success of democracy. If the people aren't interested or can't be reached, well it is just a weakness that we try to overcome. I don't know whether I am drawing this in too broad a picture, but I was trying to get fundamental for a moment.

The concept of the information function as that of a press service differs from the view that seeks a definition in terms of a more generalized public. A typical response came from one officer:

I don't understand all of the legal aspects of the board; I do understand, I believe, better than many other people in this business the problems that are faced by the newsman in attempting to get news. Our business is to aid the newsman in gathering news, to alleviate the problems he has, to try to give him the whole story, the whole picture, of what is going on. I don't mean to try to spoon-feed him, but [only to] provide a concise statement of the decisions of the board so that the newsman does not have to come in here and do all of the case work himself.

The opinions expressed by this group are remarkably like those of the press corps regarding the function of the information officer in government. Of the newsmen surveyed ($N = 35$), 80 per cent expressed the opinion that the information officer's function should be that of "bulletin board," calling attention to the routine; "traffic cop" or "card catalogue," telling the reporter where to go for information; or "buffer," providing a point of contact for the newsman and, if possible, being his ally in ferreting out the news or the official who can provide it.

Without violating the service nature of his task, another officer indicated an initial orientation of quite a different variety.

> Well, I think I do the same thing any information man
> in government does or in public relations, in business, for
> that matter—that is, I do what my boss wants me to do. I
> think that is true for any job for that matter—you do what
> your boss wants you to do; if you don't do that, it can be
> damaging to your job security. It is the same as if you
> worked for Jimmy Hoffa; you may not believe in what he
> is doing; but because you work for Jimmy Hoffa, you do
> what he tells you to do; you do what he wants you to do.
> This I suppose is a cynical attitude toward one's profession,
> but the practical aspect is one of carrying out the tasks that
> are assigned to you.

A final category of officers spoke of information personnel as
specifically obligated neither to governed nor governors, but
stressed the officer's job as a necessary ingredient of the democratic process linking citizen and policy official. It is not the informational request alone that stimulates action nor some desire
for agency promotion, but the necessity to link the two: as one
respondent expressed it, "promoting a basic democratic concept
of government." More often, this is expressed as service to both
official and citizen by reacting to the requests of both; in one case,
this function was stated as "the capacity of serving as go-between
between the official and the public, as intermediary."

Individual officers interviewed preferred to steer away from
the political nature of their service. They spoke of their responsibility as directed toward avoiding conflict and characterized it
as noncontroversial, legally prescribed, and immune to changes in
partisan control that might occur in an agency. More than once
it was stressed that "Congress forbids our being political" and,
therefore, it would follow that it must be so! On the surface it
appears that the problem is simply one of semantics—that the
information officer is speaking of party politics when he uses the
term political and to the extent that he avoids partisanship his
function is nonpolitical. Without an elaborate digression on the
nature of the political, the noteworthy fact here is the information officer's very acceptance of a narrowed view of the political

which permits him to describe the information function as non-political and conceptualize his personal role in terms which imply, to him, legitimate behavior, even if political to the observer. For example, one press chief commented, "If any story comes in over here with politics in it, we just send it back. We don't touch it!" The discretion as to whether any story has "politics," however, is his; and where he draws the line has political consequences.

Such a statement stresses an unconscious acceptance of political responsibility. Within this political context, how does the officer define his own personal performance? Four broad categories of self-analysis emerge. For example, some stress activities described as purely reportorial in nature—digging around the agency for news, saving the reporter the necessary spadework, facilitating the flow of information out of the agency, responding to questions of a routine nature, supplying the documented facts as available, and avoiding interpretation of these facts. The ideal is one of objective agency reporting with the officer as an agency reporter. This differs from the officer who views his job as that of interpreting his agency's actions, on his own volition, to public and press:

> Well, you may not know this, [but] this is not a hard-sell agency. We feel it is our job to put the information out which is relevant to public understanding and let it go at that. We don't intend that it be a hard-sell at all. This does not mean that we will not make efforts to put the best light on policy. I feel, and everyone in this office feels, that it is our duty to make this agency look good and look in its best light within the framework of the truth, but the important thing you have there is the framework of the truth. We don't engage in any promotion, but we try to render our chief responsibility to the agency and operate within the framework of the truth.

Different in kind is the information officer who regards himself as a coordinator with tasks of balancing informational needs of the citizen with the practicalities of information security in policy-making. Balance is not an automatic function, but involves varying degrees of discretion. In the coordinator framework, the information office both "initiates and responds"—in-

dicates the information that the agency wants known about programs and policies and responds to the outside stimuli of citizen
and reportorial inquisition. Or, as colorfully expressed by one
respondent, "You can see it is a big organization; it is a big can
of worms that has to stay coordinated, and the job of the information guy like me is to coordinate."

Another responsibility is explicitly recognized as promotional
and often couched in terms reflecting concern for "the public
image," or "positive publicity." This viewpoint is exemplified by
the following:

> My job is not directly service to the public so much as to the
> secretary, and my allegiance is primarily devoted to him.
> My task—well, I look at it this way. I am concerned with
> the image he creates before the public.

How much reporting, interpreting, coordinating, and promoting the officer does is related to his position in the organization he serves. He may be accepted as important by his agency or
as "just there." The degree of his acceptance by the agency influences his performance in policy formulation, revelation, and
promotion. Officers vary in opinions as to their proper role in
each.

When it comes to an explicit statement of personal responsibilities in policy-making, officers interviewed $(N = 38)$ distributed themselves in three categories: those participating directly
in the making of policy beyond mere consultation (10 per cent);
those informed, advised, and consulted on policy formulation as
a prerequisite to an effective information program (25 per cent);
and all those not recognizing any relationship between their public explanation of policy and the formulation of that policy and,
hence, a nonparticipant in policy-making (65 per cent). Recognition of direct influence on policy-making is indeed rare among
information officers, being limited to officers at the level of assistant secretaries in the department. In 65 per cent of the cases, no
such explicit role in policy-making was perceived. The remaining 35 per cent usually spoke of their part in the policy-making
process in the following manner:

> I find in my personal experience that rather than to sit at
> the conference table and attempt to throw my opinions in
> just constantly, it is sometimes more effective to see what the
> technical experts are talking about and then perhaps quietly
> to say, "Well, I would like to flag down this possibility for
> a backfire," or, "Here is an opportunity to perhaps inform
> the public a little better." But on the whole I think that
> [the information officer] should be definitely included in all
> discussions of policy, in the formulation of policy. The
> point is if he can't be thought of as a senior man whose
> advice is worthwhile, then he can't serve his superiors well,
> and I don't think they [can] serve the public well.

Officers were also reluctant to regard it as their prerogative
to reveal policy-making discussions prior to the time final policy
statements are released for the agency. Of those responding to the
problem ($N = 37$), only 21 per cent felt the premature revelation
of policy, the "leak," a legitimate part of their duties in their
relations with the press. The majority of respondents (69 per
cent) disclaimed premature revelation and, indeed, stressed that
they thought it not a legitimate portion of their responsibility.
The Cater hypothesis that the official frowns on any premature
policy revelation, whereas the reporter believes in the "purifying
powers of publicity," [7] is shared by the information officer:

> It seems to me government officials like to reach their de-
> cisions without too much outside scrutiny. This is not neces-
> sarily because they are doing anything wrong, but because
> they feel they have a better grasp of the situation than any-
> one else and should not be prevented from doing what they
> consider to be right.
> Ultimately there is one man who decides policy—the sec-
> retary—and you can't have half a dozen much lesser officials
> making policy statements that don't agree. On this kind of
> thing you sometimes have to step in and protect the de-
> partment. . . . There are situations like that where we
> sometimes have to step in.

A more surprising position is that, in rare cases, "mitigating
circumstances" necessitate such premature revelation (10 per cent).
One respondent held forth at length on his duty to act "in the

[7] Cater, *The Fourth Branch of Government*, p. 19.

public interest" by exposing policy matters for open debate in the
press, even though specific departmental restrictions prohibit
revelation. A difference is perceived by officers between legally,
personally, and situationally prescribed duties:

> We do give out things that are of a controversial nature,
> but we do that unofficially from this office. Sometimes we
> get our knuckles rapped for it, but we have to go ahead and
> do it. The officials have to clam up. This is about one of the
> few places that a man can get his information. He has to
> know that he can have confidence in us to give him the
> straight scoop, and we have to know we can give him any-
> thing and he will be trustworthy.

We would expect that information officers vary in the amount
of discretion they can exercise in the timing of information release. Interview data supports such a hypothesis. Only 32 per cent
of the officers quizzed on the matter ($N = 37$) stated that they possessed sole discretion in matters of timing releases; an additional
8 per cent share such discretion with policy-makers in the agency.
For most (60 per cent), timing is a matter over which they have
little control. The normal pattern is that information is released
as "available" and this "availability" is up to the policy-maker
to decide. Release then becomes a matter for organization scheduling, not officer decision. The exception, of course, is the on-the-
spot inquiry of the newsman which may be disposed of immediately, but only so long as the answer to such an inquiry does not
itself call for policy revelation.

In agencies and departments, sampled officers were normally
of the opinion that information release was based on routine
scheduling practices of the organization. In only 40 per cent of
the cases did officers believe the timing of a release should be purposely manipulated for publicity effects. Normally it is the officer
who does have authority over release time who most eagerly accepts the responsibility for choosing the most propitious moment
for desired effect. A case in point is the handling of the "plant":

> I will occasionally plant a story. Now this is a familiar tech-
> nique; everyone knows about it. Never in the sense of giv-
> ing one man a beat on a story that everyone else is entitled

to; but perhaps a new policy that you are trying out, a reaction or a viewpoint that you want to get across. I find no
qualms of conscience here because this is something [that,]
if you made . . . a general announcement, you couldn't
do . . . ; it would be impossible. But by perhaps planting
it with a particular organ, or a particular commentator, you
can accomplish a national purpose.

There are certain techniques of effective distribution of information which we use, but it is [sic] not manipulative; it
is mostly for effectiveness. Obviously if you have an important announcement to make to the public and you know
that it is going to conflict with something else that is being
announced the same day, then you would do better to wait
until you can get a clearer channel to the people you are
talking to.

The pattern of officers disclaiming responsibility for making
policy or for "leaking" it was finally carried to a refusal even to
accept responsibility for policy promotion. Promotion, as an explicitly legitimate activity, was recognized by only 11 per cent of
respondents. It is noteworthy, however, that 50 per cent of the
officers stated that some promotion is inherent in their performance. The man who sees no promotion connected with his role
(39 per cent) talks of distinctions—between program and policy
or between political and civil service positions. Of the two, the
former is the more common, but tied closely to the latter. In most
cases the reasoning of the information officer proceeds as follows:
policy-making is political in that it is an activity of "politicians."
The end of policy-making is partisan or self-interest. The "sale"
of policy is not legitimate, but the "explanation" of policy once
it now has become agency program is another matter. An action
about which nothing could be said when it was prospective policy
is cloaked in respectability when it becomes program: "We try to
do nothing that is political in nature; we are interested in the operation of existing programs, not in achieving the enactment of
new legislation."

Within this framework of nonpromotional program explanation are attitudes regarding the appropriate relationship of the
information officer with the press. There is the view that the newsman is "interested more in political developments—the develop-

ment of new programs and the demise of the old perhaps." Since
the officer is "nonpolitical," there is dictated for him a clear-cut
relationship with the press—the presentation of program facts.

> We have to look at the stories closely to see if they are not
> suspect of trying to influence legislation one way or another.
> That is against the law! We can't use the taxpayers' money
> to put out a press release that the current administration
> might prefer. This is an utterly forthright and straightfor-
> ward presentation of news facts, and that is all. The poli-
> ticians have their job, but ours is a factual contract with
> newspaper people to give nothing but straight goods.
>
> I must say that one thing I abhor in government informa-
> tion is public relations. As we commonly know it I would de-
> fine public relations as any attempt to make the bad smell
> sweet. We shy away from it in so far as possible; it is simply
> nothing that concerns us.

In contrast to the view that the personal task of the information officer is merely program explanation is the view of the information officer as promoter. In this framework, policy-making
is a continuing process that does not stop at the secretary's desk
or on the floors of Congress. Passage of policy is only half of the
battle; its effectiveness depends upon its public sale:

> It is impossible in government to carry through programs
> successfully unless those programs are promoted. The busi-
> ness of running government is essentially the same as that
> of a business enterprise; namely, you have to merchandise
> your product, you have to sell your goods. The programs
> that are carried on by any department must be sold to the
> public. They must be convinced that those programs are
> worthwhile and that they should be supported. Part of the
> obligation of informing is to seek that successful govern-
> mental action that requires publicity. Publicity and inform-
> ing go hand in hand.

Between these two views is a range which recognizes the difficulties connected with avowed promotion of policy, yet cites the
inherently promotional quality of information-dispensing in the
processes of politics. Officers speak of the necessity of educating

the citizen, interpreting the facts for the citizen, presenting the total picture to the citizen, or simply creating a climate of acceptable opinion among the citizenry. There are variations on the theme, but the theme itself comes through quite convincingly:

> The essence of the press-officer function is a rather simple one. It is simply to open the doors of the commission to members of the press and then see that that information is put in the right package.

> There are two theories of public relations. One is that you grind out as much stuff as you can get into the press to promote coverage of the agency. The other is that you release it only at the time that it is necessary to release it—when the public is in need of it. We try to follow the latter policy here and in so doing the scarcity of stories about the agency which are released from this office make any one of the stories that we do release far more important to the press; we can get better coverage for it. The result is I think in the long run better coverage and more stories in the press than another agency might be able to get.

The picture that emerges, therefore, is of the information officer as a servant to public, organization, and press. It is undeniable, however, that officer attitudes toward their own responsibilities reveal this "handmaiden" role as tinged with a political character. The officer is a communicator—through communication, he binds public, organization, and press in the inherently political process of dispensing information. Whether he is a civil servant or a patronage appointee, the officer is in the critical position of political appointee—a position fraught with all the problems of popular control and responsibility common to any public office in a democracy.

NEWSMEN AND POLITICAL COMMUNICATION

Research into the political functions of the newsman is not extensive. Our clues come from scholars in journalism schools and are directed primarily at defining the general social functions of the news media in society. They include the dissemination of information, opinion, interpretation, entertainment, advertising, and miscellaneous factual material. The function most often

mentioned is that attributed to the newspaper by Cooley: a bulletin board for important news and a medium for the interchange
of ideas.[8] Or, more succinctly, "the journalistic function is to describe the environment-in-change." [9]

The general definition of the reporter's purpose is left to the
newsman himself in those rare moments when he is given to self-
contemplation. The classic assessment appeared in a London
Times editorial retort to government chiding for its criticism of
government policy.[10] Its modern reformulation and adaptation
to the peculiarities of political communication in the United
States is the work of James Reston, Washington bureau chief of
The New York Times. The primary obligation of the reporter is,
argues Mr. Reston, to the people. The source of this obligation
is the First Amendment to the Constitution of the United States,
which guarantees freedom of the press as a "pledge of safety to
the people." The reporter is a servant of the public; the ultimate
test of what should be published is not the governmental interest,
the interest of the news organization, or the interest of the newsman, but the interests of the people.[11]

> He must know where his primary allegiance lies. He does
> not owe that primary allegiance to the owner of his news-
> paper, or to his managing editor, or to his government, or to
> the sources of his information: he owes it to the people, and
> if he gives it to any of the others, then he is not, in my judg-
> ment, a thoroughly honest reporter, no matter how much
> information he gathers, or how enterprising he is, or how
> well he may write.[12]

Variations by newsmen on this basic theme indicate the acceptance of the central idea itself. The responsibility of the news-

[8] Charles H. Cooley, "The Significance of Communication," in *Reader in Public Opinion and Communication,* ed. Bernard Berelson and Morris Jano-witz (Glencoe, Illinois: The Free Press, 1950), pp. 145–153.

[9] Rosten, *The Washington Correspondents,* p. 11.

[10] Francis Williams, *Dangerous Estate: The Anatomy of Newspapers* (New York: The Macmillan Co., 1958), pp. 6–9. James B. Reston, "The Job of the Reporter," in *The Newspaper: Its Making and Its Meaning* (New York: Charles Scribner's Sons, 1945), pp. 99–101.

[11] Reston, "The Job of the Reporter," pp. 93–95.

[12] *Ibid.,* p. 93.

man is "truth-telling" for society, and, for the political community, it is the telling of political truths. He may follow the precept of Lippmann and "fight for the extension of reportable truth" [13] or, as Cater urges, describe "the closest approximation to the truth that he can discover." [14] But, the basic function is to fulfill an obligation: "to see that the truth is told." [15]

Recognition of the press as a channel of information to the citizen is implicit in such statements. To newsmen, the dissemination of information has as one purpose the presentation of the political facts underlying policy-making, facts which fill citizen needs. Yet, the reporter has not been quick to point to the political nature of this role, perhaps accepting it as obvious. Certainly, such truth-telling features are not without their political implications. Several dimensions of the newsman's function indicate the inherently political nature of the activity. One line of research, for example, has treated the newsman as a "gatekeeper." Simply stated, the newsman is in a discretionary position, making basic decisions at all levels—reportorial, editorial, and managerial—as to what the citizen may read.[16] These decisions are political in nature, since they influence what issues are articulated for popular reaction, discussion, and debate. In deciding what the "truth" is and what versions of that "truth" are presented for public reading, the newsman acts in a political capacity.

A newsman's sources often act in the capacity of publicists or propagandists. The newsman serving as a channel of propagandistic information is himself engaging in publicity. The news story, the editorial, the interpretive or opinion column—all may serve as channels for persuasive messages, particularly if the program under discussion is a generally accepted one.[17] At least, such is the implication of Stanley Kelley, Jr.'s interpretation of relations between public relations men and the press; "For the public

[13] Lippmann, *Public Opinion*, p. 361.
[14] Cater, *The Fourth Branch of Government*, p. 173.
[15] Alsop and Alsop, *The Reporter's Trade*, p. 10.
[16] Roy E. Carter, Jr., "Newspaper 'Gatekeepers' and the Sources of News," *The Public Opinion Quarterly*, XXII (1958), 133–144. See also Walter Gieber, "Across the Desk: A Study of 16 Telegraph Editors," *Journalism Quarterly*, XXXIII (1956), 423–432; Alan S. Donnahoe, "Mass Communication Theory: A Macroscopic Approach," *Journalism Quarterly*, XXXIV (1957), 443–451.
[17] Pimlott, *Public Relations and American Democracy*, pp. 141–142.

relations man, the press and other media are not only distributors
of information but instruments of social control, and the media
have for various reasons been largely forced to accept this estimate
of themselves." [18]

This image of the reporter as a servant of the public who, in
fulfilling the citizens' needs for dissemination of news and explanation of policy, is inherently engaged in political activities
is reinforced by our interview data. Like information officers,
newsmen tend to think of themselves performing in an agent's capacity. Newsmen demonstrate a remarkable consensus on this
point. Of those interviewed, 94 per cent cited their responsibility
as being to some vaguely defined "people." Only 3 per cent would
speak of responsibilities both to "the people" and to "the government." The majority position on this question is represented by
the following responses from reporters:

> Well, I think the newsman's primary function is to tell what
> the government is doing, what activities are taking place in
> the government—to tell that to the public.

> I think it's his job to inform the public as best he can on
> what is going on in government, on governmental policy—
> what is made public and what is not made public. I think
> primarily he has a responsibility to the public to do that.

> We are the connective tissue; we connect the people with
> their rulers; we connect the body politic with the ruling
> body. Public officials are fond of berating the press because
> they don't understand that—that the press is an agent for
> the public, an agent that communicates to the public about
> what public officials are doing.

> I would say the task of the newsman in society is to let
> society know what is going on!

The image of the public, the people, the society, reified in
many cases, prevails in responses. Rare was the newsman (3 per
cent) who adopted the "damn the public" position and discussed
the question in less glowing terms:

---

[18] Kelley, *Professional Public Relations and Political Power*, p. 204. See also
Lasswell's groundbreaking interpretation of the propaganda potentialities of
the press in Harold D. Lasswell, "Research on the Distribution of Symbol
Specialists," *Journalism Quarterly*, XII (1935), 146–156.

> There is no idealistic job that he performs at all—not for anybody but himself maybe. It is just a living. It is a matter of survival for him and everybody does it to survive. The newspaper business is a business, just that; it is a business. Our purpose is to make money; for the business, its purpose is to make money for the organization. That's all!

Within the broad context of service, newsmen recognized three tasks performed by the news media in the communication process. Most often cited is that reportorial duty of serving as scrutinizer of governmental activities as representative, once again, of the people. The watchdog concept—the view that the newsman is obligated to criticize government as "watchdog of the public" —is encountered quite frequently. This is the classic newspaper role of the crusader; "We alone," said one respondent, "are not on any payroll, don't have any axes to grind personally, and we should inform the public of what's good, but particularly what's bad." Restated in other terms, the press is an opposition party, an inquisitor, a public prosecutor.

We also encounter the attitude that the press is secondarily an informal arm of governmental action. Implicit is the belief that reporters are the principal channels of political communication. One respondent put it curtly, "I feel that people just don't get informed about the government except through the news media of communication." When the task of explaining what officials want explained and that of scrutiny blend imperceptibly into one another, many problems of government-press conflict are revealed. Respondents, when questioned as to whether they perceived conflict between the press and government as growing out of those functions, replied as follows ($N = 32$): 83 per cent perceived conflicts as inevitable and 17 per cent as not inevitable, but probable. Information officers quizzed on the point ($N = 19$) distributed themselves as follows: conflict inevitable, 70 per cent; conflict probable, 30 per cent. On this basis, we would assume that both reporters and officers accept tension between newsmen and their sources as the normal pattern of living. One bureau chief summed the conflict up this way:

> You have this multiple obligation. You have first what I call the bulletin board obligation, that is, the routine bread

and butter news of government which government very hap-
pily turns out and the politicians are very happy to an-
nounce—the building of a post office, the acquiring of
money for a new dam in your area, all of the things that
make politicians happy. They are happy to hand them out
and you are happy to print them because your people want
to know about them. There is no trouble between government and press there.

You get into another realm where there is a question of
timing. A certain thing is going to be done, but the politician or officeholder doesn't want the preliminary steps covered because he would argue it might interfere with the
negotiations and the proper consummation of the thing.
What is your responsibility? Should you delay the announcement in order to assure its accomplishment or do you have
an obligation to let people know what is in the process of
being done so if they don't want it they might take issue and
stop it?

Then there is a third field in which the politician and the
reporter are natural enemies. Things are going on that the
public is entitled to know about. Maybe there's nothing
scandalous, maybe there's nothing wrong, but it's slightly
embarrassing to the officeholder. He would want you not
to know about it.

A final function perceived by respondents is that of assessment of public opinion. In some instances this means that the
newsman acts directly as a gauge of what opinion happens to be
at any given moment. In others it simply means that news reaction to policy—the amount of publicity—indicates to the official the public interest in a problem. Or, it means that reporters
raise issues around which public opinion forms. One reporter
spoke of the creation of awareness:

Well, I think the factor that makes governments work, that
makes the country alive, that makes the democratic system
responsive is the factor of awareness. If the officials aren't
aware of what's going on, if they are not aware of the demands of the nation, they won't act. I think that the press is
a sort of a lubricant that keeps people aware and you realize
that it creates a livelier environment and a more responsive
environment; and I think that this is an essential ingredient
of a democratic process.

The combination of functions—scrutinizer, channel, and articulator—are quite similar to those attributed to the representative process in a political system. Officers interviewed also mentioned these three activities as press functions. There was one difference, a critical one. Officers placed the channel function as primary; newsmen stressed the function of scrutinizing. To the officer, the press serves first the governor, secondly the governed. Furthermore, service to the citizen is often seen by the officer as a product of service to the citizen's government. Newsmen regard their function as something more than just the straight communication of information between governor and governed. Acting in behalf of the citizen, the newsman regards his role in the political process as not unlike that of the legislator—as an agent through whom public feelings and demands enter the policy-making arena.

Reston points out that the purpose of reporting is to report, explain, and disclose.[19] These representative tasks may or may not be adopted by any single reporter. Cater stresses that the reporter's role is self-directed and that there are no guiding principles by which it may be defined.[20] The Alsops imply as much by calling reporting not a profession, but a craft or a trade "like undertaking, which it sometimes resembles." [21] Assuming for the moment that no conventions define reporting as a professional activity, it is important nevertheless to document the manner in which the newsman himself views his personal role—his points of self-direction.

Newsmen's views of their personal responsibilities differ widely. On one point they are united. Regardless of whether he is bureau chief, editorial writer, columnist, or on a beat, the newsman discusses his primary personal task in terms of reporting—not commentary and not management. This reinforces the Cater hypothesis that Washington correspondents identify with the more humble title of reporter.[22] But, in discussing the nature of

[19] James B. Reston, "Reporting on Foreign Affairs," *Nieman Reports,* III (1949), 3–5.

[20] Cater, *The Fourth Branch of Government,* pp. 172–177.

[21] Alsop and Alsop, *The Reporter's Trade,* p. 4.

[22] Cater, *The Fourth Branch of Government,* p. 1.

reporting, both as to reportorial interest and approach, marked differences among newsmen occur.

Respondents defined the nature of the personal job by discussing the type of reporting they undertake. Reporting interest takes the form either of general reporting of a routine nature or specialized efforts of preparing special features requiring competence in a particular area. Only one-fourth of the newsmen questioned on the point ($N = 35$) thought of themselves as "generalists." Far more popular was the designation of "specialist," a term which implies a degree of expertise not often associated with the correspondent who roams the halls of several administrative agencies. This expertise, they insist, takes various forms. A few (5 per cent) prepare articles dealing with technical subject matter, such as aerospace developments or underwater exploration; others specialize in stories dealing with news items of relevance to particular geographic regions (14 per cent). Or a correspondent may be assigned the task of following the unraveling of a single significant story or perhaps covering a single individual such as the president over a long period. Ten per cent so specialized. Finally, the reporter may select an area of particular interest and spend months or years pursuing stories reflecting every angle of it (46 per cent). Newsmen covering a particular "run" of agencies cover anything that takes place in their assigned area. Hence, they regard themselves as giving general coverage to such agencies and speak of their role as that of a "general reporter." However, even they hasten to point to special skills such reporting requires, skills which must be possessed to a far higher degree than those possessed by the reporter who does not cover such agencies regularly.

> My problem is one of passing judgment. I have an obligation to my office uptown because I am supposed to be an expert in this field of passing original judgment and not bothering them with some stuff. The editor uptown will say, "I am not an expert in agriculture; I don't know what might be good and what not; that is his job down there." He can't use everything that we have down here, so you pick out what you think meets the needs; see what I mean?

The newsman calling himself a general reporter really regards himself as specially qualified to handle "my little facet of it." His orientation is different from that of the correspondent thinking of himself as a specialist in Washington reporting, concerned not with general news patterns, but with what he will write that requires a specialized approach.[23] For the specialist surveys the activities of the day, selects those that merit treatment for his particular audience, and writes only of them. He distinguishes his role from the generalist by the position he occupies in the flow of news. The general reporter, he argues, selects news from events which have taken place or are scheduled; the specialist makes news:

> You are always making news by your questions. I mean that's the value of specialists, the questions they ask. And you're always looking for a new approach to it. If you just wanted the flat news, you could just take the press associations—they do an admirable job on that. But a specialist's job is to probe and go to a press conference, to ask provocative questions, to get a man's viewpoint, and if you think he is not telling the truth, then you continue to debase him, you continue to probe. You are supposed to keep on asking questions and make news.

Specialists vary in giving reasons for their particular interest. One group points to the need in Washington reporting of obtaining information which will not duplicate that of the wire services and press associations. Others represent interests of particular regions and probe to uncover information not normally available through general news organizations. Hence, they regard themselves as specialists possessing peculiar competence to ferret out the story that has, as one respondent expressed it, "a regional angle, something that the wire services are not already going to have furnished us—that is [a] specialized, sometimes maybe a narrow, angle." Another specialist may be competent in a particular area of newsworthy activity—space technology, defense, foreign affairs. Relevant events, he feels, can be covered only

[23] Raymond P. Brandt, "The Washington Correspondent," *Journalism Quarterly*, XIII (1936), 173–176.

summarily by general news treatments. What the public demands, he points out, is "background, depth, interpretation," and it is his job to provide it:

> Well, like many others in Washington, I have a specialty. I think that there are more and more specialists appearing in Washington reporting today. My own particular specialty is science writing; I cover what happens in atomic energy, what happens in health, what happens in all areas connected with science. It is my job to inform people of the developments that are going on in science both technically and politically—the impact of science in the political world.

A final breed of specialist is the newsman never assigned a particular beat in Washington, yet not given the roaming freedom to seek targets of opportunity in quite the same manner as the free-lance specialist, the regional specialist, or the technical specialist. While on assignment, he covers specialized areas for a brief period or is assigned a special story for "coverage in depth." He is not the individualistic reporter of old; his troubleshooting is not in the name of the personal scoop, but in the name of the organizational need of the moment. He is increasingly the product of an organizational society, not the "man-in-trenchcoat-and-battered-hat" of nostalgic reminiscence:

> I cover a number of differing things here in Washington around from Capitol Hill to the State Department to the White House to the Attorney General's office. Basically the job is the same; you cover different facets. But you are checking on, reporting on, covering actions by the government, or by the various committees of Congress, or by the State Department—what it is doing and why it is doing it and trying to keep the people informed as to how their government is working.

Regardless of the specialty, this group tends to agree with the identification of one respondent, "We are specialists, and we are supposed to write what we think is important." Varying reportorial interests are only part of the story; much has to do with what "we feel is important."

Newsmen distribute themselves quite evenly according to

the service they think they are performing for the citizen in their own stories $(N = 35)$. Thirty-one per cent agree with one respondent: "My job is to cover news from the factual standpoint without interpretation, without editorializing." Here the reporter is a passive agent of the facts which need reporting—facts easily selected, dutifully recorded, and seldom in need of explanation. However, few believe that factual presentation is totally without its problems of discretion for the newsman. But, having accepted the postulate that selection is not totally automatic, they hasten to point out that this is far different from explaining the facts or offering opinions about them:

> But it seems to me that the closer you can stick to reporting what, in your opinion, is the significant news that is flowing out, the better off you are. You have got to recognize that nobody can be unbiased, especially if he covers a certain field continuously. I think the guy that can keep himself divorced from this thing with which he deals all the time, well, he is just almost nonexistent. However you have got to fight those prejudices; once you start looking for things that justify your viewpoint and ignoring the things that would knock down your viewpoint, then your value as a newsman is gone completely.

Others feel differently. As one expressed it, "The idea that you can be an intellectual eunuch is silly as can be." Those reporters agree that personal judgment is a part of news selection and that it should not be condemned. It should provide the opportunity for explanation of facts: "We live in an era where everybody makes speeches in which they say it's not enough to tell what, and who, and where; but you've got to tell why and how come." Simple selection of facts is not enough; it is essential to explain, interpret, and give significance to the facts so that citizens read more than an encyclopedic account of current events. Thirty-eight per cent share the feelings of one respondent who stated:

> I find interpretive writing very interesting; and I find news writing less interesting. . . . It's my judgment that news writing isn't as challenging as interpretive. Well, I

think it's limp, I think it's boring. I think you lose the interest of the reader. I don't think there is any justification
for being boring in the newspapers.

The remainder would go beyond this. Several newsmen
endorsed going beyond interpretation and criticizing political
action so that the citizen could become capable of informed
judgment. Such respondents act as the public conscience, responsible for criticism of what is bad, definers of the good, and
prescribers of the good life. One editorial writer spoke of his
role as providing "frank expression of opinion; he praises or he
condemns, points with pride or views with alarm, criticizes or
. . . extols." This group speaks of requirements of judgment,
conscience, and responsibility for reporters. The line between
this view and one of explaining or interpreting is only vaguely
defined. Many of the latter groups adhere to the view expressed
by one self-styled interpretive specialist:

> We are not allowed to editorialize. It's the analysis of one
> who has been here a long time and has the background and
> can remember what happened before—so that it's an inter-
> pretation. . . . The line of demarcation is when we try to
> project it as what consequences will be; then we are on our
> own. . . . We are not . . . interested in what should hap-
> pen; we are interested in what will happen. The editorial
> writer is concerned with what should happen according to
> his viewpoint. Well I'm not concerned about that; it's not
> what I hope, it's what I expect. That's the difference between
> the two.

The implication is readily apparent. As in the case of information officers, newsmen differ in their orientations regarding
personal tasks—both in reportorial interest and in selection and
treatment of news. As information officers approach their responsibilities in informing the citizen differently, newsmen differ
in their orientation in reporting to the citizen. One fact, however,
remains clear. It runs through the literature and through interview data from information officers and newsmen. The consequences of service to the citizen or to government by supplying
information to the populace are inherently political. Officers and

reporters engage in political decision-making. This decision-making may range from the negligible to the critical, but the identification of officers and newsmen at vital points in the political process is obvious. They are communicators inextricably ensnarled in politics. The critical aspect of this political process is that each set of communicators represents differing interests—interests which, in varying degrees of conflict, create that inevitable tension so characteristic of government-press relations in the United States.

CHAPTER III
SOURCES & CHANNELS
IN POLITICAL
COMMUNICATION

The character of information officers' and newsmen's activity has been defined as essentially political. Both this activity and the attitudes which underlie it are extremely complex. To simplify matters, we have constructed a classification of news sources and news channels as political communicators. Both classifications are based upon the consistent attitude patterns which emerge from analysis of the interview data.

A CLASSIFICATION OF NEWS SOURCES

Three basic attitude patterns were revealed in information officers' responses. Each group represents a differing orientation to the role of political communication. One such group may be categorized as the informers. The attitude pattern is a recurring one. The officer views the information function as one of complete service. The purpose of his service may vary; he is likely to think in terms of service to public, press, and agency:

> Well, the function of the information office of any govern-
> mental department is through the press to keep the public
> aware and acquainted with the operations of the depart-
> ment, and its programs, and its development of new pro-
> grams, and the developments within existing programs.

He views his own task as primarily reportorial, reporting to the
public and press what activities are taking place in the agency.
Such reporting is looked upon as necessarily factual, without interpretation or opinion. The reason lies in his perception of
what the press wants: "They want the facts, they want it accurate
and straight; that is all they ask—'Give us the facts and give it
to us straight.' " Preparation or editing of a news release is carried
on with extreme care:

> I never arbitrarily edit out great gobs of a story without
> calling back the originator because there is always the possi-
> bility in rapid editing that, in a more complicated program,
> you may be giving a wrong impression. We do try to get it in
> language I can understand, and I figure that if I understand
> it most anybody else can.

This source views himself as not connected with policy-making
in any fashion. He is quick to make the distinction of policy and
program, pointing out that it is the latter toward which his efforts are directed; policy matters are beyond his province. He
has no patience with those wishing to manipulate the timing of a
release for any coverage purpose. Said one such officer, "I abhor
public relations as we commonly know it either in private business
or in government; that is, any attempt to make the bad smell
sweet." Release of information is a scheduled matter determined
only by the status of the program:

> Now I have had people working in the news service who
> have come in, or people who have come in as special assist-
> ants with the idea that they would manage news, that they
> would release this piece of information but not all of it at a
> given time. They would release this item, hold others until a
> more appropriate time. This type of thing always backfires;
> I have never seen it to fail. The best rule to follow is the most
> simple—that is when the information is ready, then release.

Servant of the public, press, and organization—in that order—with minimum powers of discretion; a civil service reporter after facts; nonpromotional in nature and concerned with operating programs rather than policy—these attributes characterize the informer's view of himself and his role in the information-dispensing process. Of the officers sampled, 40 per cent have such characteristics.

Another 34 per cent of the officers can be classified as educators. The object of the educator's service is a generalized public. He speaks of service to the news media, but he does so only because he recognizes its utility in reaching a far larger audience: "We serve in an educational way in using the media; for we are charged with what you might call an educational and informational program." Service to his organization is vital, but only because it exists as popular property: "The department belongs to the people, and we approach it from that viewpoint." This is not the reporter grubbing for departmental facts to pass along without comment, but the interpreter concerned with expanding on facts to create understanding: "I would say the role is to make sure that we present a balanced picture of the activities of the department, and that we do a thorough job of reporting to the people." Tasks of interpretation combine with those of coordination in order to harmonize the agency's message with the informational needs of the citizen. The educator discusses matters in terms of policy, not of programs, and insists that the information officer must be informed in the stages of policy-making even though he is not actually participating in the decisions themselves:

> I think when the policy is made, there ought to be somebody available to know about the public impact. I would say that there were times it would appear as if Jim Hagerty were a policy-maker in the White House. I would feel that an information man should not be the policy-maker; he should transmit policy, perhaps help in making it, but not make it. I don't believe that is part of his job. But when policy considerations are being made, I think somebody who understands the public information function ought to be on hand. So that aspect of the matter should be considered right at the time the policy is being made. I don't think

you should make public policy without respect to the impact on the public, [and] . . . the public information officer should [have] . . . knowledge of that impact.

Educators prefer the concepts of "needed message" or "information" to those of "publicity" or "promotion." Yet, they recognize
the inherently promotional capacity of any message of information and accept publicity as a tool of education:

> Of course information by its very release might have some
> reflection on policy, but I should think that for the most
> part our business here is not to attempt to direct what poli-
> cies should be adopted; that is, our job is not to do that.
> But information is made available pointing up problems
> and areas where steps need to be taken. It is a little of both.

In timing releases, the educator has little more discretion than
the informer, but in those instances in which he has such discretion, he is prone to take advantage of it. As one respondent put it,
"On Valentine's Day, you fish for the love angle even in a labor
case."

The remainder of the officers interviewed fit the pattern
of the promoter. For the promoter, the orientation of service is
primarily organizational. Timing, for example, is important, for
the interest of the organization may depend upon it: "It is a
constant battle here, a battle for the timing of the release when
it will do the most good for the agency." The image of the organization or the superior is avowedly the primary concern.

The promoter is aware of the necessity to participate in
policy-making; indeed, he expressly admits doing so. Sample
responses include, "I would say yes, we are in policy," and "The
public relations man has to be close to the policy-maker." One
officer described the ideal relationship of officer and organization
this way: "The public relations man in government must be to
his department what Solomon's scribes were to him." The promoter must, according to the respondents, enjoy the full confidence of the superior:

> I think in order to be a good public information officer or a
> special assistant you to have that confidence. Some are and

some are not given freedom. I think that you have to be given that freedom if you are going to do a good job.

A CLASSIFICATION OF NEWS CHANNELS

In like manner, it is possible to categorize the performance and attitudes of newsmen by a classification of news channels. The newsman as a political communicator is a channel for information flowing to the citizen. Again three patterns emerge.

The first such pattern is that of the recorder. The recorder is the reporter, assigned to a specific "run" of agencies, whose discretion is limited to selection of events for reporting. He is the first link in the chain of reporting of a general news organization. Perhaps stemming from the nature of his position, his reportorial interests are those of the generalist, but his decisions set him apart from the routine: "This is not routine reporting at all, no; a certain amount of it is, but so [much is] not."

More telling in the differentiation of channel types is the distinction drawn of limits on interpretation. The recorder accepts some interpretation as a necessary part of the trade, but never to the point of injecting his own opinions: "My job is merely one of factually reporting with some interpretation; no opinion is involved in it." What he means by interpretation differs from what others mean by the term. He refers to selection of facts; an explanation of the background of these facts—how officials think the situation came about—a discussion of surrounding circumstances; and the opinions of officials as informed as possible on the probable consequences of policy decisions. He considers his "reportable fact" in retrospect and in prospect and describes it accordingly. He feels that his opinion of the reported situation must not impinge on the reporting itself; he calls himself objective (Table 1). Opinions as to the possibility of objectivity vary. The recorder regards such objectivity as possible—or, if not possible, still to be attempted. The following is characteristic of this point of view:

> In the wire services we are supposed to say nothing on our own, and when we do, always have a source to quote; we are not supposed to be interpretive. Other newspapers don't take this attitude, because they have realized that when a

reporter goes out to cover a story he inevitably works on only a few facts of the story. Well, when it comes to making a choice between what facts to cover, there is a purely personal selective process.

I don't believe there is such a thing as pure objectivity; we can approach objectivity as reporters, and objectivity has to be developed by training and experience. In order to guard against the element of personal interest in any story, one must have enough training and experience to recognize that element, and, if he is attempting interpretation, [to] cover both sides of any controversy.

In connecting the citizen with the government, the recorder views himself as the source of the factual information from which the citizen must choose what he wants, how he wants to view it,

TABLE 1

NEWSMAN CONCEPTS OF INTERPRETIVE
AND OBJECTIVE REPORTING

	Newsman (N = 35)
Type Interpretation (categories not mutually exclusive)	
Objective-retrospective (background, why the event occurred)	25%
Objective-descriptive (what else took place, relation to other events)	35
Objective-prospective (probable consequences)	23
Subjective-retrospective (how things should have been)	25
Subjective-descriptive (how things should be)	30
Subjective-prospective (what should take place in the future)	30
No distinction perceived or necessary	5
Possibility of Objectivity	*(N = 33)*
Complete objectivity possible	9%
Complete objectivity impossible, but must be attempted	70
Complete objectivity impossible and not even desirable	21

and how he wants to act upon it. The recorder transcribes the facts of a given event, then limits his discretion to the very sizable and subjective task of sorting from encyclopedic detail the material for his short article. He initiates the filtering process that determines what news the citizen reads or hears. Of the newsmen observed in this study, 29 per cent can appropriately be classified as recorders.

A second pattern belongs to the expositors. The expositor has more discretion than the recorder does in story selection itself, not just in the selection of relevant facts. He identifies himself as a specialist scanning Washington for stories that may serve the purpose of giving depth to reader understanding. He carves out a limited area and does not compete with general news organizations. He does more than report the facts of a story; he interprets the significance of the event for the citizen and does not leave such interpretation solely to the discretion of the reader. He feels the constraint to go beyond the routine of reporting. This calls for personal judgment, and it is not surprising to find the expositor regarding objectivity as impossible. He will, perhaps, admit to the necessity of attempting it; but often he will deny that even this is desirable. If such action limits the story or makes the story misleading in its interpretation, nonobjectivity may be necessary to balance the account:

> Subjectivity is introduced at every step of the way, and it makes it very difficult to be objective in the pure sense, but I do think that you have to make as strong attempt at objectivity as you are capable of. But you have to make sure that you are defining objectivity so it doesn't mean excluding key elements in a story.

With interpretation his reason for existence, the expositor adopts a permissive attitude in defining legitimate interpretation. The expositor is interested in more than objective interpretation in the form of retrospective, descriptive, and prospective reflection. He weaves objective and subjective interpretation into a final product which explains not only how things became a certain way but exposes any wrongdoing which may have occurred in the process. One variation of this approach is exemplified by the expositor who feels that by expressing his pre-judgments publicly, he can then proceed to interpret as he sees fit:

> The interpretation I give to a story is influenced in spite of myself, by my own feelings, and yet, I will pull back from my own feelings instinctively in order to give as fair an interpretation as I can. Everybody knows I'm an old New Deal Democrat, and yet it was my pride that Senator Taft said time and again nobody was ever fairer to him than I was, and yet I didn't believe a thing he believed in. We became great personal friends, and he said many times that he never got fairer treatment anywhere. I made no pretense to being on his side, and I interpreted things from his point of view as disadvantageous to him, but people are entitled to know my prejudices—in fact, entitled to know my views.

This reporter pulls up short at discussing how things *should* be:

> People confuse exposition with editorial comment. In my book, editorial comment is to write a story saying "John Jones was elected sheriff yesterday, and I think it was a terrible thing that he was." But if I write a story saying that John Jones was elected sheriff because he made a deal with certain factions, that's interpretation of news, and to my mind, it's fact.

Summarized, then, the expositor views himself as above the routine of limited factual reporting, responsible for interpretation of facts he reports, and responsible for making his view known. He is a specialist who normally selects the events he covers. He has far more decision-making responsibilities than the recorder. He does not compete with the latter, but as one expressed it, "we supplement the others" by explaining political reality. Forty-two per cent of the newsmen sampled fit such a descriptive pattern.

Finally, there is the newsman who does more than just report or interpret, the prescriber. Twenty-nine per cent of our sample can be described as conforming to the prescriber's pattern. He states precisely what went wrong—or right—and suggests courses of future action which will lead to the world he thinks desirable. He chooses his own subjects for comment; he is, in the parlance of the craft, a self-starter. Rarely does he see himself as a narrow specialist; he looks upon himself as a competent commentator on a broad range of problems. To a greater degree than the recorder or expositor, the prescriber views himself as an articulator of public opinion. He serves both official and citizen; the former relies on his judgment in the assessment of opinion elites,[1] and the latter is provided with possible courses of action, informed commentary, and insightful criticism. In matters of objectivity, the prescriber is quite content to recognize its impossibility and its undesirability.

> This business of objectivity has been the bugaboo of journalism for many, many years. Frankly I think that, when a reporter claims that he must be objective, that objectivity then has become a cover for cowardice more than anything else, that what we have to do is be candid. Both editor and publisher, and reporter, must be candid and say that they do in fact allow personal feelings to enter in these by-line articles. Personal in this sense—what you select to write about, what you write about, how you write it, whether you put one thing in the lead and bury something else at the end of the article.
>
> For me objectivity is no problem; I am not trying to be objective. I am a columnist. The business of the columnist is to give personal opinion about what is going on, and he makes no cover of objectivity in his business. I don't believe that you can write breaking news four days a week and then an opinion column on the fifth. You have to do one or the other; don't try to masquerade under a pseudo-objective coat.

The prescriber thinks of himself as an important transmitter of ideas and opinions which need airing. It is the prescriber who couches his definition of news media functions in the concepts of opposition party, scrutinizer, criticism, or watchdog. The following respondent represents this line of thinking:

> I believe the function of the columnist like myself is to warn the public about what governments are doing, or what they

[1] Gabriel A. Almond, *The American People and Foreign Policy* (New York: Harcourt, Brace, & Co., Inc., 1950), Ch. VII.

intend to do, what's behind the actions of the government and, of course, give also facts and news which the government attempts to suppress so frequently.

This classification, constructed on the basis of personal interviews, bears a close resemblance to the impressions of others who have attempted to specify the types of reporting that take place in the political system. Frederic E. Merwin, for example, has stressed three functions of the press in portraying governmental activities: (1) reporting (the selection of those events which should be transmitted and included in the flow of news), (2) interpreting (the ferreting out of information required to give the shape of the event in proper perspective), and (3) criticism (the pointing out of weak and questionable points in the management of public affairs).[2] It is also relevant to Richard Wilson's categorization of the Washington press corps into press association men, special correspondents, and columnists.[3] And, it poses in less intuitive terms the distinctions, so often alluded to in commentaries on the press, between facts, interpretations, and opinions.

PATTERNS AND TRENDS IN COMMUNICATOR RELATIONS

A consideration of the functions, performance, and expectations of information officers and newsmen opens certain areas of speculation regarding the nature of the source-channel relationship. These speculations are classified under three headings: (1) perceived functions and roles of reporters and officers, (2) the pattern of role definition among information officers and newsmen, and (3) trends in political communication.

Foremost are inferences drawn from the observed perceptions of function and role by the two groups. There is recognition that the processes of information-dispensing and newsgathering are political in nature and that both sources and reporters are in positions of decision-making. This recognition is not as ap-

[2] Frederic E. Merwin, "The Reporting of Government News," in *The Press and Society*, ed. George L. Bird and Frederic E. Merwin (New York: Prentice-Hall, Inc., 1951), pp. 214–219.
[3] Richard Wilson, "Reporting the Washington News," *The Annals of the American Academy of Political and Social Science*, CCXIX (1942), 128–130.

parent among the information officers typified as informers; however, even among these, there is a limited perception of tasks involving selection on the basis of personal discretion. Both information officers and newsmen define their personal behavior within
the framework of a function conceded to be inherently political.
The self-definition of the personal role of either in the communication process is one variable defining the relationship between
the two. The officer's definition of his role—what is legitimate
for him—aids in explanation of his perception of what the newsman is doing and the type of relationship he feels he should have
with the newsman; a similar assertion applies to the role definition of the newsman and his view of the information officer.

Three basic patterns emerge. The first deals with the informer. Within the broad orientation of service, he considers
himself as expediter, facilitator, or aide to the reporter. Obstruc-
tion of the newsman, either by withholding or managing news,
is anathema to him. If he does not see his primary service as being
to the press, he remains aware of his dependence on the news
media in carrying out his alternative roles—service to the vaguely
conceived public or to his agency. As one expressed it, "We find
the newsman can do the department more good than anybody
else can!" He speaks of his job in terms of aid to, and dependence
on, the newsman. He sees himself as a reporter in uniform, interested in "getting it straight and getting it right" and in ex-
pediting the flow of *information*. In this respect, his orientation
as a political communicator parallels that of the newsman characterized as the recorder. The recorder, too, is a facilitator, but
of the flow of *news*. Like the informer, he records and reports "to
let the public know what is going on in the government." His
role concept within the framework of service activities, a framework which he is as quick to identify as is the informer, is near
that of the informer himself; he even uses identical expressions
to define it. The role concepts of informers and recorders with
regard to the general function of political communication approach identity.

A second basic pattern emerges from the set of role orientations of the educator and the newsman role type identified as the
expositor. The educator looks upon his service as directed toward

the generalized public. He explains facts to create an environment of understanding. Emphasis is on the explanation of policy rather than on the factual details of what some information officers call "programs." This interest also motivates the expositor as a political communicator. Within the service context, both regard themselves as satisfying citizen needs of understanding— the perceived demand for explanation. However, the tendency for these two communicator roles to converge is not as great as in the case of the informer-recorder relationship already described. Although both commit themselves to tasks of explanation and interpretation, the product of that process may vary considerably. The decisions by the source on the event to be discussed and the explanation deemed necessary may differ markedly from those of the channel.

A final pattern is that of the promoter-prescriber. The promoter regards it his duty to create the framework of truth conducive to a favorable image for the agency, official, or policy. As political communicator, he values not information in itself or information to meet any perceived popular need for understanding, but information to serve specific purposes in the political process. Management of information or news is a legitimate enterprise; withholding of information to allay suspicions of internal agency disagreement is accepted; and exercise of discretion as to what to release and when to release it is an accepted practice. His interest is not restricted to explanation and interpretation of policy; it is the prescription of policy through promotion. This goal of prescription is also the defining quality of the prescriber. The prescriber speaks of himself in relation to the public in much the same terms as does the promoter. Both view themselves as responsible for the diagnosis of ills and the suggestion of remedies. To the promoter these remedies may be in the form of "the policy," or "the man"; to the prescriber they may be "the cogent critique," or "the truth." Regardless of form, the shared orientation is the suggestion of alternatives for reconciliation of conflict. What keeps these two communicator role types separable is the tendency for each to isolate himself as *the* communicator with *the* correct prescribed course of action. Hence, the tendency for the promoter-prescriber pattern is to be one of two separated roles which neither merge, as in the case of the informer-recorder relation, nor overlap, as in the educator-expositor situation.

Thus three patterned sets of relationships between sources and channels emerge—the informer-recorder, the educator-expositor, and the promoter-prescriber. All are political communicators; all perceive the function as service; only the first set plays down the discretionary and political nature of the service. But, the first speak of themselves as objective factual reporters, the second as interpretive communicators, and the third as articulators of action choices.

Two observations will aid us here. First, these patterns are the basic ones; they do not attempt to account for the variety that appears when other combinations appear—for example, informer-prescriber, educator-recorder, and so on. Secondly, these patterns emerge from consideration of the respondents' concepts, implied in the interviews, of political communication, personal roles, and a suggested fact-interpretation-opinion complex. The patterns suggest a sharing of role concepts as political communicators for each relationship; they do not indicate an agreement within each set as to what is to be communicated—what is news. If this particular problem is considered, one finds a partial explanation for the variety of relationships between source and channel.

It is suggested that information officers and newsmen share the same news concepts because the source adjusts to what he perceives to be the newsman's definition of news in order to gain access to the media for his message. Or, it may be a result of the newsman's adjustment to the official's definition in order to assure his access to the official's information. Both sources and channels cite interest and importance as determinants of newsworthiness in a story. Carter suggests the fruitful hypothesis that harmony and conflict in the relationship between the source and official is partially a function of differences in definition of news.[4] Our data indicates that such differences arise from (1) characteristics that make a story interesting, and (2) characteristics that make it important. Such characteristics are related to the sub-

[4] Carter, "Newspaper 'Gatekeepers' . . . ," pp. 137–141.

stantive qualities of the story itself and the audience to which it is directed.

In the case of the audience to which the news message is directed, interviews suggest that the reporter thinks of his audience in more general terms than does the information officer. The former speaks of "the public"; the latter often refers to special publics in the form of particular interests, clienteles, and so on. Insofar as story characteristics are concerned, the information officer thinks of those which make a story informative (factual material, announcement of new programs, techniques, and so on); the reporter responds with those which suggest controversy (for example, personality conflicts, covert disagreement, questionable activities). In interviews, for example, 83 per cent of the newsmen respondents ($N = 35$) cited controversy or conflict as the essential ingredient of a news story; 6 per cent of the information officers ($N = 38$) cited this as an essential ingredient. From these interviews, one may hypothesize that, in matters of news definition, actors in the informer-recorder relationship will share common concepts of news, those in the educator-expositor category will both agree and disagree on news definitions, and the promoter-prescriber communicants will often disagree as to the characteristics and appeals that determine news value.

This is not to suggest that the promoter has a false conception of the reporter's news values. Rather it indicates that with respect to this variable, he operates independently of the prescriber in his assessment and his message may be directed at the informer or expositor. Stated specifically, the choice of a news channel by a source depends on whether they share the same sense of news values in the *particular* case. Likewise, the choice of a source by a newsman is a consequence of whether that source shares the same sense of news values as he. For example, we cite a columnist's opinion of information men: "The press officer thinks that he has to put his department in the best light and his boss in the best light. If you start on that premise, most of them will give you anything that is available." Compare this to an interpretive reporter: "If it's a matter of policy, or why didn't he do so and so, or why are you doing so and so; well, then the press officer is

no good; get it from the horse's mouth!" And, finally, the man on
the beat: "If there is a good press officer, then the man in that
position will use his influence as consistently as he can for maximum disclosure of information." This helps to explain why one
reporter may accept the news judgment of one information officer (be assured of "straight facts"), fear being misled by another
(the "wrong slant," a "bad angle"), and fear being managed by a
third ("Nobody likes being used," said one respondent). It also
indicates reasons why an informer may dread the call of a columnist but work quite harmoniously with the man on the beat.

Other possibilities may be suggested for added investigation.
Interviews indicate that in covering an event about which very
little factual material is available, the reporter has a tendency to
assimilate the story into a context of past stories about similar
events or into a context of his own experiences. Although he may
correct the lack of structure in the situation by employing such
frameworks, he may also reinforce the official interpretation of
the event if that interpretation is based on an accurate assessment
of the reporter's frame of reference. Also there is a tendency for a
reporter to accept the official account of an event released in a
cover story when the event itself seems only slightly newsworthy
to the reporter or if there is very little available information from
other sources. The result may be management of news by default.

A final category relevant to the discussion of actors' role
concepts consists of certain trends in political communication
growing out of the relationships between government information staffs and media reporters. Reference is made to the political
context in which information may be considered a substitute for
legislation when used to reconcile interest conflict. One fairly
obvious implication is that the news media have a function beyond
that of simple communication; by channeling information messages of a propaganda nature designed to influence their audiences, the news media perform a policy-making function. That
is, the informational message which obviates the necessity of
formal policy-making is itself policy, and the media in transmitting it become an informal arm of policy-making.

A further trend in political communication, resulting from
the use of publicity as policy, has been recognized by the news-

men themselves—the necessity to break from objective reporting of selected facts and to interpret events in broader contexts.[5] The trend from objective to interpretive reporting, particularly in the press association and network reporting enterprises, is partially explained by the awakening awareness of the necessity to go beyond the publicity activities of government. But, in so doing, is the news media shutting itself off as a channel for official messages that require transmission in the form dictated by citizen needs or official needs rather than by media desires for independence? Also relevant is the question of whether reportorial interpretation is not in itself a form of policy-making, a form defended by the newsman on the normative argument that he is a representative of the public interest. Yet, if he is in the policy-making and representative processes, a question is legitimate, in a democratic society, regarding the nature of the popular controls over his political and representative activity.

[5] Joseph H. Mader, "Government Press Bureaus and Reporting of Public Affairs," *Journalism Quarterly*, XIX (1942), 177.

CHAPTER IV
EXTERNAL INFLUENCES
ON POLITICAL
COMMUNICATORS

Information officers and newsmen obviously interact not only with each other, but with their own organizational superiors and colleagues, other information sources and channels, their audiences, and their personal friends. Their perception of such interactions helps to shape their performance of the information-dispensing and newsgathering processes. We are concerned in this chapter with how the participants' view of these relationships influences their attitudes and behavior.

ORGANIZATIONAL INFLUENCES

The information officer and the organization

Observers point to the influence of an information officer's organizational ties on his personal performance. Carter, for example, suggests that "significant others" in the behavior of news sources generally are the source's superiors, subordinates, and peers in the formal hierarchy of authority.[1] The implication is that the mere presence of the information officer in an organizational environment publicizing organizational activities dictates his behavior, particularly his relationship with other officials of that organization. McCamy, for example, hypothesizes that the publicist role in the organization is oriented toward impressing upon the public that the organization's objective is a legitimate one. This he does through symbol manipulation. The nonpublicity official, however, posits the irrationality of the public and questions the value of information-dispensing. His desire for independence leads to a preference for secrecy, not publicity.[2] Commentary about the influence of the organization on the information officer emphasizes: (1) the influence of the organizational environment, (2) the influence of interactions with superiors and colleagues, (3) the influence of attitudes held by those outside the organization with regard to the proper function of any public information program.

One task of the information specialist is that of finding out from organization officials what is taking place. This means normal reportorial duties of conducting interviews with officials, dispensing information, and providing a screen between newsmen and the policy-maker. Such tasks imply interpretation of the activities of technician, scientist, or administrator; it may imply promotion of the policies connected with such activity. Freedom to perform such tasks is crucial to the success of an information officer and influences his own expectations of personal responsibility within the organizational framework. McCamy also points out that, in agencies in which the officer is prevented from carrying out his duties and receives no cooperation from agency officials, morale deteriorates due to the perceived insecurity of the publicity function itself. Deference and lack of certainty pose problems of status for the information officer. The tendency is for the officer to feel frustrated by what he may perceive as a hostile environment.[3]

Such frustration may effect the officer's view of those in his organization from whom he must obtain information. For ex-

---

[1] Carter, "Newspaper 'Gatekeepers.' . . ."
[2] McCamy, *Government Publicity*, pp. 175–183.
[3] *Ibid.*, 209–210; Pimlott, *Public Relations and American Democracy*, pp. 109–110.

ample, the information officer's failure to receive deference results in his viewing agency officials with a strong sense of resent-
ment. Information officers interviewed often identified problems
of information-dispensing not with the newsman, but with the
source of the officer's information, the agency official. They expressed particular criticism of the civil servant official:

> We find that politicians who come and go in the depart-
> ment and the people who you would think would be very
> bad and very reluctant to say what they are doing are the
> ones who are most eager and willing to give a public ac-
> counting of their activities. It is the administrative people
> down in the career service echelons which often are the
> ones most difficult for us to handle.

> We have people who are down in the line, administrative
> people, who, if the newspaperman gets to them and they
> have never been called before by a newspaperman, . . .
> may not be sure . . . how far this project they are getting
> questions on has been developed. And [the administrator]
> will wonder whether he has any right to talk about it at
> this point because he may not be sure of his facts. What
> [the administrator] thinks is right is only part of the pic-
> ture. If he doesn't [give answers], the newspaperman will
> call me about it; [the reporter] will still want answers.

The effects of an information officer's inferiority complex
on his performance may be several. The informed status of the
officer and, consequently, his value to the newsman as a source
will be minimal in an environment of hostility. The officer not
privy to the intelligence on which policy-makers are acting, but
forced to accept only information flowing to the general public,
is not likely to be of great value to the newsman except as a con-
duit. Newsmen operating on the assumption that political symbols circulating among the power holders "correspond more closely
to the power facts than do symbols presented to the domain," [4]
will seek out upper level policy-makers as news sources in preference to the information officer. The officer-newsman relationship is critically influenced by the degree of acceptance of the

[4] Harold D. Lasswell and Abraham Kaplan, *Power and Society* (New Haven,
Connecticut: Yale University Press, 1950), p. 110.

publicity function by members within the organization itself. The officer is useful to the reporter in direct proportion to the amount of "inside dope" which he can reveal to the press. One newsman stated it thus:

> Well, I think the most important thing is to have an information man that really knows what is going on. So that if you think maybe there is a story somewhere you can at least talk to him and get some clue as to what is going on in the area, because if you have some idea of what is going on you can better approach the officials who may be a little more hesitant about talking to you. If you have to interview blind, you are not as well off as if you can get some kind of information man who knows what it is about. That is the most helpful thing that the government can provide.

Information officers sampled were keenly aware of the necessity to be informed at all stages of policy negotiations—not after decision-making, but during that process. It is not startling to find that information officers not seeing this necessity were the informers; those committed more to explanation, interpretation, and promotion of policy could not accept policy ignorance as compatible with their roles. This fact is convincingly illustrated if we examine the distribution of officers within particular classifications with regard to their opinions of the necessity for being kept abreast of policy developments as an intrinsic part of the process of policy explanation and promotion. Of our class of informers, 40 per cent saw no such necessity; of educators, only 7 per cent were willing to remain uninformed of policy problems; and, as expected, no officer concerned primarily with promotion was willing to undertake his responsibilities without adequate information of prospective changes in policy. Both educators and promoters agreed with one officer who argued:

> If the director of information has to promote the program, has to develop the public relations behind it, it is necessary for him to know and fully understand all of the legislation that is going to be put before Congress, all of the program changes which are initiated by the commission, and all of the questions that might be asked by members of the public who are curious about those programs.

Newsmen naturally turn toward the officer given discretion by his organizational colleagues in publicity matters and kept informed of organizational decisions as they are reached. Reporters interviewed either regarded the officer as an expendable aid and hence not an integral part of their newsgathering activities or took the position that the officer was essential to their endeavor. Of those taking the first position, only 13 per cent were of the opinion that officers had any discretion in information matters; of those who viewed the information staff as necessary to their newsgathering, 68 per cent indicated that they found that officers possessed discretion regarding what information to release and when to release it. Reporters tend to regard the information officer as important to them only if the information officer is first assigned tasks of responsibility within the agency or department. An officer without discretion is expendable.

The officer's interpersonal relations with agency officials is only one factor determining his worth both to the organization and to the press. There are aspects of the officer's status dictated by his formal position within the organization hierarchy which also influence his performance. Normally the information openings within an agency or department are filled not through partisan appointment, but through civil service recruitment. The discretion of the political head of the organization regarding who shall be on the information staff is restricted to a choice of the person normally designated as "assistant secretary for public affairs." The simple fact that information staffs are normally civil servants, not political appointees, has definite implications for the degree of influence any information officer is capable of wielding within the policy-making strata of his organization.

Certainly the agency head or departmental secretary is far less hesitant to place the responsibility for being a "spokesman" on the person he has chosen for the job. Obviously, political responsibility is delegated preferentially to political appointees. Hence, the civil service-appointed information officer is less likely to be given the "agency spokesman" responsibility. But, this is not the whole of the matter. The very fact that an officer is a civil service appointee reinforces his appraisal of his own responsibilities as inherently nonpolitical. This view prevails among civil servants in information positions, even though such officers will admit to performing activities clearly political in character. For example, one such officer, on being questioned about the political nature of the task of information-dispensing, quickly took the view that, "We are all under civil service and our agreement, our policy, under which we operate, is that we are not public relations." It is interesting to note that even in this instance the respondent proceeded to point out that the civil service nature of his appointment might make it necessary for him to protect his organization and his departmental head from criticism:

> If a speech comes out that the Secretary is going to make, and it is fraught with obvious politics, it is a very fine distinction when a cabinet member is talking about this. He has to follow his views and make them known and his policies, and that gets pretty close to politics sometimes.

This fine distinction between what is politics and what is not may be difficult to make, but the officer in question went on to indicate the situation he would define as political and the course of action open to him and his colleagues in such an event:

> But if he gets up, if he has got a speech and he says, "Ladies and gentlemen, I am delighted to see on the platform with me Senator Knox from Idaho who has served you long and well" and gives him a pat on the back at the taxpayers' expense, we take it out of his speech. We say, "Mr. Secretary," and this is with the agreement of the Under Secretary through the Secretary's Press Secretary, "You say that if you want to, but you say that off the record; [then] you are free to say anything you want to." Of course, we can't tell the secretary what to say and what not to say, but we can protect him from getting himself in a jam on the Hill by having a speech published at the taxpayers' expense.

What is clearly reflected in such statements is an organizational loyalty on the part of civil servant officers—a loyalty that pushes them into protection of the agency head. If the political head perceives this transfer of loyalty from the organization to him, he may very well place added responsibilities on the information officer. But if the agency head is not given such protection by officers and is instead regarded as an interloper, the result can be that the officer is then relegated to a "cut-and-paste" function. It is in precisely this situation that the officer may ally himself with the reporter in "trying to get the stuff" out of the agency in an effort to serve as the organization's source of information for the press. Although the reporter prefers to receive his information from a trusted officer in the organization, he remains willing to ally himself with the civil servant officer who has been rejected by the agency head.

If we examine the data presented in Table 2, we are led to the generalization that those officers holding their positions as a result of political appointment are more likely to fall into the promoter classification, while civil service officers tend to be informers. On closer examination, however, it becomes apparent that career type alone is not the only formal variable in operation. For example, although some promoters are civil service appointees, this apparently does not inhibit their activities as public relations agents. Furthermore, it is interesting that civil service appointees labeled as promoters or educators are found in the upper echelons of the information service—as directors of information, news division chiefs, and so on. This suggests that two sets of institutional variables may influence the orientations of the information officer: (1) the formalized norms of career service and (2) the duties associated with a position in the agency structure.

That the organizational influences over the behavior of the officer are complex is further demonstrated when we consider that the type of organization for which the information officer works is also relevant. Officers of regulatory agencies normally view their responsibilities as those of informing the public on factual matters. This is not always the case; one such officer was explicit in viewing promotion as inherent. He looked upon publicity as a major instrument facilitating enforcement of agency decisions. In an agency without punitive powers, he stressed, publicity is vital in assuring compliance with agency demands:

> You see the commission does not have strong punitive
> powers; the commission is a rather weak thing from the
> standpoint of the punitive action it can take. The most it

can do is issue cease and desist orders, and those are rather
[impotent] tools to prevent fraud or prevent cheating of the
public. It is necessary to use persuasion in two ways—by the
timing of an announcement and the packaging of an announcement.

The timing and packaging of an announcement, the means of
persuasion, can be used as instruments to put teeth into otherwise meaningless policies of a regulatory commission. For example, the powers of publicity can be utilized even to control
fraud, an alternative involving less expense and effort than legal
action:

> There are two ways you can control fraud. There are two
> ways you can correct it. One is to prosecute the business that
> is engaged in the fraudulent action, an attack upon the
> seller himself. Another is to wise up the public in order that
> it can protect itself. This means educating the public.

The information officer quoted is quite sensitive to the value of
publicity as a tool of policy. As such, he is willing to define for
himself a rather broad role in the political process. Others, however, show considerable restraint in that definition and insist
that the nature of their position and their parent organization
dictates a restricted informational role. Notwithstanding the case
just cited, this narrow view of information responsibilities is particularly characteristic of the officer serving in a regulatory commission.

Table 2 indicates a considerable degree of consistency between officer categories and the type of organization surveyed, but,
as in the case of career type and organizational position, the
sample permits us primarily to say that the distribution of role
types on the basis of agency is highly suggestive. Several interview
statements strongly support the impression that agency type influences the officer's expectations regarding his tasks. One officer
moving to a regulatory body from an administrative agency
pointed to the difference he perceived in his position:

> Well, as a director of information at a board like this, I
> cannot participate in decisions; however, I can participate

in general functions of the board. I can participate insofar
as I know when decisions are going to be announced, and
insofar as I know who is writing decisions and generally
what attitude the board may take. But I think that a director's primary function should be to serve the board in an
information function rather than as a policy-maker about
information, so I don't think in this type of situation the
director is in on policy.

Although noting that his position within a regulatory body dictated that his service be primarily as a mouthpiece for the board
before the public rather than as a policy-maker utilizing publicity
devices, this officer hastened to add that this was not always the
case. It was not the function performed by all information officers, nor had it been his function in another agency:

> Now this varies with agencies. Where I was before, the
> director of information is taken in at all steps, that is, he is
> a director of public affairs. He is taken in on all steps of
> policy there because they are attempting to promote policy,
> and it is necessary to speculate about what public reaction
> might be. It is different here where we are not so much en-
> gaged in policy-making as such.

To the officer himself, certainly, the type of agency for which he
works dictates the type of performance which he believes to be
expected of him as an information officer. Generally, as an agency
becomes increasingly concerned with its own image as projected
to its clientele, policy-makers, and both public and private competitors, the officers employed by that agency tend to accept publicity, policy-making, and policy-enforcement tasks as dictating the
nature of their performance.

The influences of career type, position in the organizational
hierarchy, and type of organization in which the information
service is performed arise out of the relation of the officer to institutional bodies. An added factor of significance is the relationship of the information officer to his policy-making superiors, a
factor which affects his behavior as a political communicator.
Pimlott has speculated that the officer is under some pressure to
prove that he is worthy of the confidence of his superior in policy-
making; he must demonstrate that he has the capacity to advise

TABLE 2

ORGANIZATION TYPES AND ORGANIZATIONAL POSITIONS
CAREER TYPES OF INFORMATION OFFICERS

Position	Informer (N = 15)	Educator (N = 13)	Promoter (N = 10)
Organization type			
Executive department	20%	54%	20%
Executive agency	33	46	60
Regulatory agency	47	——	20
Organizational position			
Special assistant	13	——	10
Special assistant and/or director	33	8	50
Director of information	——	54	——
News service head	——	30	20
Press or information officer	54	8	20
Career type			
Political appointee	——	92	50
Schedule "C"	——	8	10
Civil service	100	——	40

on matters of high policy.[5] The authority and discretion given the information officer is certainly related to the confidence in which he is held by his policy superior, but this relationship in turn depends on several factors which include: (a) the superior's preferences, (b) the degree of delegation of authority in the organization, (c) the continuing proximity between the superior and officer, and (d) the demonstrated competence of the information officer himself.

Perhaps the central point is the ability of the information officer to obtain immediate and constant access to the policy-

[5] Pimlott, *Public Relations and American Democracy*, pp. 54–55. "The issue which is posed by those who hold that the place of the public relations practitioner is in top management is whether he is also exceptionally qualified to advise on the *substance* of policy. It cannot be decided *a priori*. The onus is on the public relations specialist, whose status as a communication expert is acknowledged, to prove that he possesses this important extra qualification."

maker.[6] The information officer with such access is the one with which the newsman prefers to deal. The degree of access to the policy-maker is one dimension along which we may distinguish different types of officers. There are definite patterns of access when measured by the degree of participation in policy formulation: informers have little; promoters have considerably more; educators are almost equally divided in the degree of preliminary participation in policy-making. As Table 3 illustrates, what is interesting here is the type of officer participation in policy-making. This varies from the most perfunctory type of advising to the more responsible role of recommending what policies must be adopted to win constituency approval for the agency. Regardless of the particular variety of advising, it should be noted that information officers often viewed themselves as defining public opinion to the agency. Some are requested to assess public opinion; others attempt such an assessment as a matter of course, although it may not be used (Table 3). The degree to which this

TABLE 3

INFORMATION OFFICER PARTICIPATION IN POLICY DECISIONS
AND IN ASSESSMENT OF PUBLIC OPINION

Degree of Participation	Informer (N = 14)	Educator (N = 13)	Promoter (N = 10)
Participates in final decision	7%	—	40%
Participates in policy advisement	8	53%	30
Does not participate in policy decisions	85	47	30

is requested of the information officer appears to increase as the officer's access to the administrator increases. The officer conducts a continuing assessment. Whether the superior uses it or not is a decision made by the policy-maker and based on factors independent of what the officer himself considers as information responsibilities. The promoter who views himself as making policy finds his skills at assessment of public opinion in demand by

[6] Dick Fitzpatrick, "Public Information Activities of Government Agencies," *The Public Opinion Quarterly*, XI (1947–1948), 534–535.

agency officials, but this is because he has already been taken into policy circles rather than because he possesses the information.

A significant organizational influence on the information officer's behavior, then, is his relationship with policy-making superiors. This relationship, in turn, feeds back and partially accounts for the value placed on the officer as a news source by the newsman. One newsman claimed it as very important:

> I think that the most important thing that the information guy needs probably is the confidence of his superior—his secretary of the department and so on. He must know what is really going on in the department. If he doesn't have the confidence of his secretary, he is no good.

What the information officer perceives that he can do, as well as his perception of what he does do, depends on the organizational environment of acceptance or hostility, his career type and position classification, and his relationship to policy superiors. Also influential in this connection is the view taken by those outside the organization of what an information officer within that particular agency should do. To some extent, this influences what the officer thinks *he* should do.

A continuing source of external influence of which the information officer is well aware is Congress. Perhaps this results from initial Congressional hostility to information units of executive agencies on the grounds that they could serve as propaganda machines. Or, perhaps Congressional limitations arise out of efforts of interests outside of Congress to curtail the administrative agencies' competing publicity programs. Whatever the reason for Congressional scrutiny, it is significant to information behavior. Officers occasionally find it expedient to ignore the newsman in the release of a story in order to allow an interested congressman or senator to release the information from his office first. Such efforts at building Congressional "good will" are criticized by members of the press. As one newsman stated:

> Well, there has been a tendency in all agencies of government that if there is a good story about to break, to get the congressman, to give it to him first, and let the congressman break it, let him release it. He'll call the house member,

maybe it might involve three or four, or he'll call two senators and let them break it. Well, obviously, the agencies are
playing up to the congressmen for more reasons than one—
appropriations, and for other reasons. I don't think they
should do it.

The newsman does not relish competing with congressmen for
news access, for in any such contest he feels he will lose. In that
contest, of course, the officer is faced with a political decision.
He must, in effect, settle a conflict of interest between reporter
and congressman—one in which each claims to be *the* representative of the people in matters of political communication and each
demands exclusive right, on the basis of that claim, to the release
of information. The information officer is subject to a crossfire
of criticism from both Congressman X and reporter Y. The result is a tendency to play a balancing game:

> If this is something of interest to some congressmen, we will
> let the congressmen know about it. If it is something that
> involved Tennessee why we would call Kefauver, Gore, and
> we would just say, "I have got the story." Now we wouldn't
> do that until the wire services have an even break. I don't
> send it down until the wire services get an even break be-
> cause we can't live in a situation where all the agriculture
> stories are announced on the Hill; the wire services must
> have an even break, [and] that is what we are doing.

Criticism of informational policies is most vocal from those
reporters of regional papers who feel they have been bypassed if
a story concerning their region is not given to them for publication first. It is upsetting, of course, to a regional reporter if the
congressman gets the information first. But it is even more upsetting to him if he learns that he has been circumvented in favor
of giving a story directly to a local paper or to the wire services.
Such action can place the information officer in an embarrassing
position. One assistant secretary for public affairs told a story
regarding the presentation of a particular award for "distin-
guished service." The title of the award bore the name of a former
secretary of the particular department, a former secretary who
had a relative connected with a local newspaper in his home area.
Said the information officer, "Now we awarded it yesterday; we

alerted the news services, wire services, metropolitan newspapers."
But, he said, the "one person we didn't alert" was the reporter of
the newspaper published by the former secretary's relative: "Well,
we fouled up, and so I called the publisher and pointed out to him
it was our fault, not the reporter's."

TABLE 4

SOURCE ROLE PARTICIPATION IN
PUBLIC OPINION ASSESSMENT

Participation in Public Opinion Assessment	Informer (N = 10)	Educator (N = 13)	Promoter (N = 8)
Assessment requested of PIO	30%	38%	88%
Assessment routine but seldom used	40	62	12
Assessment not done by PIO	30	——	——

Other information officers point to Congressional statutes as
mandates preventing promotional activities. The rationale cited
by the officer parallels Truman's view that restrictions on bureaucratic propaganda grow out of claims by legislative groups.[7] An
even more subtle "professionalizing" influence occurs when the
information officer views such restrictions as protection against
a political superior interested in advancing personal interests.
One respondent volunteered:

> In the end, it doesn't pay to use government information
> as a source to advance personal position. For one thing, it
> is dangerous because Congress is extremely jealous of this
> sort of thing—they don't like to see it. An information
> budget is vulnerable if you too obviously use it for improper
> purposes. Congressmen keep their eyes out, especially at the
> opposite party, and if you get too far out of line, you have
> to be stomped down and you know it. In a sense, that watch-
> dog nature of certain Congressional committees like the
> Moss Committee helps the government information man be-
> cause he can always say, "Well look, if you try to get away
> with that you may have to answer to the Moss Committee or
> something." So in a sense, it protects us against doing things
> which we may not want to do because we feel it is improper.

[7] Truman, *The Governmental Process,* pp. 463–467.

In their reactions to the continuing possibility of legislative oversight, information officers are much like public officials in all administrative agencies. They are sensitive to the possibility that Congress has the authority to force curtailments in programs and staffs. Lest such a possibility become reality, officers refrain from offending Congress and, through information release, sometimes cater to Congressional, not reportorial, wishes. The Moss Subcommittee, in its continuing investigation of informational policies of federal governments and agencies, serves to underscore the officer's fear that some day he may feel the sting of Congressional criticism. And, such criticism is quick in coming if reporters grow upset with an agency's policies. During the crisis over removal of Russian missiles from Cuban shores in the fall of 1962, the Department of Defense underwent criticism for withholding information on such removals and then timing releases to suit department interests. Such actions, insisted Rep. John E. Moss (D., Calif.) before the California Press Association, is news management: "We have in the past few weeks experienced a degree of news management which is unique in peacetime, a disturbing period of unplanned and unprecedented news management." [8]

Such quick reaction not only reflects the growing concern expressed by congressmen over administrative news policies but, more important for our purposes here, illustrates a weapon in the stockpile of the reporter who becomes disconcerted over informational policies of federal departments and agencies. News management is one dimension of official propaganda. Congressional criticism of the practice provides both the reporter and the information officer with a quick appeal if either thinks that the other's performance as a political communicator is becoming, as the above officer defines it, "improper" as a result of official efforts to manage, slant, or promote through information release. Hence Congressional oversight can and does exist as a factor influencing officer behavior.

The newsman and editorial influence

A charge often leveled at the American press is that reporters are tools of editorial policy. No matter what the newsman's per-

[8] Associated Press dispatch, *Lubbock Avalanche-Journal*, December 1, 1962, sec. 1, p. 1.

sonal inclinations or value system, so the indictment reads, he cannot report the news as he sees it. He must conform to editorial policy. Or if the culprit is not the editor, it is the publisher dictating policy from behind the scenes. Not all observers concur in such an indictment. Divergent views exist concerning the influence of the editor and publisher on the newsman's behavior. For example, one writer in the late thirties held the view that a reporter's superior, even though far removed from Washington, would have more influence over a correspondent than would any psychological syndrome or social-economic standing in the reporter's family background.[9] Rosten stressed the influence of psychological and sociological variables on the newsman's behavior but agreed that: "The newspaperman whose publisher has a phobia about income taxes may communicate a different version of a Congressional debate than the reporter whose publisher is crusading for government control of profits and unearned increment." [10] Finally a study of social control in the newsroom suggests that newspaper policy is an important determinant of the reporter's behavior because of the tendency to accept the values of the newsroom group.[11]

Newsmen sampled in the present study tended to bear out assertions which attribute only indirect influence over reporters by editors and publishers. In the sample of newsmen interviewed ($N = 35$), only 14 per cent were of the opinion that their reporting was directly influenced by the dictates of their news organizations. Few had ever experienced any threats of reprisal for treating a story in a particular manner. Another 16 per cent insisted they were totally free of any organizational influence whatsoever. But, the remaining 70 per cent were not willing to go to either extreme. They viewed organizational influence over their performance as existing but indirect in nature. An awareness of direct editorial influence was rare among respondents. Some were very firm on this matter:

[9] Cyril Arthur Player, "Review: The Washington Correspondents," *Journalism Quarterly*, XV (1938), 58–60.
[10] Rosten, *The Washington Correspondents*, p. 150.
[11] Warren Breed, "Social Control in the Newsroom: A Functional Analysis," *Social Forces*, XXXIII (1955), 328–332.

No, I think that has nothing to do with editorial view. Now none of the reporters that I know have had any economic sanctions leveled on them. I don't think that they have any awareness of it.

This respondent, of course, stressed the link commonly thought to exist between the economic rewards of journalism and the necessity to please the editor in order to obtain those awards. Another, however, felt that the degree of editorial influence experienced might be more correctly a function of the personal prestige of the correspondent in the business:

I've been here so long that there is no conflict of interest between me and St. Louis. I mean St. Louis is influenced just as much by my view as I'm influenced by their viewpoint. I make a hundred decisions where they make one. I'm not bothered by the editorial page; if they take an entirely different viewpoint from mine, that's their affair. I write it as I see it, and the other people in this bureau write it as they see it, and if the editorial page doesn't like it, well, that's just too bad!

The more common approach was to point out that, as reporters, they share a certain affinity with news organ policy and that attitudes expressed in editorial columns are those with which they agree. The values of the newsman are those of the organization, but not, insists the reporter, as a result of pressure brought to agree with news policy. The following is representative of this thinking:

I don't know that it gives me any particular problems. It so happens in my case . . . well, I lean; I don't claim to be independent politically, I mean I am a Democrat. And it so happens that the paper that I work for is a Democratic newspaper; and while I do disagree with them sometimes on things, I would say for the most part as far as politics is concerned I see pretty close . . . I mean our views are very similar on most things—that's just coincidence. I would say that there may have been times when the editorial policy might have affected me when it should not have, but I don't think that's happened very often.

Some reporters are quick to point to their personal freedom but view their cases as unique. Recurrent among Washington correspondents is the view that the press generally is not free but that they, as individuals, are very independent. Remarks such as the following indicate the tendency of reporters to indict other correspondents for falling victim to the "organization ethic" and to cling to the belief that they alone still represent the bygone days of journalistic individualism:

> Yes, now I have a wonderful amount of freedom in my paper. I have never had anything that I wrote downplayed or not printed that I can remember or played up too much. With maybe a few, very few exceptions, I have never had anything that's been treated back home by my office other than a pretty fair appraisal of its news value. In other words, I may be writing something rather nice and fine about a figure that the editorial page doesn't like, but it still will run. This is not like some people around this town, what they *have to* put up with.

Whether the reporter first has a value system, then finds a news organization with which he agrees, is questionable.[12] Warren Breed suggests that the newsman structures his values as a means of adjustment to the peer group composed of his newsroom colleagues.[13] In order to promote that redefinition, the organization has other means than direct editorial influence. Respondents were keenly aware of indirect editorial controls such as: (1) the type of assignment received, (2) the placement of a story, (3) the space alloted for a story, and (4) granting or withholding of the by-line. One newsman pointed to the significance of story placement as follows:

> I think where the story appears in the paper influences a great many reporters. If he is writing a story that appears on page one, then he thinks that the editors think that's important. So he writes along those lines. If that story appears on page twenty-five and continues to appear on page

[12] Marquis W. Childs, "The Interpretive Reporter's Role in a Troubled World," *Journalism Quarterly*, XXVII (1950), 134–140.
[13] Breed, "Social Control in the Newsroom . . . ," p. 335.

twenty-five, he will think, "They are not interested; and
I'm not writing for page twenty-five."

Such sanctions hold meaning for the newsman, far more
meaning than direct pressure brought by the editor or publisher.
It is interesting to note that such indirect influences are perceived
even by the columnist, the commentator, and the editorial writer.
Additionally, the editorial writer is in a position to experience
direct pressure since he is engaged in the "business of saying what
the newspaper as an institution thinks of the news." The recorder
is more impressed by sanctions of story assignment, the expositor
by sanctions concerned with by-lines, story placement, and particularly space allotment. One bureau chief, explaining the plight
of a member of his staff, suggested the nature of this sanction:

> One of our young men was complaining because, for
> space reasons, they had cut his story. He had given two rea-
> sons for enlarging the House and three reasons were ad-
> vanced for not enlarging it. Well, they cut out part of it so
> it made him look as though he had slanted the story. Those
> are practical problems you are up against, but we try to give
> the arguments on both sides.

Newsmen perceive the consequences of not being allowed to
write a news story as they wish as grave. What disturbs them is
the possibility of being led into "nonobjectivity" and a consequent drying up of news sources. Reporters were generally of the
opinion that the greater freedom given them by their news organization in reporting a story, the greater the ease of access to
news sources. Two-thirds of the reporters interviewed concur in
such a generalization; the remainder see no relationship between
their personal freedom as reporters and their access problems.
The majority of respondents agree with the reporter who
pointed out that a newsman must have freedom in writing if he
is to get news: "I don't think that most public figures of any
standing enjoy dealing with a journalistic horse!" What is involved is an element of trust between the news source and the
newsman, between the source and the channel role. The result is
an unwritten rule that states the newsman shall not misinterpret

the source's information, even at the expense of crossing editorial policy. One information officer was quite pointed in this respect:

> Yes, we don't have this very often, but we have had from time to time the kind of reporters who are always looking for some kind of sensational angle which distorts the thing beyond recognition. Some years ago we complained to one of the wire services about a fellow, and he was taken off the beat because he was completely distorted in his view on a certain subject. He was actually neurotic; no amount of explanation or reasoning would get him out of the groove that he was in. Now this is a very unusual case, but there are reporters—not many fortunately—but there are a few who distort facts to make a better story. Well, we don't like that.

Information officers are sensitive to the needs of interpersonal respect between themselves and the reporter. They are quite aware that their value goes down as they try to "peddle stuff" to correspondents. But they are firm in the conviction that this places on the newsman the responsibility to treat information which is released both faithfully and accurately. One information officer spoke of the evening in which he was called by a "rather prominent reporter" and asked for specific facts regarding a story. The next day the story "had the facts exactly opposite to what I had given him." Stated the officer, "I called him up and I said, 'Well, how did you get that? I told you the opposite!' 'Yes,' he said, 'I know you did, but it made a better story this way.' " The officer, quite obviously, was disturbed by such action:

> Well, that is a kind of cynicism we don't appreciate very much; obviously that is fiction he is writing and not fact, and we don't like to deal with people like that. When a guy gets a reputation like that, we warn our people not to cooperate with him—don't give him any confidences because he can't be trusted.

Apparently, the warning "not to cooperate" stems both from a desire on the part of the information officer to retain his reputation as a source of accurate intelligence for reputable newsmen and that of wishing to avoid trouble with his superior.

In return for accuracy and fairness, the newsman receives the assurance that the information officer will not purposely mislead him or try to force on him trivial information in exchange for the "big" story. As one information officer indicated, "Any information officer who tries to peddle stuff knowing that it is old is pretty soon going to lose his acquaintances, lose his contacts."

To the extent, then, that neither information officer nor newsman is a complete tool of his own organization, mutual understanding of the limitations under which each operates tends to develop a spirit of harmony. At the same time, the recurrent, latent sources of conflict between the two roles may break out at any time. Organizational controls are certainly one source of such conflict. The information officer forced to "peddle" or the newsman forced to "slant" create disturbances in the source-channel relationship.

ALTERNATIVE SOURCES AND CHANNELS

For neither information officer nor newsman is the other the sole source or channel available. The competent newsman builds multiple lines of access into official Washington; the information officer represents one of the more formalized of these. The information officer has other means of communicating to the citizen than through the reporter, although such news channels are perhaps the most significant. Both groups of political communicators must maximize their newsgathering and information-dispensing capabilities. This maximization requires the exploration and development of other access routes. It is helpful in explaining the relation of officer and reporter if we describe and compare other access routes with the channel and source lines which are the subject of this study.

Reporters cite the need for cultivating a vast array of news sources, both official and nonofficial. We might even suggest that the quantity and quality of a reporter's news sources are a measure of his status in the journalistic enterprise. Newsmen accept the premise that the very existence of the information officer forces the reporter to go beyond, to break through to the operating official for news.

Indeed, a fundamental set of expectations in the newsman's trade is expressed in the phrase "to go beyond." The newsman is expected to go beyond the public information staff to ferret out information, to go beyond to the civil servant, to go beyond to the upper management official, and to go beyond to the political agency head. If the information officer is the agency's outlet for news, the reporter feels compelled to hunt even harder among other sources for the unexpected angle. One correspondent summed it up this way:

> Those people are enormously busy and get an enormous number of queries, and I think they earn their salaries. I don't regard them as the answer on most of the stories I get interested in. I think they get bogged down in sort of the machinery of answering the *pro forma,* the routine questions; I don't find most of them are awfully good on the subtle stuff.

Whether the newsman does, in fact, utilize the most available source of news—the information officer—depends on several factors. One of the most significant of these is that of experience in Washington reporting. The old hands at the business place little emphasis on such officers. One correspondent who had been in the nation's capital for twenty-five years dismissed the value to him of the information establishment quite succinctly:

> That's routine. I mean when we get local queries from St. Louis, the Department of Justice or the CAB, SEC, or anything like that, why we go right through the press officer because he knows where the information is. Oh, yes! But, that's routine.

But what is routine for some is vastly more important to others. The young reporter just appearing on the Washington frontiers and anxious to learn his way around as quickly as possible is not quite so willing to dismiss the value of the officer who is eager to please. Note this expression by one neophyte Washington correspondent:

> One of the first things when I came to this city, someone said go over and do some stories on residual oil imports. Well, I never knew there was a thing called residual oil, and

> I didn't know where it came from. Not only that, I didn't
> know why there was a controversy—apparently residual oil
> is a real problem in fuel in competition with coal; and their
> people were just excellent. For instance, a fellow who is the
> oil guy, sort of oil and mineral, but particularly in oil for
> the Interior Department, and he was excellent. Unlike be-
> ing a coal lobbyist or an oil lobbyist who would have given
> me about 40 per cent of it, he sat there very objectively and
> told me what the oil people's stake in it was and what the
> coal people's stake in it was and what the Administration
> was trying to do. He was about as detached as anybody I
> have ever seen. In fact I wish all public relations guys were
> like him; I thought he was just a very honest man and, be-
> yond that, well informed.

Young, inexperienced correspondents find objective sources of
news hard to locate. The information officer with the skill to
make his messages appear nonpromotional and primarily factual
can be an important confidant of the newly arrived reporter and,
hence, build up a stock of good will to be capitalized upon in the
event that correspondent does indeed make a name for himself.

The alert information officer, however, reacts to such a reportorial attitude by seeking out the "subtle stuff" and feeding it
deliberately to the newsman. The anticipation by the officer of
what the newsman wants, the anticipation by the newsman of
what the information officer can give, and the assessment involved
in both operations form a continuing process that makes the relationship of newsman to official news source a dynamic one. The
information officer attuned to reportorial needs can capitalize on
them and turn them to his advantage in dealing with the newsman:

> I spent nine years as a newsman so I think I understand
> what he wants, and I could give him what he wants. But if
> he got the story from me and went back to his boss and said
> he interviewed the press officer, his boss would think he was
> crazy. His boss doesn't want an interview with the press
> officer; his boss wants an interview with someone in author-
> ity. We have to protect the newsman from his own bosses
> and enable him to hang the biggest names that he can on
> the story that he writes.

It is not unusual for the information officer to overestimate the depth of the newsman's probe, then become discouraged because the correspondent lacks the aggressiveness expected. Then the information officer may have more control over the total news-gathering situation than does the newsman who thinks he is "going beyond" to the real source of the news. Notice the following meticulous preparation by an information officer for such a contingency:

> A newsman shouldn't be satisfied with easy answers. I am amazed sometimes at how frequently newsmen take a simple answer and miss an opportunity to ask a more penetrating question which would develop a better story. At press conferences reporters waste an awful lot of time asking pretty superficial questions. We have found that sometimes we have to plant questions in press conferences in order to get the information out. The secretary is prepared to answer a lot of important things and he gets trivial questions.

No matter how the information officer may play the game, however, to the newsman he is not the primary and preferred source of news. Yet, as Table 5 indicates, although the information officer is not the primary source level *desired,* he is the primary source level *utilized* by reporters.

TABLE 5

PREFERRED AND UTILIZED SOURCE LEVELS OF NEWSMEN

Source Level	Preferred (N = 34)	Utilized (N = 35)
Department/agency head	46%	13%
Lower tier officials (careerists, minor political appointees, "colonel cliques")	47	39
Public information officer	7	48

It is revealing that agency heads are not necessarily the most favored sources of news. In fact, some respondents suggested that the man who really knows what is going on is not the agency head, but the official in middle management tiers. For example, one newsman put it this way:

> Well, that's where the longer you're in town, the better off you are because you know some third assistant secretary of something, who is an authority on this particular thing. Suppose I'm writing about the president's proposal for aid to education; I happen to know a guy down in the bowels of the HEW, knows all about how they work out the formula for how much each state shall get. I don't know that because I'm smart, I know that because over the years I've learned it. The same way in the Pentagon. I don't happen to do much Pentagon work, but people who do, know what man and what area and who is an authority on this and that and the other. If you can talk to them without interference of press secretaries or even through them, why you can get your questions answered quickly.

Perhaps it is because he is new to the job, perhaps because he must be secretive, perhaps because his messages are obviously promotional—all are reasons offered by newsmen as to why they avoid the agency head.

> Very often it isn't the high ones who will tell you a story. You know the trouble with those fellows at the top is that they are under tremendous pressure, and they don't always have the story. We find that often the truest information we get on the departments is down lower.

Controversy between government and the press arises out of reportorial desires to contact officials in the lower strata and agency desires to centralize control of the flow of information at one point. Many of the classic problems of freedom of information stem from this conflict. Certainly the public information office can be an organizational device for exerting such centralized control over political communication. That control, even if based upon so-called doctrines of good administration, runs afoul of the reporter's desires to get to the source he chooses. In this respect, the problem parallels centralization of other organizational functions in that certain interest groups—in this case newsmen—find access terminated. That access is vital to the promotion of news interests. The reporter quickly symbolizes those interests in such phrases as "freedom of the press" or "freedom of information." One reporter covering a sensitive agency had the following to say on the subject:

> Well, I suppose ideally if you can get access to the top officials, the top echelons, of the Pentagon, it may be best to do so; but I find very often that these people don't know what is going on. Not only sometimes do they not know, but in other cases where they do know, they will not say what is going on. The middle layers are often the best ones. There is an old cliché around here that it is the colonels who really know what is going on and they are the ones that will talk to you.

However, the reporter is reluctant to take this rule of thumb as his most valid dictum for professional living. Said the correspondent just quoted, "There is always the doubt in the back of your mind—do they really know everything or is something being withheld from them?" And, if the correspondent has that doubt, "it is difficult to rely on them; you have to rely on others."

Nonetheless, a newsman covering particular agencies as a specialty tends to build up a reserve of sources to be called upon in particular situations. This reserve is normally made up of the professionals within the department—professional civil servants, politicians, or armed forces personnel. These are people with virtually permanent status in the lower layers of a department who remain in office in spite of temporary political shifts at the top. Consequently, they are not always attuned to the current promotional dimensions of the information program, but continue in their job day-by-day and draw upon their technical expertise in conferring with newsmen:

> Newsmen around here try to do the best job they can, and they get their best help in that respect from the professionals—the people on top never seem to learn that. They just never seem to understand that if you are going to do a story about an atomic bomber, you don't want to go to someone who is a policy man who suddenly has decided the bomber is bad. You want to go to the man who is tech-

nically equipped to explain the bomber to you, but the people on top are not willing to let him talk because he might give you something that you need. They prefer to apply the lid to him. Well, that takes the professionals out of reach, yet they are the best ones because they have no interest in the political facts, they have interests only in the facts of the program itself and the information which you might want.

In stating their preferences in source levels, many newsmen pointed out that they prefer to go to the decision-maker no matter what his level may be in the agency hierarchy. One newsman of twenty-five years' experience in the covering of a highly specialized department commented this way:

I think the important thing always is to go to the man . . . who really makes the decisions. Now you can't judge in this present administration yet, but that's what really is meant by going high. Sometimes the man at the top may not know all the details that you need to know, you have to go to somebody lower down; sometimes he won't want to talk, and somebody down the line will; your job is to get out the facts, and that's what you keep your mind on. But you reach a point in every story bearing on policy in the grand scale in which you have to have a clear insight into the factors in a situation which will determine a decision, and only the man who will make the decision knows what those factors are.

Such a formula, however, may be of little use to those who know neither where the decisions are made nor where they might possibly be made. For some newsmen, the entire rationale behind their effort is the ferreting out of the decision-maker. Failing this, other, less preferred sources are utilized.

I like to go to the individual who is making the policy if I can find out who he is and if I can get to him. Both of these are not easy to accomplish. You have to accept secondary sources of many stories simply because you can't find out who it is who has laid down policy.

The public information officer is accepted as a news source in the hope that he may provide a clue as to what person in the agency is most likely to have the coveted information.

Newsmen vary on the source level utilized according to the part which they view themselves as playing in political communication. Table 6 indicates the distribution among the newsmen. The prescriber, usually of long experience in covering Washington affairs and having built personal contacts over this period, is more likely to utilize policy-making officials as information sources. Being influential as a political communicator, he may control access lines to important news channels favored by upper-level policy officials and those desirous of publicizing policy.[14] Seventy per cent of those reporters classified as prescribers revealed that their pet sources came from the middle management levels of agencies and departments. They might be career civil servants with a story to tell, minor political appointees not always

TABLE 6

CHANNEL ROLE TYPES' USE OF SOURCE LEVELS

Level Most Often Used	*Recorder* (N = *10*)	*Expositor* (N = *15*)	*Prescriber* (N = *10*)
Department/agency head	——	13%	30%
Lower tier officials (careerists, minor political appointees, "colonel cliques")	30%	44	70
Public information officers	70	43	——

happy with their superiors, or the common "colonel's clique" desirous of speaking out on departmental policy in spite of regulations to the contrary. Newsmen engaged in uncovering explanatory details apparently distribute themselves along all levels of source utilization. For the reporter interested merely in transmitting information without interpretation, the information officer and technical experts are sufficient. Seventy per cent of the recorders sampled relied on the information officer as the primary news source. It is suggested that the source levels utilized by Washington correspondents will vary with (1) their view of their role as political communicators and (2) their length of service.

[14] Worth Bingham and Ward S. Just, "The President and the Press," *The Reporter*, XXVI (1962), 18–23.

Although the public information office is not the primary source level utilized by all newsmen, it is used to some extent by each of them; for many respondents, it is a major source level. As Table 7 indicates, the information office is a major source of story ideas for newsmen surveyed, providing tips, directing the newsman to particular topics, and pointing up items that deserve particular attention. One correspondent who had recently acquired a major scoop praised the value of the information staff which had suggested the story:

> So much happens that I couldn't possibly keep up with it. Sometimes an information man will know of something, and he will call me, and he will say, "Look, here is something." And it will bear fruit.

Such responses are no longer as surprising coming from newsmen as they might have been in the past. The multitude of occurrences which the newsman finds it impossible to handle alone and which his organization can give him little assistance in covering is being reported to the newsman by the information officer. As this glut increases and the officer's function of selecting and transmitting from it grows, the correspondent finds it increasingly necessary to rely on the official news source. This is not a matter of choice, but of necessity. Hence the tendency for respondents to draw a distinction between desired and utilized source levels. The newsman desires alternative sources of news; the complexities of reporting place restrictions on his capabilities in utilizing them. The desire to "go beyond" is perhaps as influential in the form of a myth dictating reportorial behavior as an actual operation in which the newsman engages. It is small wonder that the names of James Hagerty, Pierre Salinger, Lincoln White, and Arthur Sylvester have become increasingly common in news stories —indeed, in some cases more common than those of the officials they represent.

Whereas the newsman desires other sources than information personnel, the officer looks upon the press as a principal channel for information distribution. He has several variations on the general theme, but each variation is aimed primarily at getting

TABLE 7

NEWSMEN'S SOURCES OF STORY IDEAS

Idea Sources (categories not mutually exclusive)	*Percentage Mentioning Source* (N = 34)
Government sources:	
Scheduled functions	56%
Information office (PIO, news release)	40
Congressional tip	25
Secondary officials (experts, civil servants)	43
Top level officials	15
Professional sources:	
Personal curiosity (areas in which the reporter exhibits continuing interest)	38
Colleagues (competitive and noncompetitive)	10
Assignment (beat, scheduled event)	43
Topical (in news, rewrite)	48
Other:	
Friends and informal sources	25
Special interest associates	3

the message into the news media. The most popular alternative means are agency publications and official speeches. Every officer interviewed stressed the importance of the news media as his primary means of reaching the reading, viewing, and listening public.

Other alternatives are open to serve special communication needs. The agency publication is usually directed at a limited audience as, of course, many news releases are aimed at the house organs of special groups. Information officers of regulatory commissions in particular direct their news releases to specialized publications rather than to general news organizations. Departments and agencies do the same with their marginal material— the item in which few are interested, yet requires telling. A major decision-making task is to sort those items which will command mass media attention from the chaff siphoned to trade journals,

speeches, or agency newsletters. Here the news sense of the information officer is significant. Attempts to guarantee the possession of such news sense is one reason for the requirement of news
experience in the recruitment of information personnel. The
nature of this decision-making problem was explained by one
information officer as follows:

> I'm sure that we put out a lot of marginal stuff. I would say
> that the justification is that there is a marginal area of in-
> terest. We put out some releases here that I would say are
> very technical, and we would only distribute a thousand.
> You just can't go by the numbers of pieces of paper that we
> put out; you have to analyze the market that we hope it to
> have.

Perhaps the widest range of choice for the officer deals with
the news channels he will utilize. His selection will vary directly
with his task as a political communicator. Depending on how
strongly he feels about the necessity of selling a particular idea,
he may go beyond the newsman just as the newsman may try to
go beyond him in seeking access to information. The information officer too has a problem in access—access to the maximum
number of people. To maximize his audience, he may ignore the
news media and branch out into the entertainment field. Classic
examples are the use of comic strips as vehicles of policy promotion—hence, the advent of Smokey the Bear on the American
scene. One respondent has another "gimmick" utilized by his
agency:

> We have found that we can inform people better by en-
> tertaining them. We can inform people better when there
> are 40,000,000 television sets turned on with two to three
> people in front of each one if we provide them with some
> entertainment and work our information into those pro-
> grams. When you do that, the information officer assumes
> the mantle of the salesman; it is inevitable, it is something
> that cannot be avoided.

The foregoing data shows quite clearly that neither the source
nor the channel group is wholly dependent upon the other in its

information-dispensing or newsgathering operations. For the newsman, however, the information officer remains a major contact. For the information officer, the news channels are crucial in informing, explaining, and promoting public policy. Neither has absolute freedom of action, but the reporter is seemingly less bound to the information officer than vice versa.

AUDIENCE PERCEPTIONS

Both information officers and newsmen are seemingly aware that there are many masters to be served. One of the masters which the newsman serves is his audience. Similarly, the information officer is concerned with communicating to an audience. But the audience to which newsman and officers refer is not always the same for both. They may have different targets when they work. Indeed, we may suggest that differing audience perceptions of newsmen and officers contribute to their differing views of their responsibilities in political communication.

Speculation exists regarding the influence of the reporter's audiences over his performance as a communicator. For example, the correspondent's audiences of sources, bosses, and readers has been found significant.[15] Lippmann emphasized the role played by the "constant reader" and "the buying public" in determining how the newspaper business is conducted.[16] One observer has stressed that a primary factor influencing the professional norms of the reporter is his perceived obligation to his readers.[17] Another study, approaching the problem from the psychologist's point of view, has hypothesized that what the reporter writes or says is influenced by "imaginary interlocutors"—the audience about whom the reporter is thinking when he works.[18]

The image of the newsman's audience screened from interviews is what the reporter calls the "average reader." The variations on the meaning of this phrase are several, but the following quotations yield some of the flavor and indicate the pattern that is present:

[15] Cater, *The Fourth Branch of Government,* pp. 170–171.
[16] Lippmann, *Public Opinion,* pp. 317–337.
[17] Breed, "Social Control in the Newsroom . . . ," pp. 333–334.
[18] Ithiel de Sola Pool and Irwin Schulman, "Newsmen's Fantasies, Audiences, and Newswriting," *The Public Opinion Quarterly,* XXIII (Summer 1959), 145.

My mother is now dead, but when I came down here she was alive and she was in her seventies. She was a right intelligent woman who grew up in Kentucky, but had come back after an adult life in Missouri. Well, she didn't know everything about politics; in Kentucky internal affairs she had a great gap of knowledge, but she was interested. When I would write a story, I would think of explaining this to her, somebody who had an interest, but not complete knowledge. Those who don't care aren't going to read your story anyhow. Those who are interested are entitled to have you give them full coverage, but not treat them like nincompoops, and not write down to them.

When I sit down to write, I forget all journalists, all newspapermen; I put editors completely out of my mind. What I try to do is write to an informed and interested person who might be a friend. In other words, I try to write as though I were sitting down and having a conversation with an informed friend of mine about the particular topic at hand. I could almost say that I could put at the top of my column each day, "Dear Friend," and then go ahead and write the column.

The way in which the reporter defines "his audience" or "his readers" is a very personal matter. Responses from individual newsmen offer us more than simply the perception of a generalized audience. Often in such responses we find a clue concerning a correspondent's personal reactions to his profession and the members of it. Indeed, in some instances it is abundantly clear that the readers for whom an individual is writing include his competitors in journalism. For example, one columnist took advantage of the opportunity, when discussing his audience, to give his opinions of other writers of commentary:

I'm thinking of the gasoline station attendant; I am thinking of the housewife who reads the paper in the afternoon; I am thinking about a taxi driver—and that type of people. Now Mr. Lippmann, for instance, one of the greatest, most respected columnists in the United States, thinks only of the State Department high official, the university professor, the college teacher, the philosopher; that's why his column is difficult to read for a man who is not very highly educated. When sometimes by accident I slip a five-dollar word into my column, I quickly go to the dictionary and look and find a seventy-five-cents word, because I realize that a taxi driver, and a gasoline station attendant, and the clerk in the store may not be familiar with that word or may not understand its meaning.

TABLE 8

AUDIENCE IMAGES OF SOURCE AND CHANNEL ACTORS

Audiences Perceived	*Sources* (N = *38*)	*Channels* (N = *34*)
General public	22%	33%
Regional publics	13	15
Publics of opinion leaders (influentials, students, informed laymen)	4	17
Specialized publics (clienteles, economic interests)	41	9
Policy-making publics (president, cabinet, Congress)	16	13
Organization publics (superior, editor, bosses)	4	13

One may question the importance of Dear Friend, Druggist from Omaha, Gasoline Attendant, and Folks-at-Home images when it comes to the newsman's determination of what to seek as information and what to write. Does he truly write to such audiences? What we can say is that there is a tendency to focus on interesting as wide an audience as possible in the selection and writing of news. The reporter expresses this generality of appeal in his audience image. Certainly, as Cater suggests, the "instinct" of the reporter is distributive in seeking out widespread readership.[19] Unquestionably, the concept of the general public or average reader received more mentions as a primary audience than any other. Yet, there is an observable tendency (Table 8) to distribute selections among alternative audiences as well—opinion leaders, geographically defined interests, specialized interests, policy-makers, and organizational superiors and colleagues. It appears that the reporter seeks as wide an audience

[19] Cater, *The Fourth Branch of Government,* p. 17.

as possible within the range of what he regards as his responsibility as a writer. At the same time, this determination of responsibility is itself partially a function of the interests to whom he
thinks he is communicating. For the newsman there is mutual
reinforcement between his conception of his audience and his
conception of his responsibilities.

Information officers mention the general public in its various
images to a lesser degree than newsmen do. In contrast to the
newsmen, information officers show a tendency to think of a particular clientele or the special interest of the agency. Here again
Cater's assertion is relevant: the official relates the newsworthy event "to the broad body of record on which he precari-
ously builds his policies." [20] The information officer assimilates
the newsworthy event to policies relevant to particular interests dealt with by his agency. Both his and the newsman's audience images are dependent upon their differing views as political communicators within an institutional complex. We may posit
that the newsman and news source are, in their interrelationship,
oriented toward service to differing interests as a result of differing
institutional ties. Yet one set of interests with which the newsman interacts is that of the information officer; likewise, influential interests for the information officer, those bringing "pressure" on him, are represented by the newsman. The elements of
cooperation and conflict in the source-channel relationship are
attributable not to the nature of the newsworthy event over which
they may quarrel, but to the fact that officer and newsman represent differing interests in the politics of communication. It is
the competition of interests between reporters and officers which
lends tension to government-press relations.

PERSONAL FRIENDSHIPS

Little information is available indicating what effect personal friendships between information officers and newsmen have
on their behavior as political communicators. Such conclusions
as exist are concerned with whether newsmen should or should
not cultivate personal friendships with public officials generally.
These conclusions, based sometimes on impressions of newsmen

[20] *Loc. cit.*

and sometimes on systematic measurement of the attitudes of newsmen on the question, are contradictory.[21]

A problem for the newsman is the continuing possibility that (1) he may be manipulated for promotion of agency policy or (2) he may find himself being too uncritical of agency policy, perhaps even "sitting on" a story. Because of what he regards as the inherent danger of getting "too close" to officials, a newsman may simply rule out the possibility of getting personally, rather than professionally, involved. Or, succinctly stated, "I think it would be dangerous; if you become obligated or not, you take a risk." One newsman stated the problem as follows:

> I've known people that got completely tied up—they probably knew more than the other reporters about what was going on—but their hands were tied, they couldn't write it. If they wrote it, they lost a friend. You are certainly going to find out more from a person if you know them and if you are a friend of theirs than you will if you are just a face or even a stranger.

To many reporters such friendships are primarily a means to an end. They are instruments to be used for other purposes, those of obtaining a story for the reporter's by-line. If they serve such a purpose, all is well and good. But, if they do not, then they should be discarded as quickly as possible in order that the newsman can get on with the task at hand. There is a subtle art in the making and keeping of friendships, one which requires a form of what may best be termed as realistic faith on the part of the correspondent:

> There are people that you can sit down with, and you trust them. You trust their honesty. You would be very, very surprised if you ever caught them in some kind of wrongdoing, stealing, or political skullduggery that you would have to expose. If you did, you would have to write it. But you trust them; you think that they are good public servants. With those people, . . . you can sit down occasionally and say, "Look let's just talk off the record, I want

[21] Alsop and Alsop, *The Reporter's Trade*, p. 16. William L. Rivers, "The Washington Correspondent: Significance for Government" (Ph.D. dissertation, American University, 1960).

to ask you what's going on. I will only use any part of it that you will authorize me to, or I will use it but not attribute it to you; but I've got to somehow increase my knowledge, and I can only do that by talking privately." Now this can be abused. Somebody can say, "Let me talk to you off the record," and they'll tell you something that in the public interest should be reported. Yet you've promised to keep your mouth shut about it. Well, this is dangerous. You've got to then go find it out from some other source, or find it out some other way.

The present study was designed to seek data on this question but was more limited in scope than earlier efforts. Attitudes of information officers and newsmen toward friendships with one another were sought to determine if sources and channels perceived problems arising out of a friendship relationship.

Such friendships do develop. One reason is that many officers are former newsmen and bring to public office their friendship ties from the past. When they occur, do they produce problems? Newsmen ($N = 31$) divide almost evenly in their perception of problems connected with such friendships. Some (52 per cent) avoid such friendships or at least proceed with extreme caution. For example, one newsman offered this opinion:

> Well, I think certainly it can lead to a problem, but there is no reason for it to if you follow a few simple rules. One I follow is that I try to keep this on a social plane. I think it is a perfectly natural thing to have these friends. You see them all the time, you converse with them all the time, so you inevitably have friends among them. But you can keep them on a social level and believe that anything [that] you are told by a friend as a news source should be expressed to you in his office rather than anywhere else.

Others are less cautious in the matter and perceive that friendship with the information officer may be an advantage. Friendships mean that the path for a personal interview with the agency head is made clear; it may even mean the possibility of breaking one of the fundamental tenets of the information officer's code—the release of information to all newsmen at the same time. This tenet is not always followed and, when not, it gives some newsmen a preferred position. Friendships used as tools to get the jump on competition are approved only for oneself, not for the competition:

> The public information officer who is supposed to tell every newspaperman, answer as many questions as possible for him, and to give everybody the news, naturally is going to tend to favor someone with whom he is more friendly. I think this is a human factor that you couldn't eliminate if you tried; you can't eliminate, no matter how hard you try.

TABLE 9

SOURCE AND CHANNEL PERCEPTIONS
OF FRIENDSHIP RELATIONS

View of Relation	*Sources* (N = 36)	*Channels* (N = 31)
Produces problems and should be avoided	7%	3%
Produces problems and requires caution	17	49
Produces advantages and should be encouraged	76	48

Those who perceive no problems in the relationship tend to agree with the respondent who pointed out that friendships are not something that could, or should, be avoided:

> Oh, I think the more friends the better, probably. Most newspapermen are able to judge what they can do with their friendship, and I think the relationship of the friendship is a well understood thing here in Washington. I think the officials, the people who have news, they're the guardians of the flock and the newspapermen are wolves who are trying to pull off a sheep or a lamb if they can. You can be friendly, and yet you can try to get your news. I think the relationship is pretty well understood by experienced reporters and by experienced government officials.

Information officers are much less cautious in viewing such friendships. The possibility of being "used" by the newsman appears remote to them. Faced constantly with the task of competing with other public relations officers, both within and outside the governmental structure, they perceive definite advantages to anything which will make that job easier. This is true whether the category be informer, educator, or promoter. One informer saw it this way:

> In the event that you have a person with the idea that certain news should be withheld or squelched, problems can develop through the existence of friendship. I mean the friendship might end, one or the other of them might lose the argument: neither of them could win. But as long as you have a government information specialist whose primary interest is in the dissemination of news—properly, promptly, and accurately—I doubt that you would have problems develop. I think there is a lot of room for such friendships, and they should be encouraged.

Compare the informer's statement with the following from an avowed promoter:

> I think it is completely inevitable when the newsman wants to cultivate his source and the source, unless he is a man who is completely without any human feelings, is going to want contact with the newsman. Generally speaking under our system I think this works quite well. In my experience I have never known a newsman to kill a story unless he was told, "Look, this one really is dangerous." I cannot recall a single instance of any newsman sitting on or killing a story unless it was presented to him on this national interest business. I have never tried.

All officers tend to agree that the problems that develop would be primarily over questions of when information should be withheld. Friendship with the newsman is perceived as a definite advantage in release of information and in its distribution; problems arise if the newsman is not permitted to print a story which he feels is newsworthy.

For both groups, then, a friendship relationship, although potentially fraught with problems, has certain advantages. Both perceive the crucial problem to be that of determining when a story should be printed. When the reporter perceives danger in the relationship, it is due to his fear of not getting the story; he sees advantages in the relationship if it aids him in getting his story. The information officer perceives danger only if it means a sacrifice of organizational interest by releasing information that might be damaging; advantages are perceived if the relationship helps him to inform, explain, or promote. The basic functional interest each political communicator has dictates the orientation toward the friendship relation. The source perceives the relationship as good if it furthers the interests of telling the "truth," bad if it distorts that telling. The channel perceives the friendship relation as good if it aids in uncovering the "truth," bad if it serves to withhold it.

COMPETENCE AND CONFIDENCE IN THE SOURCE-CHANNEL RELATIONSHIP

We may attempt some provisional generalizations concerning influences on the source-channel relation described in this chapter. An initial question suggests itself: Are political communicators' images of their own functions formed prior to perceptions of other influences, so that the communicator deliberately structures his views of organization, sources or channels, audiences, and friendships consistent with his self-perceived or preferred role in political communication? Or, are such images a product of these factors?

Within the organization, the degree of legitimacy of the information function and the confidence placed in the information officer by superiors bear on how the officer feels he can and should perform. As hostility changes to acceptance, the officer is better able to develop access to agency officials. Less time need be spent searching for organizational news if it is volunteered, and the officer is freed to become an agency spokesman to the press. As his position is accepted, his relations with the press corps improve. Newsmen have greater confidence in officers accepted by an agency as legitimate outlets for agency news. One newsman pointed this out by citing the difference in value to him of an old, trusted information office as opposed to a newly organized one still in its "shakedown" stages of development:

> I think Agriculture in my experience has the best in-
> formation setup; and this is not meant as a criticism of
> CAB or FAA, it is just that Agriculture has had an infor-
> mation program going for so many years and had a con-
> tinuity of personnel there. There are guys there, you go over
> and talk to them, and they have been in Agriculture since
> before the days of Henry Wallace, and they are still there
> in almost the same job. They may be appointed to a higher
> position, but for all practical purposes, they are doing the
> same thing they were back in the old days of the corn-hog
> program. Their help is just invaluable to you. You move
> into FAA and their information setup is definitely hav-
> ing growing pains; the agency now is less than three years
> old, so they had to set up an information program.

As the informational function itself is institutionalized and
legitimized, the officer can develop a distinctive set of expectations characterized by less caution, restraint, and routine. He is
oriented less toward simple reporting and more toward explanation and promotion.

The confidence of the superior is also crucial. As the information officer moves into the development of policy, his responsibility for policy explanation increases. Policy negotiations replace established programs as a frame of reference. How the degree of confidence in the information officer may change was
stressed by one respondent as follows:

> In 1953, when we were established, a man was appointed
> director of information who was a Republican. He had no
> conception of information. He had never had anything to
> do with public information or the news business. He simply
> did not know what should be done in releasing information
> to the public; consequently he was not of much value in
> talking to the administrator, and the administrator didn't
> place much confidence in him, didn't rely on him very
> much. Now we have a new director of information, and he
> is consulted on all policy matters and advises the admin-
> istrator on what policies should be because he is informed
> about public reaction and he can best determine policies
> to alleviate problems. And not only does he advise, but his
> advice is usually taken.

The extent to which confidence is placed in the officer for
policy advisement and development is a function of (1) his po-

sition in the formal information hierarchy, (2) his position in the formal agency structure, (3) his capabilities, and (4) the nature of his appointment. The political appointee is more likely to have this confidence than is the career officer looked upon as more loyal to the organization than to the regime. Imposition of a higher loyalty than to agency itself is sometimes sought. There may then be severe conflict, with the officer appealing to the newsman for support against the political superior. Such appeals are made on the basis that the career information officer will satisfy the access claims of the newsman, but the agency head will not. In this environment, the relationship of career officer and newsman is cooperative and the one between newsman and agency head or political press secretary, one of competition. The "we may get our knuckles rapped, but we do it anyway" attitude by officers may be less a reflection of willingness to serve the press than unwillingness to serve the political master. For informers, the norms of the career civil service position may be greater influence than political variables. If the newsman makes his claim for access on the basis of these norms, the information officer is a close ally of of the newsman's interests.

An example of such a situation is the continuing struggle for news control in defense and security matters. At the outset of the Kennedy Administration, the Department of Defense, faced with traditional problems of leaks, colonel's cliques, and so on, attempted the centralization of informational policies for the armed services in much the same manner as it has attempted unification of the services themselves. The unwritten rules of this centralization, however, did not permit "placing the lid on" until a recent change in administration in which the assistant secretary for public affairs was replaced as a matter of course. New policies restricting release of information from service information offices were forthcoming. This was followed by a quick reaction in the service journals protesting such policies, a reaction echoed, if not first advanced, by the information offices themselves.[22] Reactions of service information officers interviewed were as unfavorable as those of newsmen, but became more favorable to centralized

---

[22] For press reaction to the policies see "The Right to Know," *Army Times,* April 29, 1961, p. 12, and "Defense News Policy Collision Course Set," Ted Bush, *Navy Times,* April 29, 1961, p. 4.

control over information as the interviewer went higher in the department itself. The "news as weaponry" concept employed in the Cuban crisis of 1962 was more compatible with the interests of policy-makers and upper echelon information officers than with those of newsmen and lower status information staffs.

Between political and career information officers, the newsman may be faced with a dilemma in the choice of his news sources. The political appointee is on the inside of policy decisions, has discretion over information release, knows more, and seeks publicity for policy purposes. These assets, however, are offset by his tendencies to be secretive about policy negotiations and desirous of putting a good face on his work. Although the career officer knows less about the inner workings of decision-making, he can be more willing to go "to bat" for the reporter in getting information out of the agency.

Organizational influences affect the newsman also. To the extent that they force him to misinterpret the official message, these influences have a direct affect on his access to the news. Furthermore, as the newsman becomes free to select his own stories, work out his own interpretations, and inject his own opinions into his writing, his relationship with the information officer changes accordingly. Perhaps part of the happy harmony between wire service reporter and information staffs results from organizational restrictions prohibiting editorializing in news stories. The recorder is often most restricted in this respect and limits himself to recording because such restrictions permit him no other choice. In this respect, he resembles the informer, bounded by organizational restrictions in the form of hostility to the information function and lack of confidence from the agency head. In the case of both newsman and information officer, changes in organizational parameters lead to changes in orientations of what each could and should do as political communicators.

Whereas organizational influences are independently significant, orientations toward alternative sources and channels are much influenced by political communicators' views of their political roles, not vice versa. Newsmen simply reporting what government officials say they are doing—the so-called pseudo-event

—may not be overly concerned with sources other than information officers.[23] Officers can either (a) give him the answer he seeks
or (b) tell where to go to find it—encyclopedic and card catalogue
functions. The newsman expositing or prescribing courses of action takes a different view of the necessity of compiling innumer-
able news sources for emergencies. The same reasoning tends to
hold for the information officer. The informer telling only the
factual "who, what, where, when" without "why" and "how" looks
for the channel most appropriate to the transmission of routine
information. Those interested in the explanation and promotion
of policy may resort to official speeches, entertainment media, and
selling campaigns to get the point across. For both information
officers and newsmen, role perception as political communicator
influences behavior.

Orientations toward audiences are, then, directly related to
the idea of communicator role. The audience image of the information officer stems partially from his service to particular
clienteles—farmers, laborers, defense contractors, broadcasters, air
lines—in an agency established to serve or regulate such interests.
The information function of that agency is directed toward the
special interests that provide the rationale for the agency's existence. Seldom does the general news story come from such an information office unless the implications of the special interest's
activities are such as to have consequences for a larger public.[24]
A case in point is exemplified by stories arising from the information office of the Civil Aeronautics Board after a particularly dis-
astrous air crash. The newsman has a certain audience image.
This takes the form of an "average reader" to whom all things
must be made clear, never opaque. But, the science reporter writing of the political implications of changes in technology envi-
sions himself as communicating to a different "general public"
than that of the farm correspondent. Still the tendency is to gen-
eralize his special audience and think of it as the "general public"; the information officer thinks more concretely of special pub-

[23] Daniel J. Boorstin, *The Image: Or What Happened to the American
Dream* (New York: Atheneum, 1962), pp. 7–44.
[24] John Dewey, *The Public and Its Problems* (New York: Henry Holt & Co.,
1927), pp. 3–36.

lics and communicates directly to them. In choosing the newsman as a channel of his communication, the officer is forced to accept the newsman's myth of the generalized public. The result is a critical decision—when to make the message general and use news channels as means of transmission and when to specialize it for a channel other than the mass news media.

In the case of the information officer, his desire to distribute *his* agency's information leads him to accept friendship with a newsman as positive if it promotes that distribution; his desire to protect *his* agency from criticism, however, may lead him to emphasize the negative aspects of a relationship which could require premature revelation of details. The newsman, on the other hand, emphasizes the positive aspects in connection with just that possibility of obtaining secret information; he emphasizes the negative aspects if friendships endanger reporting, explaining, or prescribing. "The reporter would rather kill his friend than his story" is the form in which one newsman expressed it.

This chapter suggests that source-channel relations are both cooperative and competitive. Which is more characteristic depends partially upon the interpersonal respect between information officer and newsman. Mutual confidence and recognition of competence reflect that esteem. Each emphasizes the other's skill and integrity if (1) each has the confidence of his own organization, (2) conflicting audience images are not perceived, (3) each regards the other as a prime source or channel, and (4) there are shared attitudes toward the friendship relation. Elements of harmony and disharmony are blended through awareness of qualities and conditions of mutual trust. Government-press relations begin at just such a personal level.

CHAPTER V
THE SOURCE-CHANNEL RELATION: PATTERNS & VARIABLES

There are three basic patterns of source-channel interaction. In the first, the reporter and the information officer are in regular contact. Each is a primary source or channel for the other. Communicators—in this case informers and recorders—share views of their personal responsibilities. They cooperate to communicate to the citizen. A second pattern occurs when officers and reporters utilize each other's services less consistently and not to the exclusion of using other sources or channels. There is less harmony between actors in this relationship than in the cooperative type, but enough remains to resolve conflicts that might disrupt relations entirely. Such harmony stems from similar, although not identical, views held by communicators—for example, educators and expositors. This type of source-channel relationship is essentially compatible.[1] A third pattern is characterized by minimal

---

[1] Compare the terminology here with that of Lasswell and Kaplan, *Power and Society*, p. 7. "Compatibility is the relationship of acts neither integrated nor in conflict." Compatibility as used in this study differs from the Lasswell and Kaplan definition. Compatible acts are those which occur in a relationship even though some conflict may be present.

contact between officer and reporter. Divergent views of their roles as political communicators make this relationship basically competitive.

Such patterns arise from specific role definitions of source and channel communicators. They, in turn, affect communicator perceptions of (1) ideal news sources and newsmen,[2] (2) story values, (3) news and information as values, and (4) assessments of officer and reporter performances.

THE "GOOD" NEWS SOURCE AND THE "GOOD" NEWSMAN

Newsmen are quick to comment upon inadequacies of news sources. Sometimes sources are guilty of the cardinal sin of putting out too much information; or, they accuse sources of withholding information.[3] Underlying such criticisms are basic views of an ideal news source. Information officers, on the other hand, have their own images of ideal sources. The officer's utility to the newsman as a source is dependent partially upon how closely he fits the reportorial definition of the ideal news source. Although it was not feasible to determine whether actual information officers possess the precise qualities the newsman seeks in a source, a fruitful attempt can be made to determine how closely the images held by newsmen of their "good" news source coincide with the concepts of information officers of the "good" PIO. The question is, how closely do the characteristics information officers think they should possess for their own task compare with attributes which newsmen demand in a qualified news source?

Table 10 indicates the qualities most often attributed by newsmen to the "good" news source and by information officers to the "good" officer. Reporters emphasize that the "good" news source is likely to possess a fine sense of news values and selects the significant news item for the correspondent. The newsman is not equipped to handle a wide variety of information; pressures of time and limited talent make it difficult to search through the infinite variety of newsworthy events. Hence, he prefers the news

[2] Carter, "Newspaper 'Gatekeepers'. . . ."
[3] Fletcher Knebel, "Public Relations at the White House," *Public Relations Journal*, XII (1956), 4. See also Reston, "The Job of the Reporter," pp. 92–108.

source that makes his task easier, the source that knows what items deserve significant publicity. The following newsman's remarks are illustrative:

> It takes a certain interest in news and in the fellow himself. You find most good news sources would have been good newspapermen. They are interested in the development of the news story. You can take some people right in the middle of it, and they can be perfectly frightful news sources because they just have no consciousness of things. I think most of the people who are good news sources have done well and have a great sympathy for the people in the news business. They know what is of great value, and they notice the interesting fact.

TABLE 10

PERCEPTIONS BY NEWSMEN OF A "GOOD" NEWS SOURCE
COMPARED WITH PERCEPTIONS BY INFORMATION OFFICERS
OF A "GOOD" INFORMATION OFFICER

Attributes (categories not mutually exclusive)	*Percentage of Respondents Mentioning Attribute*	
	Newsmen $(N = 35)$	PIO's $(N = 38)$
Responsible attitude (to public and press)	22%	66%
Sense of news and publicity values	84	98
Personality attributes	38	36
Sense of responsibility to agency	17	35
Informed of agency activities	46	——
Intellectual capacity	——	36

Here we see the quality of empathy sought by the newsman in his source. To be informed, to be "in the middle of it" is not enough. There must be some capacity to see the "newsworthy" item among all of the chaff which passes through any governmental office in Washington daily. Furthermore, there is the definite implication in such responses that the source should take the lead in reporting by "being conscious of things" and by "noticing the interesting fact." To the newsman, the "good" source alerts the reporter to the significant, not vice versa. It is precisely this expectation on the part of the reporter which poses a recurring problem in government-press relations; that is, must the press always react to the leadership of the official in matters of political communication, or does the press have an independent and responsible function to perform as "fourth estate?"

Such an emphasis on the source's capacity in the development of a story is notable, for it stresses the very rationale behind the establishment of information offices—aid to the newsman in covering government developments. This aid requires that the information officer have an accurate news sense. Officers themselves are aware of this requirement. Few failed to mention a sense of news and publicity values as a vital prerequisite for their jobs. Interestingly enough, informers point to their news sense as an aid to the reporter, whereas promoters stress this sense as useful in "getting through to the American public—for instance the guy and what about his sick cow—an ability to articulate that."

Not all newsmen, however, desire this ability in their sources. Prescribers and expositors, for example, are suspicious of the officer with this ability and point out that it is far more important for the source to have a sense of responsibility to the citizen and the citizen's agent, the reporter. Too good a news sense, unless coupled with a responsible attitude, leads, they argue, to purposeful management of the news to mislead and misinform the press. Above all, stresses the reporter, the source should be willing to talk first, then worry about the news value of what he has said afterward. "I don't really care whether he has a sense of what the news is," said one expositor, "that's *my* job." One correspondent made the same point by way of analogy:

> He should have a sense of just wanting everybody to know what he knows. He just can't hold a secret; he is just like money in the pockets of a drunken sailor when he gets some choice information, he's just got to tell you about it, almost like a neighborhood gossip. Now you have to sift out the

> part that is unfounded gossip, malicious gossip; but still you have to get him talking. And he has to be somewhat loquacious. I say he has to have that sense of urgency of wanting to tell everybody everything, almost a blabbermouth.

Information officers also emphasize a responsible attitude as essential in dealing with the public and the press. In fact, they do so to a greater degree than newsmen interviewed. Informers reason that, since it is the newsman's job to determine news, the officer's primary attribute should be a sense of service to public and press, avoiding any exercise of discretion over news:

> I think perhaps if I had the last word on the matter, it would be my inclination to do away with all departmental news releases. The reason is that a news release is essentially a substitute of our judgment for the newsman's about what is news. When we write a release we are saying to him, "Here is the news of the department today." I don't think this is the best way to do it; it simply takes out of his hands the judgment which he should exercise and puts us in the job of managing the news.

Twice as many information officers as newsmen mentioned that the incumbent in the source role should possess a sense of responsibility to his own agency. The definition of this sense of responsibility varies considerably. Some information personnel insist it includes protection of the agency against negative publicity. Others feel it is simply a matter of doing "what my boss tells me to do." Less than 20 per cent of the newsmen sampled listed this sense of responsibility to agency as an attribute they prefer in their news sources. This pattern—officers viewing a sense of agency service as desirable but newsmen not recognizing it as such—is conducive to the competitive character of source-channel relations.

To newsmen, second only to "news sense" is the requirement that their sources be informed of government operations. They single out for criticism the official desiring personal publicity without a satisfactory news story to back it up. But if newsworthy, such publicizing is acceptable. Information officers fail to mention this attribute specifically. We may recall that officers were quite open in citing the necessity that officers be informed in carrying out their function properly. This is a quality so taken for granted about information personnel that officers tend to ignore it as a specific attribute. Information officers did cite intelligence and intellectual capacity as necessary in a source. A few criticize their fellows for not possessing these qualities:

> Many information people do not know a press release. The worst are former lawyers; when they get hold of a story they so completely chop it up it is laughable; you just have to sit and laugh at it when you get it back. Other information people aren't capable because they are not smart enough to be!

Newsmen failed to single out this quality of intellectual capacity, perhaps because they felt it to be included in the more general attribute of being informed. Such a tendency was revealed in several statements by reporters:

> I can't think of any attributes of a good news source. Of course knowledge of what's going on; this is very important. I suppose that might be implied too. You know there are the usual things: knowledgeability, intelligence, sensitivity, and this kind of thing. All of these I would assume you would presume, and I would too.

Newsmen speaking of source attributes and officers speaking of the characteristics they like in their colleagues mentioned the necessity of certain personality patterns. Both groups mentioned the same personality traits: "easy to get along with," "easy to talk to," "pleasant personality," "gets along well with correspondents," and "patience in dealing with people." Both groups stress the necessity for capitalizing on the "hail-fellow-well-met" image.

If one extrapolates the newsman's view of the "good" news source from the interview data, the following profile develops. Newsmen prefer the source who knows what makes a story newsworthy and publicizes his policies because he "believes in the process of communication." Preferably he should possess personality traits that enable the newsmen to "get along" well with him. As a safeguard to public and press, the source should have a necessary sense of responsibility to both—a sense of responsibility imposing restraint against temptations to overpublicize, misinform, or protect the agency's record at the expense of public knowledge. Additionally, he must be informed of what is going on in his organization.

If the governmental environment in Washington were filled with ideal information officers by the officer's own definition, would they be the ideal news sources of the newsman? In a few respects, they would. The critical sense of news values and the desire to inform or publicize would be present. They would be well informed. But, the information officers sampled often spoke of responsibility to public, press, and agency. Depending upon which of these responsibility concepts is emphasized, the information officer may qualify or disqualify himself as a "good" news source for the reporter. If the news and publicity senses of the officer are combined with a subjugation to institutional loyalty, the newsman, suspecting efforts at news management, may be wary of utilizing the officer as a news source. If the news sense of the officer is combined with a feeling of responsibility to the public and press, however, the information officer may meet the essential qualifications of the "good" news source in the newsman's eyes. Officers were acutely aware of this and indicated the necessity of balancing the interests of press and public with those of agency if maximum service to the latter was to be achieved. For example, one director of information of long experience put it this way:

> You have to practice some selection and call members of the press only on good stories; not all actions of the commission are bell ringers, so you make sure that you pick out only the bell ringers and inform the press about those. If you call them on every case, you cheapen your actions so much that newsmen are not going to be able to have any respect for what you are doing. You are not going to be of any service to them, and you are going to be less effective in your service to the commission.

At times the officer is required to place one interest over the other temporarily such that the reporter, for example, becomes a tool to secure agency interests, or vice versa. If the reporter's interest is given preference, the relationship between source and channel is cooperative; if the agency's interest is preferred, the relationship is characterized by increasing conflict. More often the officer, as the "buffer" or the "man-in-the-middle," must balance the interests of both, which leads to a dynamic relationship of tension-compatibility between officer and newsman.

These generalized images held by the newsman and the information officer of the good source and good officer respectively reflect a range of orientations by channels and sources toward their respective functions, roles, and interests. The model of the good information officer compares favorably with the newsman's "good" news source when actors share basic role concepts as communicators. The models differ when there are differing operational requirements in the roles of each. The cooperative nature of the enterprise between information officer and newsman may become so reinforced that it pervades the newsman's thinking of what qualifications the officer should have. He tends to think about the qualifications he sees in those officers of the agency he covers. Hence, informing requires a capacity for empathy:

> Yes, he has got to be, I don't know whether it is a good term or not, but you have to be a quasi-reporter. In other words, he has got to have the reporter's instinct. He needs to have it because here often you see the information man try to argue and fight with the administrator about handling some stories and some stuff like that. It has happened many a time. "Well now listen let's tell the boys this, let's tell the boys this, give them the whole hullabaloo, tell them the whole story," or "Let's don't put this out now, let's hold it back because of the timing angle." In other words, the good information man has got to project himself in the role of the reporter and of the editor.

To examine this problem from a somewhat different perspective, one may compare the perceptions of information officers of the qualities of the "good" newsman with the newsman's own perceptions of such attributes (Table 11).

Information officers place great emphasis on the professional qualifications of the newsman. The news judgment, writing ability, and experience of the newsman are items to which information officers are quite sensitive. Officers tended to agree with the expression of the following respondent linking professional qualities and knowledge of what is being covered: "Experience and a knowledge of the programs, many of which are infinitely complicated, are essential; he has to know what he is writing about." For a few information officers, the mark of whether the newsman possesses news judgment is his willingness to report unedited the information in an agency press release. Occasionally a respondent

TABLE 11

PERCEPTIONS BY INFORMATION OFFICERS OF THE "GOOD"
NEWSMAN COMPARED WITH PERCEPTIONS BY NEWSMEN
OF THE "GOOD" NEWSMAN

Attributes (categories not mutually exclusive)	*Percentage of Respondents Mentioning Attribute*	
	PIO's ($N = 38$)	Newsmen ($N = 35$)
Intellectual	69%	82%
Character	10	31
Educational	8	43
Personality	10	20
Physical	3	23
Professional	79	51
Responsible attitude	14	22

would report with pride that the stories printed in the press from his agency were those he had prepared in his handouts, "sometimes with only the lead changed."

An often mentioned characteristic of the "good" newsman cited by information personnel is that of integrity. Upon probing, this quality was defined by officers either as a basic character attribute or, more commonly, as a quality directly connected with a sense of responsibility toward a vaguely perceived public. Honesty and integrity were more often defined by officers as the newsman's recognition of the "public interest"—a definition which then should be identical with that of the information officer. Integrity in the newsman at times comes quite close to being defined as "seeing things about as responsible officials see them." A promoter expressed the following view of what is meant by reportorial integrity: "I also—and this is something which has become I think fairly important especially in recent years— I believe that the newsman has to have a certain integrity in being concerned about the public interest." Integrity, he argued, was largely a matter of printing only those things which are in the interest of the public. And, who is to determine this? For the most part, this is a governmental responsibility. The reporter's responsibility extends to making a judgment regarding what the consequences of his story will be on the public. "Good" consequences make for a good story; "bad" consequences mean the reporter is not acting with integrity. The officer added that this had not always been the case; a responsible attitude on the reporter's part—integrity—was seen as a modern phenomenon: "Now twenty years ago, I don't think it was quite as important." The reason such integrity has become necessary is apparently the increasing scope of the influence a reporter can have and the nature that influence can take:

> For example, a man discovers, or thinks he has discovered, that there are capsules of radioactive material scattered around Pennsylvania Avenue, and he rushes into print about this. He is . . . responsible for obvious reasons—impact on the public.

The qualities the information officer wants most in his newsman are those of professional skill, intellectual capacity—often to catch the subtleties of the agency program—and a responsible attitude toward the dispensing of information closely akin to the attitude held by the officer himself. Table 11 indicates that these are also attributes mentioned by newsmen themselves, but neither to the degree cited by officers nor to the exclusion of emphasis placed on other characteristics. Intellectual capacity was most often mentioned and mentioned by the highest percentage of channel respondents. There is an intense awareness among many newsmen of the growing complexities of modern reporting. Such reporting requires that the reporter: (1) be interested in his job, (2) be curious, and (3) be capable of grasping the subtleties of government operations. Of the three, interest and curiosity are considered uppermost. As one respondent put it, "If he's curious about things, if he wants to go out and find out about it, he must have initiative, he must have imagination." One newsman drew the following parallel between news reporting and reporting generally:

> You would be silly to hire a sports reporter who wasn't excited about who would win a football game. You don't necessarily have to have a sports reporter who was quarterback of the team, or who even played on the team, because participation is not necessary for interest, but if a man was bored with football, bored with basketball, bored with baseball, it would be ridiculous to put him in the sports department. And it would be equally ridiculous to put in the public affairs a man who didn't care who won the election, a man who didn't care who was going to be mayor, or what a board of aldermen was going to do tomorrow, or who didn't find the state legislature exciting, or the Congress exciting. Interest should be your first qualification!

The possibility of a reporter being competent without the possession of intense interest in his craft was considered remote. It is the essential characteristic to the profile. A single respondent found it the essence of success in the journalistic profession:

> I think that anybody that likes it is likely to do pretty good at it. This business of writing can be learned. I think that anybody who really revels in the business is very fortunate, and he will be very good. I don't think there is any other, because if you like something you can do it; then you love your work.

One Washington correspondent has pointed out that reporters are quick to emphasize "the purely physical requirements of the craft." [4] Although newsmen sampled were more likely to mention the physical qualifications of the good newsman than were information officers, such qualities were not mentioned by

[4] Cater, *The Fourth Branch of Government*, p. 1.

either group with any degree of regularity. The most often mentioned attribute, in fact, was intellectual capacity—interest, capacity to think, a quick mind, a disciplined mind, and curiosity.

The reporter in a technological age needs brains as well as shoe leather and subway fare. As in the case of other professions in an organizational society, skills tend to replace the captivating and engaging personal qualities that qualified one for success in a far simpler age. Professional skills were regarded by respondents as a necessity. The ability to write the "simple declarative sentence" was often cited as essential. Little respect exists for the "leg man" who is adept at gathering news but who must then give his story to the rewrite desk because of an inability in written expression. As one bureau chief expressed it: "I don't mean you should be necessarily a fancy writer or a colorful writer, but should be able to make what is going on in government interesting to people, something they will care about." Newsmen generally agreed that stories had to be simple enough for general comprehension as a test of their expository abilities. On the other hand, they stressed the necessity of being well versed in their particular area of competence. This is the era of the specialized reporter; gone, thought some respondents, is the day of the Jack-of-all-trades.

> The college-trained, the college-graduate type of journalist or reporter is a relatively new thing. In days past, the person could write for both the sports pages and be a political columnist. Bob Considine is a good example. He can write about anything; it doesn't make any difference whether he is covering the Olympics, the World Series, Khrushchev or the Eichmann trial; it is all the same to him. This is true of many of the old-timers.

This, said the reporter, is a situation which is changing rapidly. For one thing, the requirements of the trade are such that specialization is necessary to cover a story. But it is also necessary for another reason, and that is to keep the correspondent interested in his job. Unless the individual is an expert, reporting can "be pretty dull for him" stressed one reporter. And this is due largely to the nature of the reporter's background. No longer do newsmen learn the business by serving extended apprenticeships, but rather by going to college. A young columnist added "nowadays the college graduate comes directly into some sort of reporting, and he needs something a little more to keep him interested than simply the excitement of the profession." That something is expertise.

The newsman thinks expertise is needed not only to keep things interesting and to understand the complexities of modern reporting, but also to get the story in the first place. Working in an environment of competent people, it is argued, requires competence:

> When you go in and talk to a public official, the man should feel here is a man who knows what he is asking about and who has got the intellectual capacity to understand what I am saying to him. Well, then a reporter should not deal with public people unless he has familiarized himself with what they are doing. The worst thing in the world a reporter can do is go in and talk to a man in any field and not understand what the man is doing. You can't ask intelligent questions unless you know; you can't get answers out of the man unless you can ask intelligent questions. That is important.

The reporter does not ignore integrity. In the newsman's framework, integrity takes on the quality of a character trait, absolute in its possession or absence. As one newsman stated, "Of course you can't replace integrity; I don't know how you go about finding out whether the man has integrity or not, but honesty and integrity he must have." The newsman considers possession of this fundamental integrity as producing problems in formulating official friendships, dealing with his superiors, exposing policies prematurely, and reporting what the public does not wish to hear. The responsibility which he must bear was described by one editorial writer:

> You ought, of course, to have qualities of initiative, imagination, and of course, integrity—the ability to recognize that this calling is colored with public responsibility, that you have an obligation to use what you learn responsibly with-

out malice, without personal vindictiveness, to use it in
the public interest because it is serving in an instrument
of public welfare. He's working, it's true, for a private
business, but it's a business which affects the public interest
and which has a privileged position, which carries with it
a public responsibility.

The emphasis upon personal integrity, personal enthusiasm,
personal expertise, and personal pride in authorship expressed
by many newsmen still retains a nostalgic air about it. Perhaps,
as Cater insists, the reporter considers himself as the "supreme
individual in the age of the organization man." [5] It is interesting
that the criticism most often leveled by newsmen against their
own brethren was that "there is a certain amount of follow-the-
leader among newsmen." One sharp criticism by a newsman of
his colleagues was voiced as follows:

> Another thing a reporter should guard against in the
> press corps is writing in a pack. Some leader of the press
> corps—some well-known correspondent or columnist—he
> sounds the alarm and says, "This is the way to go, boys,"
> and they all follow in mad confusion. And he sets the tone
> and everybody seems to accept the fact that what he says is
> right, and that whoever they are writing about is wrong. I
> think that there is a mob influence or tendency among the
> press corps that's bad.

What is really posed here is the problem of a leaderless press. In a
period when highly structured organizations, gigantic in size
and scope of function dominate the American political, social,
and economic scene, the reporter still prefers to be the lone wolf.
But such an individualistic role in society increasingly requires
competence and an ability for responsible judgment from the
correspondent. If he possesses both, he may fight off the tendency
to follow the crowd. If not, he may fall victim either to writing
with the "journalistic pack" or, even worse to many a correspondent, becoming a "tool of the administration." In either event,
crowd behavior may be substituted for individual insight. The
reporter does not want to be led, but increasingly he finds no

[5] *Ibid.*, p. 2.

other choice. To many newsmen, the result of being torn in both directions is to withdraw from the conflict and unconsciously commit oneself to blandness. The failure of the press, pointed out another correspondent, is a lack of subtlety:

> I think there is a tendency to take the sort of obvious, and it becomes sort of a volley of the obvious. I think the press ought to look a little bit more for the subtler issues, to try to get away from the obvious ones. I think what we want is not stereotyped and follow-the-leader thinking; I think we want thinking individuals. I think that is the most important thing.

From the data, of course, it is not possible to tell whether only the newsman visualizes himself as an individualist or whether the information officer shares the sentiments that the "good" newsman possesses individualistic traits. Although agreeing with the reporter that professional skills and intellectual capacity are fundamental traits of the "good" newsman, officers placed less emphasis on qualities of education, personality, and character. It is suggested that information officers look for intellectual and professional characteristics in the newsman that facilitate distribution of information—curiosity in seeking information, capacity to grasp its meaning, and skills with which to communicate it. Newsmen too emphasize the necessity for the reporter to be interested, curious, informed, specialized, educated, and skilled in communication. But one cannot avoid the impression that newsmen feel the need for enthusiasm, specialization, and communication skills as personal weapons in a competition both with government and each other; they want newsgathering to be personally identified with the reporter and not with the impersonal organization by which he is employed.

Perhaps most significant is the fact that information officers and reporters share many of the same ideas about what qualities they want in a newsman. To the degree that the information officer shares the newsgatherer's definition of the model newsman, conflict between source and channel roles is lessened. In a cooperative pattern, information officer and newsman judge the actual role performance of the reporter within similar frameworks of expectation. Each can anticipate the reactions of the other to deviations from the ideal and adjust his behavior accordingly to maximize the effective use of the other as source or channel. The presence of similar or diverse concepts of the ideal newsman between actor groups indicates cooperative, compatible, or competitive patterns in the source-channel relationship.

NEWS STORY VALUES

Many students of the American press have observed that there is a difference between what a news source sees as the necessary ingredients of a good story and those characteristics the newsman perceives as significant.[6] Analysis of our data lends credence to such assertions. Information officers and newsmen were asked to choose the characteristics which they value most in a news story and to guess what they thought would be the characteristics their opposite number (reporter or officer) would name. Responses fell into categories of: (1) accuracy, (2) comprehensiveness (accurate facts reported and all facts included), (3) interest to the reader, (4) utility to the reader, (5) utility to the originating agency, and (6) topicality. The distribution of both choices and guesses by information officers and newsmen appears in Tables 12 and 13.

Is truth the number one story value shared by both the newsman and officer?[7] Accuracy and comprehensiveness are both attributes relevant to the consideration of "truth" in the study. Table 12 indicates accuracy to be the characteristic most often named by information officers as essential to a good news story. This general concept of accuracy information officers define as the statement of the facts without "dressing them up." Not only is accuracy most often mentioned by most officers, but many single it out as *the* most important attribute:

> Accurate it must be, useful it must be, interesting we try to
> make it. But unfortunately, in government, some activities

[6] Carter, "Newspaper 'Gatekeepers' . . . ," p. 137. Warren Breed, "Analyzing News: Some Questions for Research," *Journalism Quarterly*, XXXIII (1956), 477; Roy E. Carter, Jr., "The Press and Public School Superintendents in California," *Journalism Quarterly*, XXXI (1954), 175; Walter Gieber and Walter Johnson, "The City Hall 'Beat': a Study of Reporter and Source Roles," *Journalism Quarterly*, XXXVIII (1961), 290.

[7] J.Q. Mahaffey, "PR and the Press," *Public Relations Journal*, IX (1953), 12.

that are of considerable importance are not particularly exciting. They don't move you too much!

Information officers valued accuracy to a higher degree than newsmen sampled realized. Accuracy and reader utility are valued attributes of the good news story according to the information officer. Less important is reader interest, utility to agency, and topicality. Reporters guess that information officers are more interested in seeing that a story promotes agency purposes, a characteristic on which officers placed relatively little value. Superficially, information officers discourage purposeful distortion of a story to make the agency itself "look good." There is a fine distinction, however, between what the information officer calls accuracy and comprehensiveness, and what the newsman refers to as distortion and misinterpretation. That distinction often rests on "whose ox is being gored." One information officer who regarded his first loyalty as to his department head and the political administration cited an example. He published a release stressing the success of sales of a particular variety of governmental bonds. He emphasized the departmental secretary's pleasure over the success of those sales, thus identifying the secretary with the happy results of a policy decision. Was he, therefore, using the press as an instrument of administration policy, as a means of publicizing his superior's ability, and as a device for misleading the public? No, he argued:

> I put the release out saying this—the secretary being quoted in saying this. Why? Not to make him look good or the department look good, but because our financial situation as a nation is in certain difficult straits. The fact that this was such a successful bond issue reflected confidence on the part of the banking community in the policies being followed by this administration. It strikes me [as] totally legitimate, aside from the fact that I happen to be part of the New Frontier, and we were not being dishonest in any way.

Newsmen sampled also selected accuracy most often as an essential characteristic of the news story. Table 13 indicates this was not totally unanticipated by the information officer. Reader interest and accuracy were the attributes most often guessed by information officers as valued by the newsman, a guess which is not without foundation as newsmen selections indicate. As in the case of information officers, some newsmen spoke eloquently regarding the necessity of accuracy in the news story above all other ingredients. One reporter commented: "The first requirement is accuracy; if you are not right in your facts, you do a disservice to a report." But there is more involved here than simply getting the facts reported correctly. It also involves the necessity to get all the relevant facts, not just part of them. "If you can get only part of the facts," the correspondent went on to add, "then be sure you report only that part and that you make it clear that

TABLE 12

NEWSMAN "GUESSES" OF CHARACTERISTICS PIO'S WOULD
SELECT IN A "GOOD" NEWS STORY COMPARED WITH
THE ACTUAL PIO SELECTION OF
SUCH CHARACTERISTICS

Characteristics (categories not mutually exclusive)	Percentage of Respondents Mentioning Attribute	
	Newsman Guesses ($N = 31$)	PIO Selections ($N = 38$)
Accuracy	45%	92%
Comprehensiveness	13	42
Interesting to reader	3	29
Useful to reader	10	51
Useful to agency	80	14
Topical	——	9

there are some unanswered questions in your mind." Reporting to such a newsman is much more than simply the transmission of information that one happens to find interesting; it is virtually a struggle to be honest: "Neither speed, nor clarity in presentation, nor length, nor brevity—none of these things is an excuse for not being accurate." So vital is this one characteristic of accuracy in the reporter's craft that "this is the basic requirement of all journalism anywhere; if it is not right, if the facts are not correct to the degree to which human effort can eliminate error, then the story better not be written." Apparently subject only to the assumed finitude of man, accuracy is the *sine qua non* of reporting. At least this is the verbal position of correspondents; critics might suggest that other forms of behavior—the actual writing and reporting of the correspondent—indicate otherwise.

In responses, at least, both newsmen and information officers selected accuracy as essential to the news story. Although officers perceived that this would be so for newsmen, newsmen apparently were less sensitive to the accuracy concepts of information officers.

TABLE 13

PIO "GUESSES" OF CHARACTERISTICS NEWSMEN WOULD
SELECT IN A "GOOD" NEWS STORY COMPARED WITH
ACTUAL NEWSMAN SELECTION OF
SUCH CHARACTERISTICS

Characteristics (categories not mutually exclusive)	*Percentage of Respondents Mentioning Attribute*	
	PIO Guesses ($N = 38$)	Newsmen Selections ($N = 33$)
Accuracy	80%	76%
Comprehensiveness	2	36
Interesting to reader	84	60
Useful to reader	2	24
Useful to agency	—	—
Topical	4	18

Although officers feel that newsmen are interested in the accuracy of a story, they do not perceive that the newsman is more interested in accuracy than they. In fact, a scant majority (only 51 per cent) found them as interested in accuracy as the information officer; the remainder perceived that officers worry much more about the degree of accuracy than do the newsmen.

Aside from accuracy and comprehensiveness, officers and newsmen differ markedly on the story values. Reader interest is emphasized by the newsman, which is no surprise to the informa-

tion officer. Utility to the reader is emphasized by the officer, but
not by the newsman. Perhaps differing audience conceptions are
operating here. The reporter with a more generalized audience
concept thinks of news stories which will interest the maximum
number of readers, with a consequent emphasis on circulation.
The information officer concerned with more specialized publics
thinks more of the utility which the information has for these
publics. Characteristics of reader and agency utility are directly
connected. For, if information from the agency meets favorable
reaction from agency clientele, it increases support for the agency
itself. The differing emphasis of reporters and officers on reader
interest and utility, considered in the light of the audiences to
which each must communicate, reinforces the assertion that cooperation or competition in the source-channel relationship results from divergent concepts of the newsworthy event and the
audience to which it is communicated.

It is interesting that information officers' guesses of newsmen's story values tend to be more accurate than newsmen's
guesses of values held by information officers. This may reinforce
the assertion that the officer tends to recognize that, to gain access to channels of news communication, he must adjust his definitions of news to those of the newsman. This places a premium
on the officer's ability to anticipate the newsman's definition of
news and to predict the values of a news story for either the single
reporter or the reporter group. A correct assessment in both areas
increases the likelihood that the information officer will gain access for his message to news channels. The newsman is less interested in determining the news definitions and values of the
information officer since, according to the data, he does not perceive this as required in gaining access to information. He believes, perhaps correctly, that the information officer must take
his cue from the newsman, not vice versa. He feels he can ignore
the officer's criticisms of his performance, but the information
officer cannot ignore the criticisms of the newsman. As one prescriber put it:

> Government information men are in a state of constant dis-
> approval of the way reporters handle stories affecting their

department. They think the story ought to be given bigger play. They think the head of the agency ought to be put in a more laudable light. They're always dissatisfied with the newspaper reporter; it couldn't be otherwise. They see the story from a particular point of view.

There is another possibility. Since information officers and newsmen have similar backgrounds—both are, or have been, reporters—it is to be expected that they would share the same story values. However, this does not explain why one emphasizes reader interest while the other speaks of usefulness to the reader. It is suggested here that this arises out of the differing institutional connections of the two sets of actors. Even though a former reporter, the information officer is now serving in a different environment, operating in a different role. His goal is the attainment of consensus on policy built partially through the provision of useful information to constituents.[8] The reporter thrives on the revelation of conflict and controversy commanding interest among readers. Decried by some as sensationalism, this aspect of the reporter's performance is nevertheless clearly evident. Relationships of sources and channels are thus to a large extent determined by the degree to which the actors perceive their role as directed toward resolution or exploitation of conflict. This orientation toward the treatment of news connected with a conflict situation is a fundamental difference between the two sets of actors, whether or not they agree on the method of handling the newsworthy event and the values of the story written about it.

INFORMATION AND NEWS AS
PROFESSIONAL VALUES

Members of the press corps are often criticized for manufacturing news; that is, they are accused of manipulating events and people in order to produce a newsworthy story where none existed.[9] Although some observers are critical of such behavior, others look upon it as an inevitable feature of the reporter's role.

[8] "The sources' role-bound need for assimilation is the most powerful force operating in their relationships with reporters." Gieber and Johnson, "The City Hall 'Beat' . . . ," p. 292.
[9] Cater, *The Fourth Branch of Government,* pp. 108–11.

Since he works on behalf of the citizen, they argue, the newsman's function is to probe and seek out information and transmit it to people who are not "on the spot." There must be an assumption of reportorial initiative, an initiative defined as asking the right questions—the questions that make politicians and officials into sources of news.[10]

In searching out the new fact or idea, the newsman, it is argued, places more emphasis on revelation than upon the significance of the material itself or the consequences of its publication. Some reporters recognize this criticism and adjust to it. The Alsops have pointed out that they follow the rule "never to print a column lacking at least one previously unpublished and significant item of factual information." [11] Simply put, news must be new. The pressure to write the new, the novel, and to expose the hidden is one of the single most significant influences defining the newsman's performance. And, if nothing new is happening, then it becomes the responsibility of the reporter to "see that it does happen." Newsmen frequently indicate that they regard it the mark of a competent correspondent to be able to create news independently of the surface events which are routinely reported:

> A good reporter manufactures news; he can start something on his own a lot of times. But it's still news, I think, as long as he gets the facts and reports what he dug up. It happens here in Washington quite a bit.

As we shall note later, information officers are sometimes implicated by reporters in efforts to "manage" news. To this many officers, particularly those responsible for policy promotion, will admit. What is often ignored by reporters, of course, is that the reportorial emphasis on "creating" or "manufacturing" news plays directly into the hands of such "news managers." By catering to the correspondent's needs and desires for the unrevealed item, the new in news, the officer can skillfully place his agency's case before the public. Unless the reporter is sensitive to such gamesmanship, he may well become a tool for official use.

Whether good or bad, the creation of news as well as its

[10] Alsop and Alsop, *The Reporter's Trade*, p. 7.
[11] *Ibid.*, p. 6.

simple recording, explanation, and analysis is part of the news-man's task. Certainly obtaining news is "an acquisitive behavior which is approved and expected in the newsroom milieu." [12] News becomes a commodity, a product, around which the correspondent's efforts are centered. In effect, news per se is a value to the newsman.

News may become a value to the reporter for several reasons, two of which deserve particular attention. One is offered by Breed's study of the newsroom environment within which the reporter operates.[13] He concludes that the reporter must produce news even though nothing has happened. By producing, he is rewarded; he is given the approval of both his colleagues and superiors. He thus feels that there is pressure on him to produce, to get the news. The newsman is sensitized to these demands; they pervade his consciousness. Compare the following statements by two newsmen on the same staff in a Washington bureau, the first for less than a year and the other for twelve years:

> There are an awful lot of lazy reporters in town, and more of them have to get off their fanny to get news. Now on this thing last week, I went down the entire list of all the people who had been sent this letter and asked them all if they had received any cancellation. None of them had. I had a feeling that they were lying to us, but no one else in town did. Now I wanted to prove that the chief hadn't made a mistake. I am a young reporter; I want to get started in this business. I want to prove myself. So I thought the paper ought to get a little more for its money. That is why I called all these people, and then I was able to get a good and exclusive story that nobody had been called on those letters, calling them back. This is the type of reporting you just simply have to get off your fanny to do.

Note the same sensitivity to pressure even in the second respondent's statement, one who had long since "proved" himself:

> Newspapering is a very competitive business; an extremely competitive business. When you first come on a job pressure is put upon you to prove yourself every day. These pressures

[12] Carter, "Newspaper 'Gatekeepers' . . . ," p. 137.
[13] Breed, "Social Control in the Newsroom . . . ," p. 331.

are tremendous—they come from your editor, they come
from your colleagues, and they come from the pressure of
events. Because of these pressures, the business of reporting
news is a physically and mentally demanding job. On our
staff, this pressure lets up after a few years, and you are able
to pace yourself although you remain constantly busy.

Conscious feeling of pressure is one thing, but reporters also
place a value on news for other reasons. They regard news as
their basic commodity; their reason for existence is to sell it.
Even without the atmosphere of pressure from superiors and colleagues, the competitive nature of the business requires that they
come up daily with something new to offer the buying audience.
The market place of ideas to this group is a buyer's market, and
the newsman must sell his product. Here news is valued for itself
as the product inherent in the reporter's role.

The majority (55 per cent) of newsmen interviewed thought
of news as such a value in their make-up as reporters. Few (10
per cent) were vividly aware of external pressures on them to
come up with something new every day. More than a third of
reporters indicated that they felt no problem at all with coming
up with "new" material. As one respondent pointed out, "In
general, on any news about government, you wait until you have
the thing, the new development occurs." Prescribers agreed that
they are not interested in writing the news, but writing about the
news. Pressures for the new are not present.

Perhaps the most fruitful statement is that the reporter tends
to incorporate news per se, its acquisition and transmission, into
his value system as a newsman. This results from pressures of the
newsroom, from superiors, and from his competitors. He may not
be totally aware of such pressures but will still seek news as the
single commodity which provides the operating rationale for his
role in society. Provision of news justifies his existence and provides him with status. News is a value in itself for reasons of felt
demands of others and his own internal desires. One reporter respondent summed it up this way:

I think that every reporter is trying to get on the front
page, trying to get his name and his story where the reader
is most likely to see it, and this alters the way he writes

things and the way he defines news. This produces a problem for the reporter because the editor wants the hard lead
—he wants the hard facts of what has taken place, and the
reporter on the other hand may see something in the news,
may see something in the facts, that is much more important
to him. The editor, for example, thinks that a story that the
secretary of agriculture is going to do something is a much
better story than what the reporter writes if the reporter
writes that the secretary will *probably* do something.

As the newsman sometimes manufactures news, the information officer is accused of manufacturing information. The officer
is subjected to the charge that he "turns out" information simply
because he must do so. Inherent in the charge is that information
is valued for its own sake by the officer. Newsmen interviewed
felt that the officer makes information available not only on a
need-to-know basis, but simply because (1) it is his job to do so or
(2) because pressure is brought on him to do so. Responses of
information officers, on the other hand, indicate they feel no
particular compulsion to issue information either to rationalize
their existence or to placate demands of others.

This is not to say that the information officer does not perceive the necessity of producing copy favorable to the interest of
his agency or superior if the opportunity arises. Politically appointed assistant secretaries for information are constantly attuned to such possibilities. For them, favorable publicity is a
rationale for their existence. Difficulties arise when the career information officer is expected to publicize his department or superior. One press officer offered a comment on when such times
occur and what the reaction of the officer must be to them; it is
a comment echoed by other respondents speaking of pressures
brought on them to "get out" information:

> I would say that you would find the pressures tend to
> mount for this sort of thing just before election. There is
> a tendency on the part of political officers to want to crow
> and magnify their accomplishments just before an election
> period. I think that you find that tendency. I also think you
> find that the career information officer resists to the best ex-
> tent he can because, in the long run, his future depends

on transcending changes; he has to be able to live with both
parties and can't afford to get closely identified with any
maneuvers of this sort which are not legitimate.

Pressure to produce information brought about by partisan political desires is, however, a deviation from the normal routine of
the officer. On a day-to-day basis this is apparently not a critical
cause of pressuring. Indeed, a political campaign may produce
pressure on the reporter, just as it may produce pressure for an
officer. Even campaigns are carried on by newspapers, and then
the reporter must "come up with something":

> I don't think pressure is very common. I think this sort
> of thing happens when a paper is carrying on a campaign.
> Whatever you are campaigning for, then the reporter is un-
> der pressure to get a story every day.

Pressure on reporters or officers resulting from organizational or
political campaigns, while not unheard of, is uncommon. Actually, it is not the agency pressure which troubles the information officer so much as the demands of the reporters. For a second
source of pressure brought on information officers to turn out
material comes from the newsman group. The newsman is as a
member of an interest group making value demands of governmental officials in the form of requests for information. In this
framework, information is a value claim of the news media just
as a particular policy alternative is sought by any organizational
group. From this point of view, the pressures on the information
officer are those of the newsman as lobbyist, and the officer reacts
to such pressures by attempting to anticipate demands. This may
lead to his distributing information of little significance, particularly if the officer is sensitized to another demand of the newsman—that the reporter alone should be allowed to determine
what is news. Here the officer is caught in a dilemma. If he releases everything, he is accused of flooding the market place with
trivia; if he does not, he is accused of withholding information.
In either event, the tendency of the reporter is to assume that information either released or guarded by the officer is valued for
its own sake.

What is the result of such attitudes held by newsmen and officers for the source-channel relationship? Several possibilities suggest themselves. For one, the newsman tends to accept the information officer's performance if it is not directed at putting out more information than the reporter can use. The newsman can ally himself with the officer who releases information on the basis of news value rather than to impress the agency head. The recorder is more inclined to see news in released information; the expositor, being more selective, finds more "guff" in the information officer's release. The prescriber writing and commenting upon that which is often already published news cares little about the information officer's effort and finds him useful only for facts:

> Well, mechanically they are very valuable. If I want to get some information on the Treasury—like statistics—I just call the man over there. Yes, they're valuable that way, but that is about it.

The officer views the newsman somewhat differently. To the newsman, the information officer's acceptance of information per se as a value is bad. But the information officer finding the newsman under some self-imposed or external pressure to get news can capitalize on it and does so. If the reporter must find news, the information officer can supply the commodity; if the newsman is not under this pressure, he can be more selective in dealing with information officers. The officer can help the reporter "manufacture" or "create" news by use of the plant, leak, or backgrounder. The officer can become the "spokesman" for an agency if (1) he has discretion over news release and (2) the reporter *must* have news of that agency. A case in point, of course, is the "man-into-space" program of the National Aeronautics and Space Administration. Demands are made on the reporter —from his audiences, his superiors, his colleagues, and his competition—to find every new change in the program. This has provided the information staff of NASA with an opportunity not unique in the activities of governmental publicity. The staff controls access to information for the press. We need only cite the periodic rise to fame of Colonel "Shorty" Powers before each launching in the "man-into-space" program. The promoter is most often in the position to take an advantage, for he is dealing with information in which the newsman is most interested—information of broad audience appeal about personalities and controversial issues. But the educator, profiting from the increased demand for "interpretive" and "background" information, also is able to anticipate reportorial value demands and reacts accordingly. Even the informer may manipulate information if it is in the guise of the new item which the correspondent must have:

> Since we have a particular program to publicize continually, it is difficult to publicize one program over and over again. Once you write a story about something in most instances in the news field that ends it, the story is finished, and you move on to something else. But here we can't move on to something else; we have to keep publicizing the story as much as possible. What we have to do is let a story go for a while, then pick it up again and again [and] present it to editors throughout the country as a news story. We must write in a different way, with a different angle, yet getting basically the same information across to the groups to whom we are communicating.

It may be hypothesized that, to the extent that the information officer is perceived to have a vested interest in getting out information, the newsman will tend to ignore him as a news source and seek unpremeditated revelations elsewhere. And to the extent that the source perceives that the newsman demands news for its own sake, the officer may manipulate his release for purposes of extending the scope of his publicity. In short, the degree to which either actor values his particular commodity, and the extent to which the other is aware of it, are constant influences upon the course and direction of the source-channel relationship.

PERFORMANCE JUDGMENTS

The variable that would seem most directly related to the quality of the source-channel relationship is the degree of satisfaction expressed by officers of the newsman's performance and of newsmen toward the official news source. One researcher has hypothesized that the favorability of a news source toward the reporter and vice versa is promoted by frequency of contact.[14] Although it was not possible to assess the frequency of contact of information officer and newsman, it was feasible to determine the types of newsmen both preferred and contacted by information officers (Table 14). The type of newsman most preferred is the routine reporter. Although looked upon with favor by information officers generally, he is not their exclusive channel. Contact is distributed among all reportorial types; preference, however, is centered upon the routine reporter. This is as expected, for the reporter least likely to change the factual and interpretive message of the officer is the one most favored. Hence the explanation

TABLE 14

PREFERENCES EXPRESSED BY INFORMATION OFFICERS FOR
TYPES OF NEWSMEN WITH WHOM TO HAVE CONTACT
COMPARED WITH TYPES ACTUALLY CONTACTED

Newsman Types	Type Preferred (N = 38)	Type Contacted (N = 38)
Routine reporters (regulars on the beat)	92%	40%
Specialists (feature writers, interpretive reporters)	4	34
Editorial writers, columnists, commentators	4	26

for data in Table 15. The informer interested primarily in transmission of factual material seldom approves of interpretations by the specialist or columnist; the educator prefers his own interpretations to those of reporters and hence desires to utilize the reporter who changes that interpretation the least; finally, the promoter can utilize the routine reporting of the mass circulation media most effectively for widest circulation of publicity messages. Obviously cooperation in source-channel relations is reinforced when sources interact with reporters who share their communication goals of informing, educating, or promoting.

[14] Carter, "Newspaper 'Gatekeepers' . . . ," p. 133.

The information officer's satisfaction with the newsman's performance is positively related to his perception of the degree to which the reporter treats information without basic changes in fact or interpretation. Conversely, the reporter's favorability toward the information officer is related to the freedom given him to freely interpret "off-the-cuff" tips. Officers willing and in a position to speculate about the course of policy are those who become known in the trade as "official spokesmen" or "authoritative sources." One respondent quipped: "My ambition as a press officer is to become known as an unimpeachable source in the press; I have only been that on one occasion that I can think of." But the reporter is disenchanted with the officer who releases

TABLE 15

SOURCE ROLE TYPE PREFERENCES FOR NEWSMEN
AS CHANNELS OF INFORMATION

Newsman Type Preferred	Informers (N = 9)	Educators (N = 10)	Promoters (N = 6)
Routine reporters	86%	90%	100%
Specialists	——	10	——
Editorial writers, columnists, commentators	14	——	——

his purposive message in such detail that no license for speculation remains. Publicity itself is not frowned on so much as the nature of it. The reporter's dissatisfaction with publicity activities is related directly to the degree of specificity that appears in the publicity program released to him. Highly detailed messages not subject to reportorial interpretation are frowned upon by newsmen.

This refers directly to the type of information sought by newsmen of officers (Table 16). Both factual and speculative material was sought by newsmen sampled. Factual material included the routine of policy and program information; the search for the

speculative involved an appeal to the officer for statements regarding how a policy was chosen, what alternatives were open,
why was one selected, and what would be the probable course of
future policy. Officers themselves perceive that newsmen ask
them about what course policy should take more often than newsmen admit. Moreover, some information officers take any request
for background information as an effort to expose their personal
opinion of policy. This tendency to regard speculation about
policy determination as inherently beyond the capacity of the
information officer is particularly relevant in the regulatory agencies. The following is a typical comment from one such information officer:

> Even in a minor matter of whether the board is going to let
> a certain tariff go into effect—until such time as the board
> either does or does not indicate by an order or the lack of
> an order as to what it is going to do—I am not in a position
> to comment because second guessing them is not my busi-
> ness. I wait until I get a piece of paper or the word that
> they have either approved it or denied it, and then the
> information is available.

TABLE 16

SOURCE-CHANNEL VIEWS ON TYPE OF INFORMATION
SOUGHT FROM PIO BY NEWSMAN

Information Type	PIO Listing (N = 37)	Newsman Listing (N = 35)
Factual material	49%	51%
Speculative material	37	45
Prescriptive material	14	4

Whether the newsman contacts an information officer or
not, and for what, is largely dependent upon the newsman's
purpose. The correspondent interested in a story revealing controversy within a decision-making group seeks access at those

points at which information is most likely available. In few agencies, this is at the information officer's desk. But the information staff may be able to open doors permitting the newsman to talk to the official who has the information. A cooperative source-channel relationship is characterized by the officer yielding both information and access sought by the newsman; competition stems from refusals to supply requested information or access to the officials who can provide it.

TABLE 17

NEWSMAN AND PIO SATISFACTION WITH PERFORMANCE

Expression	Satisfaction with PIO		Satisfaction with Newsman	
	Expressed by PIO ($N = 33$)	Expressed by Newsman ($N = 33$)	Expressed by PIO ($N = 30$)	Expressed by Newsman ($N = 35$)
Satisfaction with performance	70%	65%	86%	60%
Dissatisfaction with performance	30	35	14	40

Information officers sampled tended to be more satisfied with the performance of newsmen than vice versa (Table 17). This satisfaction was expressed toward the amount, type, and accuracy of coverage given the agency by newsmen. Information officers also are satisfied with the performance of their own brethren, although not to as high a degree as they are with newsmen. Some receive censure for violating certain "rules of the game." Officers are particularly critical of staffs which put out too many press releases or make attempts to manage the release of information for favorable timing. Information staffs are in competition with one another for time and space in the news media. For one agency to maximize its circulation through timing releases works a hardship on those which do not manipulate or are not permitted to do so. Newsmen sometimes are critical of information staffs for just the opposite reason—failure to manipulate timing of the release. This is particularly true of the reporter who thinks he might maximize his own output of stories if the agency he covers would just cooperate:

> But our biggest difficulty in trying to perform this service of informing the public about what this department does is a question of what I call timing. Often the time you say something or issue a press release may be more important than what is in the press release. What I am saying is, if you say it at a time when, because of the competition of other news stories for news space in the newspapers and the radio, your story may be of minor importance, [it] will get lost. In other words, if you say it at the wrong time, it gets thrown in the wastepaper basket in the newspaper office, and maybe it doesn't even get moved on our wire.

Newsmen are not always satisfied with information officers and also are in a state of dismay regarding their fellow reporters. Criticisms of the information officer have been mentioned: they put out too much information, they try to sell policy, they act in self-interest, their information is routine, and so on. In spite of such criticism, however, only two respondents stated they would prefer having no information staffs. Both were columnists of more than forty years experience in Washington reporting. Both voiced the same criticism: "Information people don't help you much because they want to make all the news public and very little of it is exclusive." Experienced in the tradition of the self-starting, individualistic reporter, neither had use for arrangements for making information available to all reporters at the same time—information offices, press conferences, press releases, and so on. "The time existed," said one, "when if you wanted to find out what was going on, you talked to Wilson or Coolidge; you can't do that with a president or even a cabinet member now."

Interestingly enough, fewer reporters expressed satisfaction with fellow newsmen than they did with information officers. Members of the press corps are apparently their own worst critics. Views varied considerably. Prominent was criticism of the follow-the-leader aspect mentioned earlier. Also condemned was the tendency of reporters to become favored by news sources in exchange for making the source look favorable in the news—"the closed society of the backgrounder." Manufacturing and coloration of news also came in for comment. One columnist even charged his fellows with purchasing news from sources in exchange for favorable publicity:

> Why, some buy their information from underlings, and they admit frankly that they do when they do it. This in my book is unethical; it's bribery and corruption. Oh, I'm not opposed to bribery; I am not "holier than thou," but I don't think that will work in the end. They are bound to manufacture news in order to get your $100 that you pay him for a piece of information—and you would be in the hole, that's my own main objection to buying information.

One interesting suggestion emerges from such comparison of newsmen's and officers' satisfactions with their own and the others' performance. Restraints over the information officer's behavior consist of administrative regulations on unwritten procedures. Officers in a bureaucratic environment appear to incorporate such standards in judging the performance of information staffs.[15] As the information function is increasingly accepted and specialized, such standards become even more explicit. For the newsman, however, formalized standards do not exist. Newsmen judge their own performance by applying vague formulas connected with service to the public interest, keeping the public informed, and scrutinizing the official. The definitions of what are acceptable standards are largely individual. How far the reporter can go in revelation, interpretation, and prescription before he disrupts policy-making, misinterprets, and misinforms are questions of government-press relations which as yet have no definitive answer. When sources and channels judge their own and each other's performance by similar standards, a potential for cooperation develops; divergent standards foster competitive behavior.

[15] For example, see Federal Power Commission, *Rules of Practice and Procedure (Including General Policy and Interpretations)*, 1958.

COOPERATION, COMPATIBILITY,
AND COMPETITION

The bases of officer-newsman role orientations were suggested previously: (1) actors' concepts of function and purpose, (2) orientations toward superiors and organizations, (3) orientations toward alternative sources and channels, (4) orientations toward audiences, and (5) orientations toward friendships. In this chapter, some effects of these role concepts on the source-channel relationship have been discussed. Actors' self/other images, story values, professional values, and performance judgments are also influenced by role concepts of sources and channels. Although treated separately, the significance of these variables lies in their blending with independent variables described in the preceding chapter to reinforce the qualities of cooperation, compatibility, and competition in the source-channel relationship.

The likelihood of cooperation between source and channel actor increases as information officers and newsmen share common images of the "good" newsman, the "good" news source, and the "good" information officer. When these images diverge, the relationship takes on characteristics of compatibility, involving activities which are neither completely in cooperation nor in open conflict. If divergent enough, the images contribute to competition. The placement of source-channel relationships on the cooperative-compatible-competitive continuum is also directly related to the degree to which officers and newsmen share common story values. The data reveals that both actor sets place emphasis on accuracy but differ on other values depending upon their audience and function orientations. News itself as a basic value in the reporter's framework may lead to cooperation if the officer adroitly takes advantage of it but to competition if the newsman perceives manipulation. The newsman's concept that information is an end in itself to the information officer tends to increase misunderstanding between the political communicators. Finally, the satisfaction of each actor group with the other has direct effects on the source-channel relationship, as well as being an outgrowth of it.

The last mentioned point is significant for it raises the com-

plex question of cause and effect in the source-channel relationship. Do the role orientations mold source-channel relationship
types of cooperation, compatiblility, and competition? Or do
officers and newsmen comprise vital categories of "significant
others" for one another such that the type of source-channel relationship determines the role orientations? The evidence indicates that, although the source-channel relationship itself influences actors' perceptions of and behavior toward one another,
the greater likelihood is that cooperation, compatibility, and
competition result from their generalized role orientations. Primary in the behavior of the political communicator is his evaluation of his role within the institutional complex of which he is
a part.

Furthermore, the interests toward which officers and reporters
orient themselves are sometimes similar, sometimes different. One
newsman summed it up this way:

> None of us can cover all of the beats in town that exist;
> you have to start somewhere, and the information officers
> are there, and they will give you a great deal of help. I think
> that probably the best policy to adopt is to leave the in-
> formation officer behind as soon as possible because he
> usually has a certain policy to sell or defend and your in-
> terest and his are divergent. It is in the nature of the beast!

Service to the same or similar interests promotes cooperation between communicators; service to unrelated or only superficially
opposed interests tends to create compatible relations; service to
basically opposed interests contributes to competition in the
source-channel relationship. Such interest orientations are, of
course, the precise orientations reflected in actors' role concepts.

So crucial are the role concepts of political communicators
in determining basic relations between sources and channels that
one may construct a typology of source-channel relationships by
drawing upon the recurrent role patterns developed in the preceding chapter. A specific type of relationship can then be explained by referring to actor role orientations and significant dependent variables. For example, cooperation is the characteristic
quality of informer-recorder relations. Role orientations and op-

erative influences provide an explanation. Actors share common role definitions as political communicators, tend to share definitions of "good" newsmen and "good" news sources, share common story values, and contact one another regularly. Their audiences overlap. For example, the audience of the agricultural correspondent of the wire services is approximately that of the agricultural information officer—farmers, consumers, and so on. Audience-sharing holds for Commerce and Treasury information staffs and reporters covering the "financial run" or between officers in regulatory commissions and reporters on the "commission beat." But compatibility characterizes the interaction of educator and expositor. Differing concepts reflected in interpretive reporting and policy explanation produce elements of disagreement. However, sufficient consensus prevails on perceived goals as political communicators to minimize disruptive conflict. In promoter-prescriber relations, actors' prescriptions are seldom the same, but each views it as within his purview to offer that prescription. Actors compete for the ear of the citizen. Their actions, rather than reinforcing one another, conflict openly. Estrangement between the two is immediate and, in extreme cases, permanent. The prescriber perceives the promoter's story values to be entirely self-centered; the promoter fails to trust the prescriber to transmit the agency story unchanged and uncritically.

The most probable type of source-channel relationship is that of compatibility. Officers and newsmen seldom share identical orientations toward interests, goals, and purposes—which is to say, the same role concepts. Role behavior is not integrated; some conflict inheres in the relationship. But, in an age of complex reporting, the newsman can no longer ignore the aid of the information expert. Seldom are the communicative acts of officer and reporter totally divorced, and seldom are role orientations absolutely divergent. There is sufficient sharing of role concepts by sources and channels to permit continuance of the relationship. Neither absolute harmony nor disharmony characterizes source-channel relations; rather there are varying degrees of tension.

Cooperation, compatibility, and competition in the source-channel relationship highlight qualities of stability and dynamism that characterize a viable process of political communication. Conflict there is, but conflict resolved within boundaries excluding total integration or disintegration of source-channel relations.

CHAPTER VI
TOOLS OF THE TRADE: THE PRACTITIONERS' VIEWS

Neither governmental publicity nor political reporting occurs at random. Both information officers and reporters have regularized techniques for political communication. Moreover, the techniques utilized by each are often the same; what the official news source uses to dispense information, the correspondent relies on as a method of gathering the news. Techniques of officers and reporters do not differ; it is the orientation of each toward the purpose and nature of any technique on which there is divergence. It is the purpose of this chapter to explore the attitudes of political communicators toward those techniques that are the tools of their trade.

EXPRESSED PREFERENCES OF PIO'S AND NEWSMEN

The brothers Alsop in their "inside" account of the reportorial craft urge that there can be no regularized pattern of newsgathering in Washington. For example, they insist, "A Washing-

ton correspondent does not get his news from a series of delight-
fully convenient pipelines; each reporter must rely on his own
initiative, genius, and imagination to ferret out needed information." [1] One respondent agreed, "I just don't think there is any
generalizing about gathering news; you get it, you know, it just
depends, circumstances, etc." Convenient pipelines there may not
be, but regularly relied upon techniques of newsgathering have
become virtually institutionalized procedures for the transmission
of information. In the present study, respondents were questioned
on the use and abuse of six of these techniques: the news release,
the news inquiry, the news conference, the background conference, the interview, and the use of the informal release.

An initial question involves the relative preferences expressed
for each of these devices and the comparison of such preferences
with the degree to which each technique is actually used by political communicators. As Table 18 indicates, information officers and newsmen do not agree on the techniques they prefer.
With few exceptions officers interviewed selected the news release
as the most favored way of releasing information. Underlying this
general consensus is the assumption that the news release is the
means of distribution least open to misinterpretation. Officers
are particularly disturbed concerning the possibility of being mis-
quoted or misinterpreted in the press; this is as true of the press
secretary as it is of the information specialist. The news release is
viewed as a protection against this eventuality. Once given to
the press, it is a matter of public record, to be filed and integrated
into the organization memory like any other data connected with
agency activities. As such, it (1) is a permanent protection or indictment of the performance of the information staff and (2) provides one of a continuing series of statements of agency position.
The release represents security to the officer—security before his
superior, security before Congress, and security in the face of the
reportorial inquisition. Some departments have elaborate techniques for the administration of the news release alone. One press
officer was quite proud of his procedures:

> After the stories are issued, we keep them on file by year,
> and then a basic copy is sent to the archives and kept on

[1] Alsop and Alsop, *The Reporter's Trade*, p. 4.

tap. I believe that they are in the process of microfilming that stuff in the archives. I will just go then to the file and look up that number, and I can find a copy of a story. I can also find a distribution sheet that would tell where that story went. So if you wanted to know just what distribution that story got, I will be able to tell you!

Of course, the attitude reflected in such a statement is often the very one decried by the reporter. This filing is the "routine stuff" which reporters often refuse to have anything to do with at all. The file clerk concept of public information is precisely what sends many reporters scurrying to find other sources of news than the information officer.

To reporters surveyed, the preferred way of gathering news was the interview. More than three-fourths of news respondents spoke of the advantages of this technique above all others. Its prime merit, they point out, is that it is exclusive. In the modern age in which most of the daily routine is standardized through release of information through identical channels simultaneously, the reporter longs for the opportunity to differentiate himself from his brethren with the "scoop." Although the desire for the exclusive angle is perhaps becoming a nostalgic bit of journalistic folklore, it retains much of its influence as a convention over the behavior of the reporter. The interview characterized as private, confidential, and intimate provides the newsman with an all-important "peg" for his story. The body of material may not differ from what every other reporter is writing, but nonetheless, an exclusive quotation in the lead is a much sought symbol of reportorial initiative. The adroit information officer recognizes this trait and plays up to the resourceful reporter by placing him in contact with agency officials for purpose of interviews. Reportorial resourcefulness thus becomes a tool for official use.

It is interesting to compare these preferences of official news sources and newsmen with the techniques which they actually use (Table 18). The release and the inquiry response are utilized extensively by information officers. They are followed closely by the use of the interview, either an interview with the information officer himself or an arranged interview with an agency official. Although officers overwhelmingly favor one particular means of distribution, they appear to utilize all six methods available to

them. Preference for a particular technique does not foreclose
the practical use of all means at the officer's disposal. The same
is true of the reporter. No newsman selected the news release as
his preferred manner for gathering information; yet, 41 per cent
of the reporters use it. Likewise, none chose the official inquiry
or the background conference as a preferred method of newsgathering; however, this did not preclude the use of each by
almost two-thirds of the newsmen sampled.

TABLE 18

INFORMATION-DISPENSING AND NEWSGATHERING TECHNIQUES
PREFERRED COMPARED WITH TECHNIQUES UTILIZED

	Preferred		Used (nonexclusive categories)	
	Newsmen	PIO's	Newsmen	PIO's
Technique	(N = 35)	(N = 38)	(N = 35)	(N = 38)
News release	——	82%	41%	89%
Interview	76%	——	83	78
News inquiry (to PIO)	——	12	65	90
News conference	20	3	71	79
Background conference	——	——	65	11
Informal release (leaks)	4	3	17	13

Another interesting comparison is that between the communicator role type of the information officer or newsman and
his preference for methods of information-dispensing and newsgathering (Table 19). The prescriber, as is expected, is the newsman who most favors the interview as a means of obtaining information. Established contacts in Washington, recognized status
among colleagues and public officials—both give the columnist,
commentator, or editorial writer "convenient pipelines" to interviews with the decision-maker. Many frown on the use of an alternative procedure:

> I prefer the interview only; in the first place, it livens up
> the story, and the second point is it brings it right up to
> date. Like, "So and so told me, today."

Informers prefer the use of the news release more than do information officers generally. This reflects their reluctance to go beyond transmission of factual program data, a purpose to which the release is admirably suited. As one stated, "We like the release; we try to keep them in a format for newspapers because we realize that a newspaper format is the most easily understood type." Educators prefer the informal release and news conference to a greater degree than information officers generally. The conference places the agency official before the press with the opportunity to "explain to the American people the activities of the department; it's a chance to educate them to problems that arise." The informal release is a means of doing the same to the individual reporter. Strangely enough, those interested in direct pro-

TABLE 19

COMPARISON OF CHANNEL AND SOURCE ROLE TYPE
PREFERENCES FOR INFORMATION-DISPENSING
AND NEWSGATHERING TECHNIQUES

	Channel Role Types		
Technique	Recorder (N = 10)	Expositor (N = 12)	Prescriber (N = 10)
News release	——	——	——
Interview	70%	75%	90%
News inquiry	——	——	——
News conference	30	16	10
Background conference	——	——	——
Informal release	——	9	——
	Source Role Types		
Technique	Informer (N = 15)	Educator (N = 13)	Promoter (N = 10)
News release	93%	77%	80%
Interview	——	——	——
News inquiry	7	——	20
News conference	——	12	——
Background conference	——	——	——
Informal release	——	11	——

motion of policy prefer the information techniques of officers generally—the release and the inquiry. It is through the use of the inquiry that the officer can place in the ear of the reporter an idea which will promote agency programs:

> Here is the way I handle the thing. The AP and the UPI men came in the other day. They had heard about a particular program we are going to try, and they said, "Look, what is going on; we would like to know about this thing." So I filled them in, gave them a complete rundown on the origination of the program, what was going to happen and everything. I said, "Now you know what is going to happen, but don't handle it until the right time." I then handed them a release and said, "Print this." They did, and later we got a good story out of the other thing.

Although information officers generally favor the news release, they differ among themselves over what should be in that release. As would be expected, officers tend to distribute themselves as to whether (1) the release should be factual only, (2) be both factual and interpretive, or (3) be primarily promotional. Informers are hesitant to interpret in their releases; 60 per cent expressed the opinion that releases should be factual, the remainder were willing to include interpretive material but no promotional "gimmicks." Educators shy away from promotional "handouts," apparently feeling that the problems of informing and educating go hand in hand and are best solved by combining factual and interpretive material. Eighty-seven per cent of such officers took this view, and only 13 per cent felt releases should be restricted to factual nature. Officers desiring to promote policy see the release more as a means of prescribing courses of action to the public. Twenty per cent felt this should be the sole purpose of information dispensed, and the remainder emphasized the value of the release as a factual and interpretive tool to give the public the agency's "framework of truth."

APPRAISALS OF INDIVIDUAL TECHNIQUES

The news release

"Government by press release" has been a common phrase used to criticize the activities of public information offices. Reporters have expressed fears of being "flooded" with paper. Such concern promoted attempts to measure the inundation from federal departments and agencies. Studies conclude that government press releases certainly have not increased to the same degree as have the numbers of individuals employed in the federal government or the budget of that government.[2] Other critics have directed their dismay not at the quantity, but the quality of government "handouts." Raymond Brandt, Washington Bureau Chief of the *St. Louis Post-Dispatch*, has written that handouts are minor aids in assemblying news; they contain the routine trivia of Washington reporting utilized primarily by wire services.[3] Arthur Krock of *The New York Times* also has been unimpressed with governmental press releases.[4]

Newsmen surveyed were equally without praise for the release as a technique for gathering news in Washington. As noted in Table 18 none preferred it as a device for gaining information, 40 per cent however did make some use of it. The primary criticism leveled against it was that the news release is simply an instrument of governmental publicity, of utility to government but not to the press (Table 20). It is criticized as being misleading, full of routine, or "just program stuff" as one respondent expressed it. Another called it "flak" and a few respondents were even less kind, although more colorful, in descriptive phrases. A representative criticism is the following:

> A sort of Parkinson's law is operating in information staffs whereby, having been created, they must make work for themselves in order to justify their own existence. They do this by turning out releases. I think these releases can be looked upon as dazzle camouflage—that is, they are released in order to keep the newsman busy in going through them so that he will have neither the time nor the opportunity to probe underneath the surface.

This is the complaint most often stressed. There are so many releases, argues the reporter, that it is impossible to sift through them all in order to distinguish the significant. To the correspond-

---

[2] Fitzpatrick, "Measuring Government Publicity . . . ," p. 50.

[3] Brandt, "The Washington Correspondent," pp. 173–174

[4] Arthur Krock, "The Gathering of the News," in *The Newspaper: Its Making and Its Meaning* (New York: Charles Scribner's Sons, 1945), pp. 48–49.

TABLE 20

PERCEPTIONS BY INFORMATION OFFICERS AND NEWSMEN OF
THE UTILITY OF VARIOUS TECHNIQUES OF INFORMATION-
DISPENSING AND NEWSGATHERING

	PIO's (N = 38)		Newsmen (N = 35)	
	Prime Utility Is to Government	Prime Utility Is to Press	Prime Utility Is to Government	Prime Utility Is to Press
Technique				
News release	85%	15%	70%	30%
News inquiry	79	21	37	63
News conference	69	31	33	67
Background conference	70	30	36	64
Interview	40	60	8	92
Informal release	67	33	25	75

ent the releases "operate against his interests by taking so much
of his time that he can't do as good a job as he might." With no
time to filter out the significant releases, the alternative is to ignore them completely.

Furthermore, reporters see the news release as a device by
which government tries to peddle to the correspondent rather
than aid him. Finally, releases may not appeal to the reporter's
individual temperament:

> Well, I don't like the governmental release; that is the one
> I like the least. I'm a little bit lazy when it comes to digging
> out statistics, digging out stories out of statistics, although
> you often find them there.

Excessive reliance on the press release may even contribute to the
"institutionalization" of the reporter—a process by which the
newsman's thought patterns become identical to those of the
agency officials serving as news sources. The result is a sacrifice
of reportorial independence of judgment in exchange for simpli-
fied access to information. One respondent put the problem as
follows:

> People who begin to report from a particular beat begin to think in the lingo of the institution which they are covering. They soon get institutionalized. They begin to find that they are reporting for the people of the institution rather than for the layman out in the field.

The critical problem is that the interests of the reporter become all too easily identified with those of the organization which he is covering. As this occurs, criticism of the agency's activities becomes increasingly remote for the newsman, and he finds himself becoming an agency ambassador without portfolio.

Rare was the newsman who found much to praise in the "handout" as a tool of newsgathering. Those few cited the possibility that the release may call the attention of the reporter to something previously unknown and hence lead to a good story. This is an aid, not a hindrance, pointed out one newsman:

> You receive this information in package form, and you don't have to do the digging—the running down of all the angles. Government has reached a size where there are thousands, and thousands, and thousands of reasonably good stories that never see the light of day. On the other hand, it has also reached the size and has those layers of command that if you have to spend your time trying to ferret out with no help, no guidance, all of the stories even that are of minor importance, you have to spend many hours a day, many hours, weeks, months, to get one story which whether it is timely or not does come to you in the press release form.

If the reporter calls for "guidance" as did the respondent, officers are eager to please. Revelation of the unknown fact by means of the press release is the virtue cited most by the information officer. They too appear convinced that there are many good stories never printed and many others that would never be if it were not for releases. Information personnel agree that the prime utility of the release is to the agency. It provides the facts of agency activity, on agency terms, with agency interpretation. Release is usually on agency initiative. That initiative can form the story structure for the press, and the agency does not have to face criticisms of confused reporters if something breaks unexpectedly.

One information officer indicated the manner in which his organization prepares for such unforeseen circumstances:

> If an atom bomb accidentally falls out of an airplane, the planning staff has to think far in advance of that event. The SOP that is going to be used in calming the public down and keeping the event from damaging the Air Force. We know who is going to be sent at any given time; a general officer will be sent to cover it, to act as spokesman for the Air Force in the event. It is things like this that the planning staff has to perform, to look ahead and say what are all the possible things that can happen with respect to this policy, and then prepare for every contingency that may develop.

It is, of course, precisely this practice of preparing for the unexpected which smacks of news management to the reporter and increases his distrust of the press release. In major stories, he argues, the release is misinformation; in less critical instances, it is simply trivial information. Many newsmen became gun-shy following their experiences dealing with the now infamous affair of Francis Gary Powers and his U-2 flight over the Soviet Union in May, 1960. As we now know, information specialists prepared what are termed "cover stories" to be used in the event that such a disaster should befall a reconnaisance flight like the one over Sverdlosk. The purpose of such a story is to reveal such news as governmental officials think is proper covering the event, partially to satisfy reportorial demands for a full explanation when no such explanation is either desirable or possible. All works out satisfactorily if the cover story does in fact cover the unexpected event. In the Powers case, the release of the cover story by the National Aeronautics and Space Administration explained the flight of the U-2 as one seeking meteorological data.[5] Reporters, having little else to go on, were inclined to accept such an explanation. In a confused, unstable, and highly fluid situation such as faced newsmen in that period it is small wonder that they tend to grasp at any straw of leadership available. The cover story provided such a straw. It structured what was beyond their immediate comprehension. Unfortunately, however, it did not cover the

[5] Francis E. Rourke, *Secrecy and Publicity: Dilemmas of Democracy* (Baltimore: The Johns Hopkins Press, 1961), pp. 5–6.

even more unexpected event which took place when Khrushchev offered evidence that the flight was not for purposes of gathering weather data and that, in fact, the pilot had been captured alive. What followed was even more confusion for officials, for the press, and for the reading and viewing public.

The affair of Powers illustrates two critical problems arising out of the purposeful use of the news release in government-press relations. First, it indicates the danger the reporter daily faces of being unwittingly used for official purposes. In periods of calm deliberation, he can fight such manipulation of his reportorial function by checking his sources, probing more deeply into the surface interpretation, and scrutinizing governmental statements. But in periods of flux he has no such opportunity; he has not the time. Then, the weaponry concept of news can be used to the advantage of the official, not to that of the correspondent.

But in using the reporter as his channel to the citizen, the official is faced with a problem equally as critical. As many citizens look to the news media for information in such a crisis situation, so does the correspondent look to the official. The newsman is dependent upon the official for leadership in information-dispensing. If official leadership is confused, so will be reporters in their efforts to find out what is taking place. In a chaotic situation such as the Powers case, correspondents cannot clear away public confusion as long as they are confused themselves. The cover story, designed to allay such chaos, instead contributed directly to it. The episode raises the question: is no information at all better than misinformation? Stated in terms of press responsibility the question becomes simply, do newsmen in their constant efforts to avoid being shut out in policy matters lay the groundwork for being misinformed because of their very eagerness to "ferret out the unrevealed?" Press members are faced with a dilemma: they desire to exert leadership in obtaining news for the citizen, yet are largely dependent on official leadership for the revelation and interpretation of that news. The norms of the journalistic craft offer few guidelines. Indeed, the myth of individualism to which the reporter is often devoted may very well dictate that no such guidelines can or should exist. As we will note again at a later point, the reporter, when caught in an un-

structured situation, seeks leadership; can he then get that leadership from the information establishment? The Powers affair
makes it appear doubtful.

Information officers interviewed take direct part in the is-
suance of the news release, either writing it, editing it, or clearing
it. These tasks separate the various source role types. Informers
are more often authorized to write releases (61 per cent)—releases
which others edit and clear. Educators perform all duties; 54 per
cent had authorship responsibilities and 46 per cent had only
editing and clearance duties. Promoters tend to be editors on the
information staff, with 70 per cent of those interviewed confining
themselves to editing releases, then clearing them for distribution.

The news inquiry

The information officer also likes to think of himself as a
repository of information which the reporter can have for the
asking. Many describe themselves as on the phone all day answering questions. Attitudes of newsmen toward inquiries of the information staff as a means of obtaining news, of course, are directly related to their concept of the utility of the public information officer's service in political communication. The Alsops main-
tain that the telephone is not a "direct channel of information." [6]
It is, they point out, in the same category as the public relations
man:

> It, or they, may be employed to make arrangements for get-
> ting information; but neither it, nor they, should be used as
> a direct channel of information. This sub-clause of the rule
> of the feet tends to pain public relations men, who always
> wish to speak for their masters. Fortunately it gives no pain
> to the telephone company.[7]

Regardless of their feelings in the matter, however, two-
thirds of the newsmen surveyed stated that they made some use
of the inquiry directed to the public information officer. The
relevant question is, to what purpose? Expressions vary, but the
consensus remains that the inquiry is addressed to the information officer when the reporter is working on the "routine" story:

[6] Alsop and Alsop, *The Reporter's Trade*, p. 6.
[7] *Loc. cit.*

> I would say on the routine story you start with the information man, and if he is a good information man he will try to get an honest answer to your question. There are a lot of people in government who don't like to talk to reporters and are fearful of what they say, but usually if the information man in their department calls him up and says, "Look this guy wants to talk to you," it helps.

How far beyond this the newsman may want to go in obtaining information from the officer will depend on many factors previously discussed. One of the most critical is the relationship the officer has with his organization. If he has the discretion to be the spokesman for the agency, the newsman may seek him out for information either because he is the only available source or because the officer is recognized as the official source of that agency. Inquiries to the officer increase in an agency that cracks down on the information release, especially when the information officer fails to cooperate in the crackdown. In those instances an informal arrangement arises out of the fact that the information officer and reporter form a permanent dyad within any agency. The political head may change; the chances are that the assigned reporter will outlast several changes in administration as will the career information officer. The information staff and the regular reportorial staff comprise a group with similar interests of communicating information from the agency. The result is an interest group which may or may not be in harmony with changes in information policies initiated by the political agency head. The formation of such a group is illustrated by the following reporter's comment:

> Of course you have an information man who is more or less perennial here, he is a career man. Of course we reporters are more or less permanent; we stay here regardless of changes in the administration. We have a new job every time we have a change in administration. About the time you get one educated about how to handle things then you have a new bunch come in, and you have to start in all over on them.

In cases such as this, the officer becomes what one recent account calls the correspondent's "Chinaman"—a low-level source who

knows what is going on in a limited area.[8] This same study suggests that, as political superiors eagerly become spokesmen to the
press, their subordinates tend to "clam up." [9] This reinforces the
hypothesis that reporters seek out officers—"Chinamen"—that
will talk when high-level crackdown on information develops.

A relationship of this highly cooperative nature is more
likely to develop when the newsman and information officer perform essentially the same role as political communicators with
common purposes. Among vocational types, this congruence is
most probable when the officer is of the informer type, the newsman of the recorder type. Both are satisfied with "getting the
information out." Differences over what to interpret and how to
do it, or what to promote and how to do it, and make such relationships between other officers and reporters unlikely.

Few of the information officers interviewed were under any
illusions regarding the degree to which their services are utilized
by columnists or commentators. Most would agree with the officer who stated that, "I would say the so-called pundits do not
use the government information men very much." And, they
would probably agree with his reasoning, for he went on to point
out that these pundits "are successful to the extent that they have
inside tracks to the top officers of government." Columnists and
commentators, he argued, simply "do not traffic with this daily
news budget that we put out." Apparently, according to this
officer, the use made by the "pundit" of the information staff is
limited to matters of a routine nature. On matters of more general significance, of "broad policy questions," pointed out the
officer, "They are more apt to have direct access to the cabinet
officers or the big wheels in government." This means that the information officer is relegated to a rather insignificant role in his
service to the columnist or commentator, and this was the role
which this particular officer had experienced most: "But, every
one of the leading correspondents has at some time or other called
us for some information to round out a story—statistics or something to fill in the gaps."

The officer normally feels that his responses to newsmen's

[8] Bingham and Just, "The President and the Press."
[9] *Ibid.,* p. 21.

inquiries offer a useful means of serving agency purposes. Inquiry responses permit revelation of specific facts, save the official's time in answering questions, and permit the officer to give his personal interpretation when, in a release, he would be prohibited from doing so. Finally, as several officers pointed out, it is an opportunity to find out what is on the reporter's mind. Then, having found out, the officer can go to "staff people" and "light fires under them and get them to do something in order to avoid a lousy press":

> I find that I am asked to give advice and join in the assessment of a problem and to join in the assessment of what to do about it. I can do this well because in talking to newsmen and sitting with newsmen, I can see what worries the press and what is on their minds. I can then go to a staff member and point out to them that we are going to get hit with something very soon if we don't take some action on it.

If a technique's significance is measured by its use, then in spite of a tendency to frown upon the inquiry, it is a principal vehicle of information-dispensing and newsgathering. It represents the one line of access most continuously open to official Washington. It weathers official crackdowns on information policy, legalized restraints, and news blackouts. The very informality of the inquiry to the officer lends itself to a personalized treatment in which the alliance of officer and reporter can triumph over the "bureaucratic closed-mouths" at the top.

The news conference

Perhaps the most publicized method of newsgathering is the news conference. Although it has come in for its share of criticism by newsmen [10] as being misleading, incomplete, or dull, it remains one of their most popular techniques (Table 18). It too is looked upon as of primary utility to the newsman (Table 20). But reporters also think it serves the political head of a department or agency. In fact, newsmen tended to agree that this is the entire rationale behind the news conference and should be so. The con-

[10] Krock, "The Gathering of the News," p. 48.

ference is vital, argued one correspondent, for it serves two purposes for the policy-maker.

> One is that it makes the policy-maker available so that the
> newsman can get to him and ask him questions—ask him
> things on the newsman's initiative. At the same time, it
> gives the policy-maker a sounding board for his own ideas
> and permits him a channel for self-expression to the public.

This reporter went on to point out another function served
by the news conference. It can serve as a means by which the
president is able to exert control over executive departments and
agencies. Cabinet members, for example, when they hold regular
news conferences, are forced to take positions on administrative
policies being pushed by the president. The news conference, according to this respondent, "allows the cabinet officers to indicate
their conformity to the views of the president." The press conference then serves as a means by which a "united front" is presented to the public. Said the correspondent, "Now this is very
proper, for the president alone should be the exponent of policy;
each cabinet officer then expresses publicly what that policy is
and his agreement with it."

The implications of such a view, of course, are that the president should utilize the press conference to become chief news-
maker. If he does this, he allows very little latitude among his
subordinates for variations of opinion. If regularized conferences
are being held, then the likelihood that the reporter will find it
expedient or necessary to rely on "Chinamen" or "colonel's
cliques" for his headline stories is diminished. Adroit use of the
press conference by officials, then, promotes a centralization of
information policies within departments and agencies and de-
creases the tendency for dispersion of information functions that
are so characteristic of news and information crackdowns.

Newsmen prefer the "peg" of the big name—either president
or cabinet officer—if they can get it. To the reporter, of course,
the news conference offers this regularized access to agency and
department heads so necessary to his livelihood. There is a security and dependability in press conferences, for news is often
available from them, and they are regularly held.

Criticisms of press conferences abound nonetheless. Many newsmen do not like the mass atmosphere of the conference, particularly the nonexclusive quality coupled with the small likelihood of being permitted the time to ask questions. Others insist there are too many press conferences and the newsman cannot, attend them all. And, they urge, conferences are propagandistic on the very face. They permit direct appeals to the citizen and bypass the newsman entirely. Two-thirds of the newsman respondents offered such criticisms. Yet, criticisms could not offset one outstanding advantage—the chance for face-to-face contact with the official. The regularized press conference is assured access to the policy-maker, the dream of any reporter in Washington. One reporter was elated over the announcement from the Kennedy Administration in the early days of the New Frontier that there would be regular conferences held with the press:

> We believe very much in the press conference. We have asked all cabinet members and all the agency heads please to schedule regular conferences on the theory that there is no substitute for knowing that a man will be available on a regular basis, and you can bring up the questions that you have in mind. It is all well and good to say, "Well I will always be accessible, my door is always open." Well it isn't, and these guys are busy as hell and can't see you. The press conference eases the situation.

Officers vary in their attitude toward the press conference. The promoter, as is expected, relishes the possibility of having the agency official speak directly on policy and thereby command news space. The official has the opportunity to project policy without disagreement from his underlings. This is the crucial time for exerting political control over the agency publicly. Some officers frown on the news conference for the very reason that it eliminates their opportunity to be sole agency spokesmen. On the plus side, officers see the conference as cutting down the need for interviews, allowing the official the opportunity to hear the press, and giving the agency head initiative in significant news release.

Satisfaction with the news conference apparently is a function of the vantage point from which one views it. One newsman who had recently accepted a position as a departmental assistant secretary for public affairs expressed his astonishment with his former colleagues this way:

> We are markedly surprised by how superficial reporters can be. I would say that is the thing that is most surprising from this side of the desk as it was different from the other side. Of course I am much more well informed now than I was as a reporter so I know many of these programs—the secretary keeps me informed about them. Reporters ask questions that seem remarkably superficial and accept information which is only surface information. The result is that they print only what government officials want them to print.

This, again, points up a function which any technique of news release must apparently serve in Washington reporting—that of providing guidance to the correspondent. If it be true that reporters print only "what government wants them to print," the explanation may lie in the fact that the press conference provides a leadership in defining news which the reporter no longer can provide alone. An official announcement at a press conference is one way of revealing the new in the news "directly from the horse's mouth."

Information officers utilize the press conference to varying degrees; no definite pattern common to all officers was revealed in interview responses. The greatest percentage of respondents (38 per cent) volunteered that the conference was a seldom used technique. Many could not remember its use in the "last five years." "Oh, we have one occasionally, when a new head man comes into the agency; but that's pretty seldom" was one such response. Only 20 per cent of officers were located in agencies making a regular use of the press conference—weekly, monthly, or such. Another 21 per cent used the conference "often, but not regularly." The remainder never had acquaintance with the conference as a means of information-distribution.

Indications are that the conference is primarily a device used to put a political figure heading an agency in contact with the press. It is a technique more adaptable to purposes of personal publicity, not agency or departmental publicity. Consequently, its use is limited to those organizations of political significance in the administration—those with cabinet rank or key agencies. As reporters emphasized, it is a technique for publicizing policies and personnel of the administration in power. Since the majority of information officers in Washington do not move in such circles, it is not unusual that they have no consistent experience in dealing with the press conference.

TABLE 21

FUNCTION PERFORMED BY INFORMATION OFFICERS
IN HOLDING NEWS CONFERENCES

	PIO's in general ($N = 35$)	*Source Role Types* Informers ($N = 13$)	Educators ($N = 12$)	Promoters ($N = 10$)
Function				
Arranges news conferences only	56%	72%	50%	40%
Holds news conferences with press	16	14	33	10
Advises official in news conference	20	——	——	50
No function	8	14	17	——

Those officers taking a part in press conferences perform varied services in that connection (Table 21). As indicated, officers make arrangements for holding such conferences, are present at the conference, and advise the official. Some information officers—as in the Department of State—are given continuing responsibility for holding news conferences themselves. The part played in the utilization of the news conference will, of course, vary with the amount of confidence placed in an information officer by the political superior. Advice from an officer to an official will be heeded only to the extent that the officer's skills in public relations and his policy sense are recognized by the official.

The fact that an officer may serve as "spokesman" for his agency before the press, either in interviews or conferences, does not necessarily mean that he is a useful news source for the reporter. In fact, one of the causes of dissatisfaction among newsmen in their relations with officers lies in the fact that the "agency's spokesman" is too often a mere puppet of superiors. Correspondents grow disconcerted when press secretaries do nothing but read prepared copy, refuse to answer questions dealing with sensitive matters, and respond to questions with "no comment" or "not for publication" phrases. The arrangement in an agency is often to allow the officer to speak to the general press on specific issues and with "canned" comments, then to utilize the background conference—the "backgrounder"—or the "leak" as a means of giving information to more preferred reporters. The press conference then becomes a mere facade cloaking the more vital means of information release.

A good example of the use of the news conference for meeting the general press while retaining other lines of expression to the citizen was that of President Kennedy and the press. Upon taking office in January, 1960, John F. Kennedy stressed that frequent news conferences would be held—more frequently than in the case of his predecessor—and that such conferences would, upon occasion, be televised. This was to herald the dawning of continuing open relations with the news media with full public exposure. But, open press conferences represented only one facet of the "new" era in executive-press relations. For example, if Worth Bingham and Ward S. Just are correct in their interpretation,[11] a new device was thus developed for dealing with the press—the executive backgrounder. This involved the invitation to specific reporters to interview privately both the president and, in some cases, his cabinet members and key officials. In such interviews, information was made available on an exclusive basis to specifically chosen reporters willing to accept the responsibility for publishing. The mass press conference under such conditions was, again, a device for personal public relations. And if fewer conferences were held and the pace of weekly conferences did slacken, as was the case during the latter months of the Kennedy Adminis-

[11] Bingham and Just, "The President and the Press."

tration, the use of the exclusive backgrounder may well indicate that John F. Kennedy's approach to press relations represented an increasing institutionalization of a unique departure from the past.[12]

Although the technique of the exclusive backgrounder offers the opportunity for the official, through adroit private release of information, to utilize the reporter as a tool of public policy,[13] it was not without its hazards. It did, at different periods of the Kennedy Administration, produce confusion regarding the "high-level speculation" on the demotion of Chester Bowles and the more publicized issue of Ambassador Adlai Stevenson's position regarding support of the naval blockade in the Cuban crisis of October, 1962. Furthermore, this technique of the exclusive backgrounder was used by a wide variety of officials in Washington. This opening of top-level official sources of which the change in White House-press corps relation was symbolic had its effects on source-channel relations at lower levels. As top-level sources speaking in exclusive backgrounders became primary to the newsman, lower level sources, such as the information officer, grew less significant. Furthermore, other newsgathering techniques tended to fade into relative obscurity along with the press conference, the release, and the mass backgrounder.

The background conference

Of course, the technique of the backgrounder itself is not new. Its use dates from the earliest days of Washington reporting. Modern Washington reporters have gradually grown accustomed to the use of the "backgrounder" as a major device for newsgathering. Although newsmen are quick to remark about the shortcomings of the background conference, they nevertheless look upon it as having prime utility to their own interests (Table 20). The assets of the backgrounder to newsmen are several. It provides an opportunity to get official commentary on matters never covered in public press conferences; officials in private are willing to make remarks for which they refuse to be held responsible. But it is this very characteristic that some newsmen look

[12] *Ibid.,* p. 18.
[13] *Loc. cit.*

upon as a fundamental defect in the technique. This dissatisfaction was expressed by one reporter:

> I think as many things should be kept in the open before the public eye as possible. There is no need to have a background conference when a press conference will do just as well. I think the backgrounders perhaps are more important just for filling people in than giving them some information, but making it clear that there are not going to be any stories written about what went on there.

Whether newsmen favor the background conference depends on three factors. First, if all other sources of information are closed, the background conference may be essential to newsgathering. Secondly, the number of people invited appears to have some bearing on attitudes toward the use of the backgrounder. Some newsmen (25 per cent) dislike background conferences unless the number in attendance is kept small. Others dislike such an exclusive backgrounder intensely and get upset, particularly if they are not among the elite. The former point of view is reflected in the following statement:

> Well, I think the background conference in a mass situation is a rather dubious device. I feel that some of these things seem to get blown up and if there is any news in it it doesn't stay buried as long as it should. I think that the small intimate background where there may be two or three, or a handful of people, then I think that can be useful, if the people are trustworthy. The trouble with newspapermen, if they do get a piece of news they're apt to blow their lids.

Third, the rules that apply to the conference are relevant. The backgrounder from which direct quotes are permitted is favored; the conferences in which statements are not "for attribution" are distinctly condemned. The newsman praises background conferences designed to give very general information touching on general economic questions, foreign policy matters, and so forth. One reporter stated the critical function of the backgrounder this way: "Well, the backgrounder is, and I will have to go against what some of my colleagues say, indispensable, absolutely indispensable in my area; if I couldn't go to background briefings or get information from some of my contacts, I would never have any stories."

Few information officers interviewed were directly connected with background conferences. Those that were offered opinions that the device permits presentation of the agency's case without the necessity of taking specific responsibility for what is said. One respondent looked upon the background conference as absolutely necessary to distribution of information:

> We have open conferences, open to all press members. We get all types, not only members of the American press, but the foreign press, Communist reporters as well as friendly ones. All have the privileges of newsmen. The backgrounder prevents this. We can invite who we want to invite. When it comes to a story in which we invite not only the American press but the foreign press, we do not invite Communist reporters.

But the official or the officer using the backgrounder to leak information to the press in order to avoid personal responsibility must always be wary. Of all techniques for gathering news in Washington and for dispensing it, the ground rules for the backgrounder remain the most vague. Whether the background session is to be "off-the-record" or for "background-use-only" is not always clear. Officials have one impression; reporters may have another. Newsmen share the attitude of one correspondent that "off-the-record stuff is a lot of hooey." It too often means that the reporter, not the official, gets left holding the bag when a controversy develops over what was said at a backgrounder. The reporter is no more eager than the official to take responsibility for reporting classified information, engaging in "trial balloons," or trying to "ax" an administrative official. The popularity of the backgrounder places the responsibility for both policy-making and reporting on both official and newsman. It makes the reporter an informal tool of policy-making to be used by the official; it makes the official an informal tool of administrative reporting to be used by the newsman. As the backgrounder becomes "indispensable" it contributes to the complexity of government-press relations and re-emphasizes the basic problem: where is leadership in political communications to exist in the United States?

The interview

Reporters perceive several advantages connected with the opportunity to interview an agency official exclusively: it allows a "peg" for the story, increases story interest, lends topicality, adds information to the story, and gives the reporter the opportunity to stay in front of his competitors. The value of the interview is largely unquestioned by the newsman. Of our sample, 89 per cent expressed the opinion that the interview is valuable as a continuing source of news. Only 7 per cent saw it as of no value, and such responses represent reporters who either do little leg work of their own in Washington any more or who find it difficult to obtain access to officials for interviews. A few newsmen (4 per cent) argued that the interview was really too valuable to be used frequently. It should be used only for top stories in order that the newsman does not run the risk of overusing his news sources. He does not want to wear out his welcome.

The role played by information officers in interviews varies. Some officers merely make agency officials available to members of the press and do not interfere with access; others attempt to ease the way for the newsman in talking to the agency official. In some agencies, the officer has nothing to do with the interviews conducted with agency officials. A final group of officers serve in agencies which permit no interviews at all. Table 22 indicates the varying degrees of control exercised by information officers over interviews with agency officials.

A significant problem regarding the interview is the officer's responsibility for it. Consensus among officers appears to be that they should be informed by all officials of what takes place in the interview. With responsibility for the information program, it is argued, there should be commensurate recognition that the information office must be informed of what is said to the reporter. So goes the information officer's argument:

I personally think that it is a good idea if the director of information is made aware of what went on in interviews or is even invited to participate in order that he can have a better idea of what the type of publicity might be coming out of an interview. We don't do that type of thing here, but I do believe that it is a good idea to do so.

TABLE 22

INFORMATION OFFICERS' DEGREE OF CONTROL OVER
GRANTING NEWSMEN ACCESS TO
INTERVIEWS WITH OFFICIALS

Type of Control	Percentage of PIO's (N = 35)
It is necessary to arrange the interview with the PIO	23%
It is not necessary to arrange interview with PIO but most newsmen do so	32
It is not necessary to arrange interview with PIO and most newsmen who are regulars do not	29
It is not necessary to arrange interview with PIO and no newsmen do so	9
No interviews permitted in agency	7

Officers emphasize that it is to the advantage of the reporter to make his interview arrangements with the office of information. By so doing, it is easier to talk to officials even if there is no such requirement in the informational policy of the agency. One respondent stressed it this way: "It isn't necessary to come in here to this officer, but most reporters do, and we arrange an appointment with anyone with whom they want to talk; I think this eases the way for the people dealing with the press and for the reporter himself." This is the buffer function attributed by newsmen to the information specialist. As long as this is his role in the interview, no objections are made. It is only when he is authorized to control access to agency officials and does so that the relationship of officer and reporter shifts from compatibility to competition.

The informal source

The normalized procedures for releasing and gathering information discussed thus far differ somewhat from the use of the informal source of release. Few information officers or newsmen admit to using means of distributing information other than the official ones. Yet they did speak of certain "informal" procedures. Cater has offered that the "leak" is an institutionalized feature of Washington reportage.[14] Evidence from interviews is far too sketchy to determine whether such a regularized pattern of activity exists. The backgrounder, of course, is a relevant form of informal release that is becoming increasingly patterned. However, the informal source described here is distinct from the backgrounder. Because it was rarely commented upon by respondents, the following generalizations are highly tentative.

For those reporters who are "outsiders" among the Washington press corps, the informal news source is an imperative. The outsider is that correspondent who finds the more normalized lines of communication with official Washington closed to him or desires not to use them. He is usually the prescriber in great competition with officials in recommending action—the columnist, for example, who no longer has the close contacts with government officials that he had in the early period of the New Deal and refuses to utilize official lines of access to the news retains few devices for gathering information. But a few old friendships with officials still survive:

> As far as the government itself—I mean the agencies of the government—they won't give me the time of day; and, if they do, I know it's fifteen minutes late. So it has become important that I have personal friends who trust me. Having been on the Washington scene now for over thirty years, I formed a lot of friendships in the past. Some of my friends in spite of the edicts which have been issued, once in a while do come by in the evening to my house in ci-

---

[14] Cater, *The Fourth Branch of Government*, pp. 138–141.

vilian clothes or in taxies and sit down and we have some chow, and we talk without him giving me news. But, they can give me views which, if you read between the lines, the news is in them.

The few newsmen who employ such techniques insist that they find it necessary to check any information obtained with other sources before it is used. If informal procedures, however, are the only way that they may get unchanneled information, it is hard to see where the other sources would come from as a test of reliability. This approach, relying on informalized sources of information because all other sources have dried up, received little sympathy from most reporters. Most agreed that use of informal procedures is really the mark of a poor newsman. Most would agree with the statement of one bureau chief: "Right now there is no reason why the newsman should have any trouble getting information."

Information officers have few means of informal release of information. Those encountered were three in number: (1) the planting of a story with a particular reporter, (2) utilizing personal friendships with reporters to plant editorials favoring a given policy, and (3) releasing information to reporters by means of responses to inquiries even though such release is prohibited by agency policy. As Table 18 indicates, the use of the informal release by the information officer was cited as rarely as the reliance on the informal source was by the newsman.

THE INSTITUTIONALIZING OF POLITICAL COMMUNICATION

An obvious generalization from this survey of news and information techniques is that information personnel favor a particular technique when they regard it as useful to the distribution of their particular message; newsmen are fond of those techniques which appear useful to them in gathering information. Political communicators perceived specific techniques as primarily useful to their own cause and not more so to the interest of their sources or channels. Exceptions are that both reporters and officers view the interview as more useful to the press than government interests and the news release as more useful to government officials than newsmen. Both groups are critical of a particular technique to the extent that they perceive such a technique to be detrimental to their interests. Newsmen dislike methods which permit official management of the news; officers find fault with those which permit reportorial management of information.

To the information officer, it is within his special province to manage the release of information. A technique of political communication such as the interview or the news conference restricts the freedom of the officer in such management by increasing the alternatives open to the newsman. In the interview, it is the newsman who can articulate the issues which will be newsworthy; he does so by the adroit use of interrogation. In the open press conference, he still possesses this freedom of action, but to a somewhat lesser degree. Reporters prefer the technique which maximizes their control over selection of newsworthy issues. It is just this control which the information officer is reluctant to surrender. Hence he prefers the news release or inquiry for they assure control over issue determination and permit official initiative in such articulation.

This is not to suggest that there is anything venal in the motivations of either newsman or officer. The contention is that the function each sees himself performing as a political communicator dictates the necessity to exert a degree of control over information-dispensing or newsgathering. Management of news and information is inherent in the role performance of either variety of communicator. To the officer, it implies control over the issues raised and the harmonizing of conflict over policy between the bureaucracy and its external environment. To the reporter, such management connotes the statement of new issues, the revelation of conflict, and the continuing exposure of agency activities for public appraisal and, perhaps, controversy.

Essentially the techniques of political communication described are insitiutionalized patterns of interaction between news sources and newsmen. The contacts have become increasingly stylized in both written rules and informal agreements. The effects of institutional devices in politics for changing, ending, or reinforcing patterns of political behavior is a continually fascinating question for the political scientist.[15] As in other areas of political behavior, present evidence indicates that the structure of communication techniques tends to reinforce, and is reinforced by, the attitudes of communicators themselves. Historically new techniques of information-dispensing and newsgathering have been initiated by officials desiring to increase agency or personal access to the news media.[16] Adoption of news techniques led to a commitment to their use with an increasing channelization of official information. Each technique has become an accepted norm of official communication; both reporters and information officers have increasingly relied upon such techniques and adjusted to them. The increasingly technical character of news dissemination and the swelling numbers of newsmen have also fostered the institutionalization of newsgathering. Personalized reporting, represented by the virtuoso playing several quickly available news sources, has been replaced by management of information and news. The modern reporter distinguishes himself by "manufacturing" news as much as by "scooping" his competitiors. The result is an increasingly formalized pattern of political communication between officials and citizens, with reporters becoming a part of the official information establishment.

[15] V.O. Key, Jr., *American State Politics: An Introduction* (New York: Alfred A. Knopf, 1956), pp. 85–216. Truman, *The Governmental Process*, pp. 322–332. David Easton, *The Political System: An Inquiry into the State of Political Science* (New York: Alfred A. Knopf, 1953), pp. 149–199.

[16] Rosten, *The Washington Correspondents*, pp. 19–77. James E. Pollard, *The Presidents and the Press* (New York: The Macmillan Co., 1947).

CHAPTER VII
SIGNIFICANT ISSUES OF POLITICAL COMMUNICATION

It is but a small step from discussions of institutionalized controls over information and news release—of managed information, managed news, and manufactured news—to the consideration of major issues traditionally associated with government and the press in the United States. The bulk of scholarly and polemical material in the area of political communication deals in preferential terms with such problems as freedom of the press, freedom of information, the right to know, and official and press responsibilities to public opinion. Scholars, congressmen, journalists, and administrators—all at some time or another have been included on the roll of those concerned with such issues. We may assume that the perceptions of information officers and newsmen of such problems of governmental secrecy, political reporting, governmental publicity, and the shaping of public opinion are influences on their performance as political communicators. What, then, are these problems and attitudes?

THE POLITICS OF SECRECY AND PUBLICITY

From several fronts, attacks have been mounted on informational practices of federal departments and agencies. Underlying such criticism is a chain of assumptions regarding the relationship of government and public opinion in a democracy: (1) public officials in a democracy are responsible to popular control; (2) effective control requires an informed populace; (3) citizens have a "right to know"; (4) it is incumbent upon officials freely to avail citizens of the opportunity to obtain information about governmental activities; and (5) if officials fail to make available information needed for effecting popular control, then the "right to know" has been violated. In the wake of growing criticism of informational policies of departments and agencies by congressmen, scientists, administrators, and members of the press, the House Committee on Government Operations chartered a Special Subcommittee on Government Information in 1955. Committee findings are well summarized and documented in the volumes of hearings and reports of the Committee itself. Scholars and newsmen have devoted efforts to analyzing such reports.[1] We may compare their findings on governmental secrecy and publicity with the attitudes of persons interviewed about those issues.

The newsman's case was summed up by witnesses appearing at hearings of the Special Subcommittee on Government Information (the Moss Subcommittee). Reporters have reinforced this case in their own publications.[2] They postulate that a "paper curtain" screens governmental activities from the public view. According to the subcommittee report, a view shared by reporters

[1] See, for example, House Committee on Government Operations, *Availability of Information from Federal Departments and Agencies*, H. R. Rep. No. 2084, 86th Cong., 2d Sess. (1960); House Committee on Government Operations, *Executive Branch Practices in Withholding Information from Congressional Committees*, H. R. Rep. No. 2207, 86th Cong., 2d Sess. (1960); Rourke, *Secrecy and Publicity: Dilemmas of Democracy;* James Russell Wiggins, *Freedom or Secrecy* (New York: Oxford University Press, 1956); Harold L. Cross, *The People's Right to Know* (New York: Columbia University Press, 1953).

[2] House Committee on Government Operations, *Availability of Information from Federal Departments and Agencies*, H. R. Rep. No. 2947, 84th Cong., 2d Sess. (1956), pp. 81–89; Alsop and Alsop, *The Reporter's Trade*, pp. 19–39; Wiggins, *Freedom or Secrecy, passim.*

testifying, "Behind this curtain lies an attitude novel to democratic govenrment—an attitude which says that we, the officials,
not you, the people, will determine how much you are to be told
about your own Government." [3] No single administration or
political party is held responsible for such secrecy; the trend
characterizes all administrations after World War II.[4] It consists of increasing resort to overclassification of documents for
purposes of national security, the extensive use of the doctrine
of executive privilege, and the development of "an 'attitude'
toward concealment rather than dissemination of nonclassified
information." [5]

Correspondents and the committee majority agreed that the
"paper curtain" has contributed to the complexity of reporting
governmental activities. The size of the executive establishment
has increased faster than reportorial potential for covering it.
The press corps, unable to cope with the expansion of federal
activities, has relinquished its traditional function of day-to-day
scrutiny of official actions. In this new environment, officials
simply overlook their responsibilities to inform the public, and
"[t]he people's government is nowadays less and less the people's
business . . ." [6]

It is as a representative of "the people's business" that the
newsman makes his claim that administrative agencies should
reveal matters of public concern to reporters in order that they
be transmitted to the citizen. Since the public has a "right to
know," so do newsmen acting on behalf of the public. Reporters
appearing before the Moss Subcommittee argued that the newsman is the agent of the citizen, for such a grant of authority is
implicit in the First Amendment of the United States Constitution. The guarantee of freedom of the press, they argued, belongs
to all citizens. It is made operational when the newsman is permitted to find out for the citizen what he cannot discover directly

[3] *Availability of Information*, H. R. Rep. No. 2947, 84th Cong., 2d Sess.
(1956), p. 81.
[4] *Ibid.*, p. 3; Alsop and Alsop, *The Reporter's Trade*, pp. 19–39.
[5] *Availability of Information*, H. R. Rep. No. 2947, 84th Cong., 2d Sess.
(1956), p. 4.
[6] Alsop and Alsop, *The Reporter's Trade*, p. 25; *Availability of Information*, H. R. Rep. No. 2947, 84th Cong., 2d Sess. (1956), pp. 81–88.

for himself. Hence, refusal to inform the newsman is a refusal to reveal matters to a public which has a constitutional right to know about governmental affairs. If the reporter receives such a refusal, it is then the duty of the congressman to lend assistance by opening inquiry into executive informational practices. The Moss Subcommittee tended to concur with this generalization of Congressional responsibility:

> Congress should everywhere specify exact limitations on withholding by the departments and agencies it has created.
> Congress should clearly enunciate the fundamental principle that the public business is the public's business.
> Congress should effectively implement this principle.[7]

The line of reasoning voiced by reporters before the Moss Subcommittee was adopted by congressmen serving in the investigation, at least by a majority of the subcommittee. This meant that the original conflict between press and executive departments and agencies soon became a struggle in executive-legislative relations with the interests of press and Congress allied against those of the bureaucracy. Since the opening of the investigation, claims of newsmen against federal informational procedures have often been given active support by this subcommittee. In fact, the majority of claims made against information practices have arisen either from press or Congress (Table 23). The arguments adopted in committee reports to support such claims have been those stressing "freedom of information" and the "right to know" originating with newsmen. The legislative and "fourth" branches have often united against the executive.

The principal defense of the official point of view, developed in the hearings, was that, as there is a right to know on the citizen's part, so there is a right to withhold information in the interests of orderly administration. It is the official, not the reporter, who is to make the judgment as to whether such withholding, or the timing of its release, is in the interests of orderly governmental processes:

[7] *Availability of Information*, H. R. Rep. No. 2947, 84th Cong., 2d Sess. (1956), p. 94.

TABLE 23

SOURCES OF COMPLAINTS LEVELED AGAINST INFORMATION
PRACTICES OF FEDERAL DEPARTMENTS
AND AGENCIES, 1955–60*

Source of Complaint	Percentage of Cases (N = 174)
Press	36%
Committee of congress	35
Member of congress	9
Private individual or scientist	8
Federal official	6
Private organization	4
State agency	2

* Compiled from House Committee on Government Operations, *Availability of Information from Federal Departments and Agencies,* House Report No. 2084, 86th Cong., 2d Sess., 1960, p. 36.

We have a right under the Constitution, in carrying out our functions, to make a determination in the best interests of the public, and for the purposes for which it was organized, and the Commission would, under the Constitution, have that inherent power.[8]

Such is the outline of the way that "governmental secrecy" was defined at hearings of the Special Subcommittee on Government Information—the issues raised and the opposing justifications. The present research afforded the opportunity to interrogate a sample of information officers and newsmen regarding their personal views on these matters.

From the interest and time expended on the problem by Congressional committees and organizations of editors and publishers, one would expect both information officers and newsmen to have

[8] Lawrence V. Meloy, acting general counsel of the United States Civil Service Commission, testifying before the Special Subcommittee of Government Information of the House Committee on Government Operations. *Availability of Information,* H. R. Rep. No. 2947, 84th Cong., 2d Sess. (1956), pp. 13–14.

experienced severe problems of government secrecy. However, interview data indicate that secrecy is not a big problem. Only 36 per cent of the officers interviewed and 40 per cent of the newsmen reported that withholding of information by government officials had ever been a problem to them in their jobs. Officers citing instances in which questions of secrecy had arisen seldom found such cases of any significance. What upset the information officer was the tendency for withholding to be accepted by newsmen until that moment when they were denied a story which they were particularly anxious to print. It was at this point that the newsman grew upset. At least, this was the argument offered by officers.

Many information respondents agreed with the general opinion stressed by one officer who emphasized what he thought was the hypocrisy underlying the whole struggle over freedom of information. He stated rather testily, "Well it is my opinion that the problem of withholding of information is largely a myth and is highly overplayed." As far as this officer was concerned, there was entirely too much insincerity underlying the whole argument used by reporters in attempting to justify their claims against withholding of information. The problem, he stressed, is not one of principle, not one of rationality, but rather "is emotional and stimulated by a very small group of individuals who spend a great deal of time hollering about whether information is getting out to the public." Hypocrisy abounds, he emphasized:

> I don't believe that members of the press have a genuine feeling about the public's right to know when they protest that information is being withheld. I rather believe that they are only concerned with it when that withholding produces for them individual problems of getting a story. It becomes an emotional thing because they can't get their own little story.

We should note that such arguments were not used to justify particular withholding practices, but rather to indicate that officers were not troubled by governmental secrecy. In those few instances in which they were, the event was of little importance. Officers feel that there is a gentleman's agreement between them-

selves and reporters. That agreement is violated when the newsman raises a cry that his "right to know" is being infringed upon
simply because he is denied what to the officer is trivial information and not even worth a story in the first place. What really
galls the information officer is to undergo ridicule for denying
access to a particular slice of information, then find that after he
has made it available, the reporter no longer wants it! One officer
told this story:

> I think it was about last year, by law certain files of some
> exempt organizations, charitable organizations and things
> of that kind, were open to public inspection upon request.
> Surprisingly enough, even though at the time there was
> what seemed to be at least a small hue and cry about keep-
> ing these things secret, once they were opened up there has
> not been too much interest in them.

Officers disagreed rather sharply with the press's basic argument for justifying access to information—the identification of
the reporter as the representative of the citizen. Officers contended
that the reporter is a channel of governmental information, but
only one such channel. Just because information is not given to
the newsman, it is argued, does not mean that information is not
being made public. Rather it is made public, but to an entirely
different representative of the citizen, one which the citizen himself has chosen:

> No information is withheld. It is made available to Con-
> gress, and Congress happens to represent the duly elected
> officials of the public who are acting in the public's name
> in governing the country. If information were withheld
> from Congress there might be a legitimate gripe, but simply
> because information is withheld from the press does not
> mean that information is not being made available to the
> American people. It is being made available to the Ameri-
> can people through Congress, and the question is whether
> the press in this country is going to attempt to supplant
> Congress. I believe that is the duty of Congress as an insti-
> tution and not the press!

The majority of information respondents, however, sympa-
thized with the newsman's problems in gathering intelligence.

Such officers could not accept their superiors' rationalizing the withholding of information. Regarding their primary function as that of "getting the information out," such officers share the newsman's view that withholding of information is evil. They tend to approve of the informal alliance of reporter and congressmen used to pry information out of federal departments and agencies. The Moss Subcommittee is a form of protection for an officer against his superiors:

> I think the Moss Committee has been a good thing. Five years ago when I came here, it was very difficult to get information out to the public. I think it has improved primarily because of the Moss Committee. Now a newsman, if something is withheld from him, can go to the Moss Committee and say, "Look, such and such agency is withholding this, what can be done about it?" Then we have to answer to them; so it helps us too as information people. When we think something should be released to the public, we can go to the Commission and say, "These should be released; if we don't release it, we are going to have trouble with the Moss Committee." It is sort of a leverage that both newsmen and information people use.

Another officer defined the struggle over withholding of information as one of officers and reporters versus politically appointed agency officials. In that struggle the Moss Subcommittee aids the reporter and, hence, also does a service for the information officer. The respondent stressed,

> I think they have done a great service simply by existing; they are sitting there in Washington as a kind of court of appeals for the newsmen who find that information is classified; when they suspect that it is classified for political reasons rather than for legitimate security reasons, they can at least go to the Moss Committee and ask for them to look into it.

Hence, as far as officers are concerned, the Moss investigations are often as much help to them as to the newsman. Officers shy away from withholding information because they fear either the ridicule of reporters or the scrutiny of Congress. They would prefer to "get it out into the open" and thus avoid the limelight which focuses on an agency when information policies are questioned. Hence, they regard the Moss Subcommittee not only as the reporter's court of appeal but also their own—a weapon to be used against the superior in the bureaucracy.

Newsmen divided on the problem of governmental secrecy primarily on the basis of the department or agency they covered regularly. Those covering sensitive agencies, for example, were more outspoken about the dangers of governmental withholding than were agricultural, interior, or financial correspondents. What appears to rankle the newsman is not the withholding of information for security reasons, but the tendency to rationalize marginal withholding on that basis. One correspondent who makes his livelihood by specializing in defense reporting put the matter in the following way:

> We point out at every opportunity incidents of ridiculous withholding of information that obviously has no military security aspect attached to it. The Moss Committee has done a good job of that; they have used ridicule from time to time to point up the fact that the information security mill is such a vast thing now that nobody is really in control of it, and that it leads to classification of everything but the weather report from time to time, and it even did that in the Pentagon. So you know this is one we have a particular bee in our bonnet about.

Such remarks are seldom echoed by newsmen concerned with less sensitive areas of reporting. They do not agree with the respondent just quoted that withholding is something that "we have a particular bee in our bonnet about." Since their reportorial goals are not directly tied to the conflict over freedom of information, they indicate considerably less interest in the matter. Many deny any knowledge of withholding problems and treat the subject as completely foreign to their experience. One put it this way, "I am not interested in it because I believe if you go after news, you get it; there is no way in the world they can withhold something if you make up your mind to get it."

Both sets of political communicators agreed that withholding of information from the public view is an evil. As Table 24 indicates, however, there is greater consensus among officers on the reason that it is evil than there is among newsmen. This is interesting in light of the united front presented by the members of the press corps at hearings by the special subcommittee looking into the problem.

TABLE 24

COMPARISON OF REASONS OFFERED BY INFORMATION OFFICERS AND NEWSMEN AS TO WHY WITHHOLDING OF INFORMATION SHOULD NOT BE PERMITTED

Reasons	PIO's (N = 35)	Newsmen (N = 28)
Withholding is bad because officials have a responsibility to the public to inform	64%	25%
Withholding is bad because the newsman as a representative of the public has a right to information	8	28
Withholding is considered bad only when the newsman's interests are directly involved	16	10
Withholding is not a significant problem	12	37

Furthermore, the data in Table 24 provides an interesting comparison with that in Table 25. Neither set of communicators visualizes the obligation to inform as unrestrained. Limits, it is agreed, are placed by the necessities of decision-making, national security, and so on. It is noteworthy that newsmen, however, see the practical necessity of limiting the obligation more than the officers do. This, combined with the fact that 60 per cent of newsmen respondents experienced no difficulty with governmental secrecy and 37 per cent thought the question not sufficiently critical to merit attention, raises the question of why any concern at all was expressed in committee hearings.

In Congressional hearings, newsmen raised another complaint against governmental information practices. James Reston, Washington bureau chief of *The New York Times,* pointed out

TABLE 25

COMPARISON OF ATTITUDES OF INFORMATION OFFICERS
AND NEWSMEN TOWARD THE OBLIGATION OF
GOVERNMENTAL OFFICIALS TO INFORM
CITIZENS OF ACTIVITIES

Attitude	PIO's (N = 38)	Newsmen (N = 35)
Obligation to inform is complete (newsman retains right to decide what to print)	44%	36%
Obligation to inform is limited by necessities of decision-making, national security, etc.	53	64
Obligation to inform is at official's discretion in all matters	3	——

the growing tendency of governmental officials to use the news media as an instrument of policy, a process which contributes to misleading the reading and viewing public.[9] This problem of the management of news is a reflection of the more comprehensive question of governmental publicity and the relationship of officials to public opinion.

Among newsmen surveyed, governmental publicity per se was not viewed as the monolithic evil that one would expect from reading the Congressional hearings. Table 26, for example, indicates that respondents generally regard governmental publicity as an inherent, necessary, and positive function of the official. Among channel role types, the prescriber is least impressed by this function, which conflicts directly with his own defined role of recommending alternative courses of action for public consideration.

Newsmen sampled also insisted that officials should take primary responsibility for the leadership of public opinion. They are especially sensitive to the responsibility of political agency heads to make use of particular publicity techniques for this purpose.

---

[9] *Availability of Information,* H. R. Rep. No. 2947, 84th Cong., 2d Sess. (1956), p. 5.

TABLE 26

ATTITUDES OF NEWSMEN TOWARD GOVERNMENT PUBLICITY

Attitude	Total Newsman Percentages (N = 30)	Recorder (N = 8)	Expositor (N = 13)	Prescriber (N = 9)
Government publicity is a necessary and positive function	80%	100%	77%	66%
Government publicity is a necessary but negative function	10	——	15	22
Government publicity is an unnecessary function	10	——	8	12

One editorial writer voiced a common opinion when he stated, "I think that the policy-maker ought to use the press conference consciously, determinedly, skillfully to promote public understanding of his programs; it's a tremendous opportunity that a leadership ought not to miss." But not all newsmen agreed; some felt it the newsman's responsibility to lead opinion:

> A policy-maker who protests loudest about what the public is thinking is a liar. But what he means actually is that the public should know what he wants them to know. I haven't found a policy-maker yet who had any of this fervor in him to tell the public every problem which is serious and is unpleasant. They always try to coat it with sugar coating, and the louder you protest that, the more of a liar he is.

However, this view was not encountered very often among newsmen. At most, the respondents would insist that the leadership responsibility is joint between newsman and official; two-thirds, however, were willing to leave it primarily to the official and either simply report that or explain it (Table 27). This, of course, introduces a problem in press responsibility. How far can newsmen go in foregoing leadership of public opinion before, by default, they surrender the classic role of scrutiny of official leadership? If the newsman is a representative of the citizen, enjoying the advantage of being "on the spot," does he have any responsibility for providing leadership for the citizen's opinions?

TABLE 27

ATTITUDES OF INFORMATION OFFICERS AND NEWSMEN
TOWARD LEADERSHIP OF PUBLIC OPINION BY
GOVERNMENT AND THE NEWS MEDIA

Attitude	PIO's (N = 33)	Newsmen (N = 30)
Government officials are primarily responsible for leadership	70%	66%
Leadership of public opinion is a joint responsibility of officials and newsmen	11	18
Newsmen alone are responsible for leadership as representatives of the public	19	16

The complexity of the problem is magnified if the question is asked, should public opinion be considered in official decision-making and is the official responsible to public opinion in his behavior? Table 28 indicates that newsmen and information officers assert that the public official must give some consideration to public opinion in governing. Many regard such consideration as essential, for they feel that either the success of agency programs or the political success of the official himself depends on an ability to curry public favor. One-fourth of both samples expressed the view that any official is only a "rubber stamp"; that is, he merely converts into policy the direct dictates of his constituents.

To the information officer, governmental publicity is regarded as a necessary function, a tool of leadership in public opinion. In being committed to public opinion for self- and program survival, it is incumbent on the official to provide leadership as a means of enlisting support. The pattern of newsman attitudes is similar: government publicity is a necessary and positive function; the official is primarily responsible for leadership of public opinion and is in turn dependent upon favorable opinion for success. "News management" is implicitly accepted

TABLE 28

COMPARISON OF CONCEPTS OF NEWSMEN AND
INFORMATION OFFICERS OF THE OFFICIAL'S
RESPONSIBILITY TO PUBLIC OPINION

Concept	PIO's (N = 32)	Newsmen (N = 28)
Official has no responsibility to public opinion	18%	13%
Official considers public opinion for his survival and the success of his programs	57	61
Official should act on the dictates of public opinion	25	26

as legitimate except by that 50 per cent of prescribers who insist that newsmen have the leadership responsibility. This suggests that such management is acceptable when it does not pose a threat to the newsman's perceived role.

Attempting to define public opinion is a complex process. To the information officer, the sources for the assessment of public opinion are several. Primary sources (Table 29) are editorials, columns, the amount of play a story receives in the news media, and reactions of clientele groups. This does not mean, however, that all editorial, columnist, and story reaction is considered to be of equal value. Certain newspapers are favored over others. One information officer pointed out the selectivity in using editorial and story reaction as an assessment of public opinion:

> Every morning at five o'clock I have men come in the office and go through the following newspapers: *The Washington Post, The* [Washington] *Evening Star,* the Washington *Daily News,* the New York *Herald Tribune, The New York Times,* and *The Wall Street Journal.* We have found

that stories being run in these newspapers are generally those important in many other areas of the country. Furthermore, from the standpoint of editorial opinion, these six or seven newspapers cover the entire spectrum politically from conservative on through the liberal. We can find out what editorial reaction is to bills and policies throughout the spectrum, and that is the second reason that we choose these particular newspapers. Furthermore, they represent an opinion of particular importance to policy officials, that is those that will be read by many officials other than those in this department and by many segments of the public which will be interested in departmental policy.

Attempts are even devoted to soliciting favorable editorial and story reaction in certain media. As one officer indicated, there is a tendency to seek as wide a dissemination of agency policy as possible. Such wide dissemination depends on utilization of the "prestige" press:

> Again if you have a program you want it to get the widest possible dissemination—the information get the widest possible dissemination. I think it is unfortunately true. We tend to prefer the morning releases for economics over releases, for example, in the afternoon because we get wider coverage than the morning papers on economics. We used to have a secretary who thought we had failed if *The New York Times* didn't give us a big play on everything we did. We had an awful time because we couldn't succeed very well without *The New York Times*.

Newsmen not connected with news media receiving this official seal of approval are critical of the practice of gaining wide distribution through elite news organs. They charge that officers are inclined to yield far greater access to the reporter from one of the prestigious papers than to one coming from a newspaper in the "boondocks." One newsman insisted that information officers play favorites in exchange for distribution: "If you can get a story on the front page of *The New York Times,* you don't have to worry thereafter; it will get into every paper in the country."

Interestingly enough, what one reporter criticizes another praises, particularly if he is a newsman of a favored journal:

TABLE 29

COMPARISON OF THE SOURCES OF PUBLIC OPINION
USED BY THE OFFICIAL AS PERCEIVED BY
INFORMATION OFFICERS AND NEWSMEN

Source	PIO's (N = 38)	Newsmen (N = 35)
Editorials	63%	50%
Columnists	23	35
Story play	70	40
Congress	13	20
Newsmen's questions	16	30
Letters	13	——
Interest groups	50	10
Public opinion samples	6	——

I think it helps to be working for my paper. In Washington I may seldom see anyone I know personally when working on a story, but because I am from *The Times* it helps me because they will give me things that they would never give to an unknown reporter from some other paper in this town. They will give me things and open doors to me because I am from *The Times*. That happens to be a fact of life in this town.

Role expectations of information officers and newsmen toward public opinion, its leadership, and its assessment are influential in the relationship between source and channel. To the extent that newsmen concur with officers that responsibility for opinion leadership rests with governmental officials, there is promotion of compatibility and perhaps cooperation; if, however, the newsman believes he is responsible for such leadership and perceives his leadership as contrary to that of the government official, competition is fostered. The degree of compatibility also appears to be a function of the degree of overlap in definition of public opinion between sources and channels and the assessment of the direction and intensity of such opinion. Although a vague concept to many, political communicators perceive the existence of public opinion; they would define it in approximately the terms of the following newsman: "I think that public opinion is always uppermost in the minds of most people in government; that is, you want to take, whatever the action is, you want a good public face." It is within this general framework of definition that political communicators may agree, or disagree, on the acceptable leadership for the promotion of that opinion.

Hearings of the Special Subcommittee on Government Information dealt, almost by accident, with another issue of consequence. Because it is a problem which has existed since the origin of a free press, it is rather remarkable that it was brushed aside with such quickness. Officials and minority members of the subcommittee urged that the assumption of governmental responsibility for information release must be accompanied by an equally vital recognition that such information will be treated responsibly by members of the press. Disagreement of the newsman panel before the subcommittee was immediate. Unfortunately— at least for those interested in obtaining documented views of officials and newsmen on this point—the question of press responsibility was quietly dropped, but not, however, until after the following exchange occurred between Rep. Clare E. Hoffman (R., Mich.) and James S. Pope, the publisher of *The Louisville Courier-Journal:*

> MR. HOFFMAN: I take it also that you gentlemen contend that the right to know has coupled with it the right to accurate information?
>
> MR. POPE: The right to accurate information on whose part? I don't quite follow your question.
>
> MR. HOFFMAN: The press claims the right to have information from the executive departments. That is what we are concerned with at the moment.
>
> MR. POPE: That is right.
>
> MR. HOFFMAN: That right is the right to transmit accurate information.
>
> MR. POPE: I think that I see what is coming. I would say yes, but I would like to answer the question when you get through with it.
>
> MR. HOFFMAN: Then, Mr. Pope, if it should be so unfortunate that numbered with those seeking information there is an individual who is, shall we say, a chronically inaccurate individual, should he have the same right to information

when his past record indicates that he has consistently mis-stated the facts that were given him as do those who have been accurate in transmitting to the public the information they receive from the departments. [*Sic.*]

MR. POPE: Yes; I would say he has the same right. I would like, if I may, [to] separate in all of our minds two different things. We have run across this question a good many times. It is a legitimate question and it is an important question, and that is: How accurate and decent and fair and respon-sible is the press? I would hate to have to answer that. There are nearly 1,800 daily newspapers in the United States. I find it almost impossible to read everything in the two that I am supposed to supervise. The only point that I would like to make to you is, these are 2 intensely important and 2 entirely separate questions, just like 2 railroad tracks, and if you confuse them I think you can damage both.

MR. HOFFMAN: Your two tracks run down the same right-of-way, sir.

MR. POPE: The right to access to public information is, as we have said—and I am sure that you agree—the right of the people. Therefore, no matter how "lousy" the press gets, there is never in my mind any justification for foreclosing the sources of any information because always there is the right of any individual who wants to and in a democracy like ours to go and find out for himself. We could have a long session here and a very interesting one on the irre-sponsibility of the press and I would be glad to contribute to it. I still insist that it is an entirely separate problem from freedom of information, and if we confuse them we may damage both. In other words, your committee would never, I am sure, undertake as one of its directive [*sic*], or functions, the disciplining of the press. All we can do is to try to keep it free and hope as we go along—and I believe history will prove this is true—it improves a little gradually. But whatever I can do about the press, or whatever you can do about the press is more or less personal.

As a Member of Congress, there is very little that you can do about it as long as we have the first amendment. If I admit that the press is as bad as you probably think it is, I still think that is basically irrelevant to the question of whether the people of this country should have access to Government information. As long as you do not try to shut off any information on the basis of the press being pretty bad occasionally, I will agree with you it is pretty bad.[10]

[10] *Availability of Information*, H. R. Rep. No. 2947, 84th Cong., 2d Sess. (1956), pp. 8–9.

Many government officials, including information officers, are forced to agree, however, with Representative Hoffman that the "two tracks run down the same right-of-way." Officials demand the right to screen information to assure that intelligence released to the press will be used responsibly; yet members of the press demand that they decide what is responsible performance. The problem is a continuing one. In no area has it been so dramatically demonstrated recently as in the first two years of the Kennedy Administration's handling of the recurring Cuban crisis. Both the administration and the press complained vigorously that the other was acting irresponsibly in information policies. The first outcry came from the administration forces following the ill-fated landings at the Bay of Pigs in April, 1961. Much official dismay was expressed over reports in the news media which warned of build-ups for a Cuban invasion that spring. Following the failure of the episode, President Kennedy was prompted in his speech in New York before the American Newspaper Publishers Association on the night of April 27, 1961, to lecture the group on problems of press responsibilities in a continuing crisis situation such as that fostered by the Cold War. The problem, he said, is twofold and paradoxical:

> This deadly challenge imposes upon our society two requirements of direct concern to both the press and the President—two requirements that may seem almost contradictory in tone, but which must be reconciled and fulfilled if we are to meet this national peril. I refer, first, to the need for far greater public information; and, second, to the need for far greater official secrecy.[11]

Present events offer a "clear and present danger," he argued, one in which the press must accept responsibility for the national interest. Without attempting an excuse for censorship, the president offered the formula for press responsibility: "Every newspaper now asks itself, with respect to every story: 'Is it news?' All I suggest is that you add the question: 'Is it in the national interest?' "[12]

[11] *The New York Times*, April 28, 1961, p. 14.
[12] *Loc. cit.*

Faced with the demands for official secrecy and public information, the president stressed the necessity for self-restraint on the part of the press. But his formula is not easily applied by newsmen themselves. The definition of the national interest is no easier to make for the reporter than it is for the official, indeed perhaps less so. The typical response of newsmen advocating greater freedom of information is that there is no distinction between what is news and what is the national interest; all news is in the national interest. Note the following from a Washington editor:

> Well, all information that the public should have can be news. Now, it is my opinion that all news when it is printed is in the national interest. No piece of information that is withheld is withheld because it is in the national interest to withhold it. All news that is printed is in the national interest. If they will give us particular items of news or particular events or particular pieces of information, then we can say specifically and make a judgment on our own part as to whether it is in the national interest or not.

Members of the press, when faced with the problem of defining personal responsibilities, insist first "give us the news" and, then, "we shall make the judgment of responsibility." They concur with Mr. Pope's statement before the Moss Subcommittee, that "no matter how 'lousy' the press gets, there is never in my mind any justification for foreclosing the sources of any information because always there is the right of any individual who wants to and in a democracy like ours to go and find out for himself." [13] The rationale employed by the news media for an open society is reminiscent of that of defenders of a court system in a free society regarding the right to judicial processes—it is better that a thousand guilty go free than that one innocent man be convicted. Or, as Mr. Pope stated, "As long as you do not try to shut off any information on the basis of the press being pretty bad occasionally, I will agree with you it is pretty bad." [14] An open society is essen-

---

[13] *Availability of Information*, H. R. Rep. No. 2947, 84th Cong., 2d Sess. (1956), p. 9.
[14] *Loc. cit.*

tial, argue reporters, regardless of the consequences for the so-
called national interest.

Officials can accept this rationale only to a point. For in the
Cold War, argued the president, perhaps additional tests should
be adopted rather than recognizing "only the tests of journalism
and not the tests of national security." Although no such additional tests should be applied to "censor the news," stated the
president, they must be found.[15] Newsmen doubted that, by the
time the Cuban crisis had erupted in October, 1962, such non-
censorship tests had been discovered. For it was during that period
that the Kennedy Administration, through the mouthpiece of
Arthur Sylvester, assistant secretary for public affairs of the
Department of Defense, announced the "news as weaponry" concept to be used in the Cold War. Simply defined, it meant that
"in the kind of world we live in, the generation of news by actions
taken by the government becomes a weapon in a strained situation." [16]

Newsmen reacted both immediately and negatively. The
weaponry concept, to them, implies a combination of the worst
of both worlds—the use of secrecy to avoid letting the reporter
in on what is going on and the use of planned publicity (news
management) in order to exploit the correspondent as a tool of
the bureaucracy. *The New York Times* editorialized that "there
is no doubt that 'management' or 'control' of the news is censorship described by a sweeter term." [17] Arthur Krock felt it necessary
to comment. His view was that "there is a basic functional conflict involved." That conflict is between the responsible use of
information by the press and the responsible release of it by the
administration whether its policy is liberal or otherwise.[18] Editorials and commentary were aimed at arousing public opinion;
the other course of action was to appeal to the Moss Committee,
an alternative quickly grasped and to which there was quick response, at least verbally, from Representative Moss: "We have

[15] *The New York Times,* April 28, 1961, p. 14.
[16] Associated Press dispatch, *Lubbock Avalanche-Journal,* November 1, 1962,
sec. 3, p. 14.
[17] *The New York Times,* October 31, 1962, p. 34.
[18] Arthur Krock, "National Security and the 'Flow' of Information," *The
New York Times,* November 22, 1962, p. 28.

in the past few weeks experienced a degree of news management which is unique in peacetime, a disturbing period of unplanned and unprecedented news management." [19]

The final publicized event was the president's news conference of November 20, 1962, in which he publicly defended the administration's posture before the press:

> I can assure you that our only interest has been, first, during this period of crisis, and over a longer period, to try to —not to have coming out of the Pentagon information which is highly sensitive, particularly in the intelligence areas, which I can assure you in my own not too distant experience, has been extremely inimical to the interest of the United States.[20]

The open controversy between president and press during the drawn-out Cuban crisis illustrated the extremely fine line that is continually drawn between press and official responsibilities in informing the citizenry. Although waged within the context of a "national interest" to which both official and newsmen groups appeal for justification of their own case, the underlying conflict is basically one of particular interests which can be only partially reconciled in a free society. The responsibilities of the press in scrutinizing government officials and, as Jefferson insisted, in providing a "censor of government" [21] must always run counter to the basic interest of a bureaucracy in pushing through programs for the satisfaction of varied clienteles. The press interest is often that of getting the news for sake of the news itself, an interest often conflicting with that of a bureaucracy either in (a) preventing publicity altogether or (b) manipulating publicity to the advantage of individual programs. Both press and bureaucracy are parts of the same political process, a process in which tension and strife are inescapable by definition.

No statement so clearly summarizes the nature of the disagreement that exists between newsmen and information officers over the issues of governmental secrecy than does that of Rep.

[19] Associated Press dispatch, *Lubbock Avalanche-Journal,* December 1, 1962, sec. 1, p. 1.

[20] *The New York Times,* November 21, 1962, p. 10.

[21] *The Works of Thomas Jefferson,* p. 146.

Clare E. Hoffman (R., Mich.) in his dissent from the majority report of the Moss Subcommittee. Here he implied what is truly at the heart of the controversy. Mr. Hoffman agreed that "insofar as the press or its employees represent the public, it certainly is entitled to all information which can, within reason, be furnished and the giving of which would not adversely affect the national security." If information is denied the public, "assuming the foregoing conclusions to be sound, it follows that a congressional committee may ask pertinent questions." If information required by Congress is refused, argued Mr. Hoffman, then "contempt proceedings may be instituted and the courts become the final arbitrators of the soundness of the request, the reasonableness of the refusal." [22]

If Congress is denied information by the executive, Congress can take some form of action. But, here is where Congress differs from the press, for the press has no such recourse. The press can only enlist the aid of Congress in the battle for freedom of information, or seek the aid of "public opinion":

> No such remedy exists for the private citizen or for the representative of the press who is denied information to which he thinks he is entitled. In this field, the remedy would seem to be through an expression of public opinion or, if a legal remedy is sought, the court might be constrained to adopt the doctrine of reasonableness, that is, balance the importance of the information sought against the cost and difficulty of making it available.[23]

What is significant for us is the underlying assumption in this view, that of a concept of "balance." Someone must balance "the soundness of the request" with the "reasonableness of the refusal." What is implicit in such a statement is that what is truly in conflict are the interests of the administration and those of the press. The struggle over "freedom of information" is basically one of a conflict of interests, conflicts which are inherently political in nature, not necessarily matters of differing principle.

[22] *Availability of Information,* H. R. Rep. No. 2947, 84th Cong., 2d Sess. (1956), p. 97.
[23] *Loc. cit.*

Without undue cynicism, we may suggest that both newsmen and information officers become intensely concerned with governmental secrecy and publicity when they believe that their own interests in political communication are being threatened. This is not to say that problems of governmental secrecy and public persuasion per se are not of significance, rather that neither reporters nor officers think of such problems in the frameworks of inherent "rights to know" or needs for "orderly government." Such concepts are introduced *after* the perceived interests of the actor are jeopardized by the withholding of information or claim for access. When reportorial interests in obtaining news are threatened, there is immediate and loud appeal for Congressional assistance on the grounds that the "right to know" is being subjugated to the whims of capricious administrators. And, if bureaucratic interests in policy formulation are threatened by publicity, policy-makers voice concern for the future of the "national security."

In these matters of interest conflict, the newsman has found it expedient to seek an alliance with members of Congress against executive privilege. Information officers recognize the alliance and approve or disapprove of it depending upon their own goal orientation within their organization. The reportorial rationalization—being a representative of the people—is accepted by officers if they perceive that the newsman's claim for access is at least compatible with their own role in information-dispensing. It is noteworthy that those officers most skeptical of the reporter's claim to being identified as agent of the public were political appointees directly responsible for the image of the agency in the press. It is among such promoters that the justification of an inherent right to withhold is encountered. At the same time it is among editors, publishers, and columnists that the claim of the people's "right to know" is prevalent. It was a prescriber who was most concerned with governmental officials "sitting on the lid":

> There is a great desire on the part of the officials to use the press for their own purposes. And unless the press is very much alive, as it isn't any more and as it used to be in my younger days, it is more and more an instrument of the government. And that is done, particularly now, by the

> muzzling of high officials—particularly generals, admirals, and so on down the line—who do not give you any secrets, but give you a picture of the strength or the weakness of the country in their respective fields. And they give you the background information; if you were not a moron or an imbecile you could draw your own conclusion and come out with a real story. Now the muzzling of these men was a great disservice because then you get channeled through only one source, the public relations officer, whose only scope is lying and whose only objective is "Everything is perfect because my boss is at the head of it."

Such an extreme attitude is rarely encountered.

Behind the debate that is waged with symbols such as "right to know," "freedom of information," "representative of the public," "freedom of the press," "demands of orderly government," and "national security" is a conflict between differing goal perceptions of newsmen and information personnel. In most cases, the goals do not conflict in concrete situations, and problems of official secrecy and publicity are perceived by respondents as either nonexistent or trivial; in the few cases where divergent purposes develop, interest conflict emerges and such problems are magnified. Policies of governmental secrecy or information management are not the primary cause of source-channel conflict. Rather it is an attitudinal conflict arising out of differing role definitions of political communicators representing divergent interests. Concern over the public's right to know or right to orderly government are used as justifications for specific positions in an interest conflict. Perhaps this is an example of the more generalized phenomena of "trivialization of ideology." Officer and reporter interests are attached to symbols generally acceptable to a wider audience to which appeals are being made—Congress, the president, and the public.[24]

PRESS PERFORMANCE AND POLITICAL ADMINISTRATIONS

Another irritant in government-press relations is that of accuracy of the press. Problems of reportorial inaccuracy are often laid at the door of the one-party press. We cannot here prove,

[24] Lasswell and Kaplan, *Power and Society*, p. 105.

disprove, or even test the assertion that a one-party press exists. This requires another study with different research techniques. However, in the present study, the attitudes of newsmen but, unfortunately, not those of information officers were surveyed regarding (1) any differences in the performances of the correspondent in his political reporting resulting from changes in political administrations, and (2) any differences encountered by newsmen in the ease of obtaining news from differing political administrations.

Newsmen vary in their opinions regarding the effect of a particular political administration—Republican or Democrat—on the performance of the newsman. Many (43 per cent) agree that it makes no difference what party is in office.

> It is my impression that for eight years . . . Eisenhower
> . . . was guarded very carefully. I think he had an eight-
> year honeymoon; I think he got better treatment from the
> press than any other American who was president. I think
> it is much safer when there is good criticism of a president;
> I think a president deserves criticism; it helps him. I think
> Eisenhower would have been a better president if he had
> had criticism. He wouldn't have got into this trouble with
> Sherman Adams, for example, with a good staunch press
> criticism of accepting gifts, etc.

Others (31 per cent) insisted that the political administration has nothing to do with the newsman's performance because either the newsman pays no attention to the political label or, as 26 per cent of respondents thought, because of the inherent trait of newsmen is to grow more critical of any administration once the honeymoon is over.

Newsmen also vary in their attitudes regarding differences in ease of gathering news between political administrations. One view held by 43 per cent of respondents is that there are differences which vary directly with the type of leadership of the administration. Active leadership exploits conflict as a means of publicity to promote a political administration. Reporters thought this exploitation of controversy characteristic of the Roosevelt and Truman administrations and absent in the era of Harding, Coo-

lidge, and Hoover. A reporter expressed how vital such active
official leadership is to the newsman in his efforts to discover
material that will make interesting copy:

> In 1938 I was assigned to Washington. I came down here
> and found a great number of New Dealers who were eating,
> drinking, and sleeping, when they slept, the jobs they were
> doing. They were so full of their business, so full of a sense
> of involvement in an important social movement, so con-
> vinced each of them that what he was doing was the most
> important job in the solar system that it was an enchant-
> ment to talk to them, a newsman's paradise. Of course you
> had to discount what they said. Of course you had to rec-
> ognize that each of them was overenthusiastic about his own
> function, his own agency. Of course you had to recognize
> that each of them was trying to tout his own particular pol-
> icy, his own solution for a particular problem. Each was
> competing with the other for advancement, and very often
> they were floating trial balloons, very often they would be
> backbiting, very often they would be leaking stories that
> they oughtn't to leak. But they were involved in what they
> were doing, they were interested. They made news and be-
> cause of that excitement they were really carrying forward
> the function of government. I wish we had more of that in
> government.

Such a statement is typical of many responses of newsmen.
A correspondent can write only as interestingly as the event which
he is covering will allow. If events are dull, the reporter's continuing efforts to create interest in them takes on the characteristics of "news manufacturing." He prefers to have ready-made
interest conveniently available to him. This removes an obligation from his shoulders, the obligation to be interesting, even to
be sensational. Reporters repeatedly offered the opinion that
controversy creates interest and, hence, the administration which
exploits controversy is the most interesting. This indicates that a
reporter's judgment of a political administration is as much
colored by the demands of his own craft as by any partisan view
regarding the accomplishments of such an administration. The
working press has often been charged with "progressive" or
"liberal" biases rather than with "conservatism." It is certainly

possible that the continuing advocacy of change which sometimes characterizes "progressive" administrations is more conducive to the revelation of controversy than are the more stable and routinized administrative procedures of an administration committed to "normalcy." Given the alternative, reporters choose that political environment of clash and conflict in preference to one in which the norm is "business as usual." This also accounts for the view that later periods in a presidential administration are less newsworthy than the first two years. Newsworthiness is a function of political productivity.

Furthermore, given a choice between the danger of being used by political officials for partisan purposes and being spared such danger by being shut out of policy matters, reporters consistently prefer the hazards of being manipulated. Reporters can be quite specific on the point:

> I think that good newspapermen will be able to take care of themselves against the excessive enthusiasm in government people. What they have to fear is laxitude [*sic*], indifference, and, of course, above all else, the desire to conceal. I'm not worried about what government agencies put out, I am worried about what they fail to put out. I think that the newsman has to be as sophisticated about what they hear and vigilant about what is kept from them and be engaged in a constant tug of war, or battle if you like, with government officials and see to it that the public business is not kept private business.

This preference for publicity as opposed to secrecy is, of course, what often creates problems for the newsman. The correspondent may be able to ally himself with Congress to get information from agencies, but he must depend upon his own sense of responsibility to judge the danger signals that warn of his being used by officials for promotional purposes.

So committed are reporters to the idea that controversy is essential to good reporting that they also emphasize the indispensable part which controversy plays in promoting good government. Reporters are often quick to stress the necessity for public controversy in a democratic government. They again tend to form their values of governmental action on the basis of their

particular interests in the governmental process. One correspondent demonstrated this point in his response:

> Another point that I sometimes try to make to these peo-
> ple is that controversy creates an opportunity. Controversy
> is normal and natural in any kind of democratic political
> system, whether it's ours or the parliamentary system of
> Britain. Controversy always stimulates public interest. If the
> people in government have something for which they need
> public support, controversy is not something that they
> should run away from, but something which, being forced
> upon them, they should welcome. This doesn't mean that
> they ought to seek controversy, but it is a fact always pres-
> ent; the question is simply to admit that it's there.

Other newsmen (25 per cent) insisted that ease or difficulty
of political reporting does not vary with political regimes. Some
felt officials have the same goals in information policy in any administration, and others (10 per cent) insisted that newsgathering
gets progressively harder under any administration. The latter
group stresses the growth of secrecy which continues regardless
of the nature of executive leadership. It is among this group that
we find our staunchest advocates of "freedom of information."
They stress that revelation of controversy is really management
of the news, a technique which, when combined with concealment and secrecy, removes the capability of a free press to report
to its citizenry.

The problem of political objectivity is critical to the reporter
and the officer. The evidence indicates that to the extent that the
newsman believes that a particular political administration is
favored by "the mass press," his personal reaction to that administration is effected. If, for example, he is opposed to the administration, his own criticism of it may be more severe as he works
under the assumption that he is the sole remaining sane reporter,
surrounded by those who have been "taken in." At the same time,
the information officer may perceive that the body of the press
corps is opposed to his superior's administration and may grow
defensive. Or, it may mean added problems for the career information officer in getting information from officials into the press:

As the political situation changes with new officials, new problems come along. With different people coming in, then you have got new problems because you have to train them all over again. You've got people coming in from business who are apt to want to hide what they do; they don't feel the public responsiveness, or they may be altogether in the advertising way of publicity where you get what you pay for. If you are an advertiser, you get stories in the news columns because they owe it to you, and so they feel that you can dictate the amount of coverage that you get in the public press.

Partisan political preferences of communicators affect the source-channel relationship by reinforcing already existing patterns of conflict. Severe turnabouts in source-channel relations from cooperation to competition, or vice versa, are not to be expected from shifts in political administrations. Changes in emphasis and quality in source-channel relations can be expected, but they are of a moderate, not cataclysmic, character. The reporter's emphasis is on news, and he will often forego personal convictions in order to get it.

NEWS DEFINITION AS INTEREST CONFLICT

In our survey of the problems of governmental performance in matters of secrecy and publicity and press performance in matters of responsibility, we concluded that the continuing government-press controversy is largely a basic conflict of two interests continually and unavoidably at war with one another. This is a controversy reflecting the deeper, inherent tension between government and press in a free society. We, as members of the reading and viewing public, catch glimpses of the struggle only in its most sensational stages—when a United States plane is shot down in Russia, when an invasion fails in Cuba, or when a naval quarantine is announced.

But, on a continuing and less sensational basis, the conflict is over the dual question "What is news, and who is to decide what is news?" News is the central concept around which the reporter functions; to supply information in the form of news is the rationale for the information officer's existence. Both groups must continuously define what is news. But they do not share the same definition. Divergences in news definition illustrate more clearly than any other factor the divergence of interest of reporter and officer.

The information officer and the newsman make basic decisions regarding what information is to be dispensed and what news is to be gathered and transmitted. Cater points out that publicity is both the means by which government explains itself to the citizen and the product of "the news-forming habits and techniques" of the media which transmit most of the public explanation.[25] If information officers are to transmit information through the news media, their definitions of news must be consistent with those of newsmen making selections of what is newsworthy. James L. McCamy has pointed to the anticipatory effect this has on the information officer; the officer assumes the habit of pushing only the stories with genuine news value—bell ringers—which would fit the news conventions of the media.[26] Compatibility, cooperation, or competition characterizes the officer-newsman relationship, depending on agreement between the two on the definition of news. Press complaints regarding nonavailability of information result from failure to regard available information as news; official complaints regarding an irresponsible press often result from failure to supply information in terms sufficiently familiar to the newsman's news definition.

Reporters insist that selection of the newsworthy item follows no automatic formula. "There are no objective standards here," argues Lippmann; "there are conventions." [27] Or, reporting is dependent upon the subjective "hunches" of the newsman.[28] The discovery of these conventions is central to the relationship of government and press. Information officers and newsmen discussed their personal ideas of what is news and what makes an event newsworthy. A few expressed surprise, dismay, or disbelief. Sample reactions of newsmen were: "Oh, that's a difficult ques-

[25] Cater, *The Fourth Branch of Government*, pp. 10–13.

[26] McCamy, *Government Publicity*, p. 111.

[27] Lippmann, *Public Opinion*, p. 354.

[28] David Manning White, "The 'Gate Keeper': A Case Study in the Selection of News," *Journalism Quarterly*, XXVII (1950), 383. Herring, "Publicizing Administrative Activities," pp. 228–232.

tion; I suppose I wouldn't have anything profound to say about that"; or, "Boy, if you can get a definition of news you have got it made." And, from information officers, "None of us know that"; or, "Just never thought of it before"; or, "I very seldom think of that; I have no real idea about what news is; I couldn't define news, but I know what it is." Most, however, were willing to venture a definition. Among information officers there were virtually as many definitions as there were respondents; among newsmen, definitions varied less. Table 30 indicates the phrases most often used to define news with a comparison of information officer and newsman distributions. Notice that both officers and newsmen concentrated on qualities of interest and importance in defining the newsworthy item. Two points may be noted. Information officers spoke occasionally of the context of governmental activity—news is "anything in government." Newsmen,

TABLE 30

DEFINITION OF NEWS CONCEPT

Definition	PIO's (N = 37)	Newsmen (N = 35)
Anything that happens	5%	11%
Anything that happens that is new	8	8
Any information about what is happening in government or any agency of government	13	—
Anything that happens that is of interest to people	24	35
Anything that happens that is of importance to people	10	8
Anything that happens in government or a government agency that is of interest to people	6	—
Anything that happens in government or a government agency that is of importance to people and they should know about	13	—
Anything that happens of importance and interest to people	13	38
Anything that happens in government of importance and interest to people	8	—

however, never mentioned the governmental context in defining news. Also, consensus on a single definition was greater among newsmen than among information officers.

More interesting than the differences in definitions, perhaps, is the similiarity between information officers and newsmen in mentioning factors of interest and importance which make for newsworthiness. Table 30 also indicates this tendency. Emphasis on the two factors differs little between the two groups; officers recognize that the news media stress interest, for example, and adapt their information-dispensing behavior accordingly. There is also a tendency for information officers to perceive their own agency's information as newsworthy and, in some cases, information is released deliberately for its news effect (Table 31). Representative expressions were: "I release only when I think they have genuine news value"; or, "Any information officer who tries to peddle stuff knowing that it is old is pretty soon going to lose his acquaintances, lose his contacts; I think in general we are very sensitive as to what is news and what isn't"; or, finally, "The only way you can build a reputation among newsmen as an information officer is to give them the information that they will really be interested in using. You will have no reputation at all unless you are able to do that."

Between the two sets of actors, there is a general tendency toward agreement on the definition of the concept of news, the factors of importance and interest which make for newsworthiness, and that the final determination of newsworthiness must lie with the newsman. It appears that the information officer adapts his definitions of news to the newsman's. This adaptation determines the officer's success in gaining access to the press as a channel for government information. As one information officer expressed it, "We tailor our product to the needs of the media that we deal with." The newsman himself gauges his requests for information so that he seeks what is regarded by the information officer as legitimate news. This problem is less critical for the newsman, however, when it comes to agencies that release information, not on the basis of its newsworthiness, but because it should be released automatically or because the newsman requests it.

Now, occasionally we do get people in here and asking a lot of questions about a story, something that they think is a story, and I will not think that it is a story. I try to point out that there is really no story here, but they have an interest in pursuing the idea, and I go ahead and give them the information. Often it turns out that they realize their particular angle has exploded, and it doesn't exist at all.

Although interest and importance are factors of newsworthiness for both groups, there is sharp difference as to the objects of this interest and importance. News for the information officer is of interest and importance to particular publics, often permanent publics. The following examples indicate this expression:

Anything that involves air service or the possibilities of getting air service, or the curtailment of air service—anything like that is of interest to any city.

Anything that explains or furthers an activity of the department is newsworthy to somebody.

Any important action of the board is news, to somebody at least that is a client of the board.

TABLE 31

PIO CONCEPTS OF INFORMATION AS NEWS

Newsworthiness	*Percentage* (N = 34)
Information regarded as always newsworthy	41%
Information regarded as often newsworthy	53
Information regarded as seldom newsworthy	6
Information regarded as never newsworthy	——
Necessity of Making News	(N = 35)
Information released must be newsworthy	60%
Information released need not be newsworthy	——
Release all information regardless of its newsworthiness	40

The newsman speaks of broad appeal, wide interest, or universal interest. Items which the information officer may find of intense interest to a restricted audience are ignored by the newsman. This forces the officer to select only items which have a broad appeal and shuttle others to trade journals, government publications, or other channels. For example, a story of limited interest is cited by one information officer in a manner intended partly facetiously, partly seriously. It posits the problem officers must face daily:

> Sometimes we get a very lightweight story, it will be about standards for grades of dandelion grains or something like that. Now that is one that we just wouldn't put out unless the originating agency, which in this case would be Agriculture Marketing Service, could go to their statisticians, and they could find out that last year dandelion grains in Ohio, Indiana, and Georgia amount to a surprising amount of money, several millions of dollars. If they could do that, we would send that story to those states because it would be worth something to somebody in those states. But if it is just somebody who is a packager of dandelion grains, and he has a hearing, and they decide on what are the standards to keep the quality uniform so a competitor can't put a poorer grade or a lesser price. . . . But the whole thing doesn't amount to much except to a few individuals; it is not worth a story, not worth spending the taxpayers' money to get that story out.

This narrow- versus broad-scale interest concept parallels the assimilative-distributive pattern cited by Cater.[29] The question is always "What is of interest to whom?"

Along with the question of agreement between information officers and newsmen on the nature of news and its determination, there is the question of agreement within each group. The variety of definitions by officers and newsmen makes any attempt at comparing source and channel role types with definitions meaningless and profitless. Within both source and channel groups there is a tendency to adjust to what is perceived to be news in the media at a particular time. For example, a source, be he informer, ed-

[29] Cater, *The Fourth Branch of Government*, p. 17.

ucator, or promoter, carries out his role only if he correctly an-
ticipates the media definition of the news concept. On the basis of
the data, it does not appear that this anticipation is primarily a
matter of the communicator type involved; rather it is common
to all officers. There does appear to be a correlation, however,
between the source role type and expressed attitudes concerning
whether information should be released even if it is not deemed
newsworthy by media standards. There is a tendency among
promoters, having anticipated the newsman's definition of news,
to release information only if it meets that definition; among
educators, to attempt the same adjustment to a lesser degree; and
among informers, to release all information even if the chances
for its transmission are small. This adjustment versus nonadjust-
ment pattern among officers parallels their manipulative-passive
perceptions of the informational role itself.

If there is not a divergence in definition as to what is news
and what is not between officers and newsmen, there must be some
consensus on what governmental items are interesting and to
whom they are interesting. It is the representation of differing
clienteles in political communication which make such consensus
likely among informers and recorders, only possible among educators and expositors, and highly improbable among promoters
and prescribers. The fact that there are differing probabilities of
such consensus of definition, based upon overlapping clienteles,
leads to a difference of opinion between officers and newsmen as
to who should determine whether a particular item is news.
Neither officers nor newsmen interviewed were of the opinion
that the official alone should make such a decision. But newsmen
(94 per cent) were then quite adamant on the point that they and
they alone should determine what is news. Officers, on the other
hand, concurred (6o per cent) that this is primarily the newsman's
function but held that the process of definition should really be
one of cooperation between the two groups. Officers, realizing
that newsmen are unyielding on this point tend, to adjust to
the news conventions used by the press. The publicity expert
must anticipate correctly the reporter's ideas of what news ought
to be and then tailor messages to meet the demands of the news
craft. The relationship of newsman with official is a function

of several factors and not simply defined by the newsman's "ability to select—to define what is news and what isn't." [30] Equally crucial is the information officer's anticipation of that selection and his adjustment to it. Who is to be leader and who is to be follower is a continuing question in political communication.

THE ORIGIN OF GOVERNMENT-PRESS TENSION IN THE SOURCE-CHANNEL RELATIONSHIP

This chapter has been concerned with the attitudes of information officers and newsmen toward traditional problems existing between government and the press—governmental secrecy and governmental publicity. It is the conclusion of this survey that, although such issues charge the atmosphere in which relations between sources and channels take place, they are as much a reflection of these relationships as they are causes of them. Patterns of cooperation, compatibility, and competition are reflected in agreements and disagreements over questions of government candor, manipulation of information, and discrimination against members of the press. The newsman's charges of governmental cover-ups, news management, and partisanship are indicative of the conflict that may exist between himself and his news sources. At the heart of these tensions are the differing role orientations of the actors—orientations toward differing goals and differing interests. When goals and interests overlap, the likelihood of source-channel cooperation is increased; as these role orientations diverge, the probability of conflict grows. The result is tension contributing to compatibility, perhaps to competition. Significant issues in political communication have their origins at the personal level of source-channel interaction. Intensification or resolution of government-press conflict must be understood by reference to that personal level as well as to ideological conflicts over freedom of the press.

[30] *Ibid.*, p. 14.

CHAPTER VIII
THE SOURCE-CHANNEL
RELATION BETWEEN
GOVERNMENT & PRESS

This study has explored dimensions of the relationship between official news sources and newsmen. It has analyzed the responses of information officers and newsmen to questions aimed at disclosing the self-role orientation and self-concepts of these two sets of political communicators. It is now appropriate to review our findings by directly relating them to the two objectives set out at the beginning of the study: (1) the statement of significant hypotheses in the officer-reporter relationship, and (2) the assessment of consequences of that relationship for the opinion processes of American democracy.

COOPERATION, COMPATIBILITY, AND COMPETITION

The explanation of governmental activities is the official responsibility of the public information officer. Varieties of designation within the general classification—specialist, director, press officer, and so on—do not cloud this central function of information-dispensing. That function is inherently political; it involves both the explanation of public policy and the use of publicity as a policy instrument in its own right. The feeding of information through the political system affects explicitly the resolution of interest conflict in society; the information officer's direct involvement in that distribution inevitably projects him into the political process. Information behavior is political behavior, crucial in a democratic system in which governmental publicity provides that essential intelligence making for popular control. The source role in this study is viewed as activity directed toward suggesting, explaining, and advocating policy through publicity.

The perspective applied to reportorial behavior in this study is also political. The news media are channels of political communication which connect the citizen and official as surely as do political parties, bureaucratic structures, or interest groups. Although the media may at times be subsumed under or allied with these other structures, on a continuing basis the media role is sufficiently distinct to warrant investigation as an autonomous political complex performing functions sometimes cooperative, sometimes compatible, and sometimes competitive with the bureaucratic, party, and interest structures.[1] The newsman performs an informal role as channel between the formal, impersonal levels of decision-making and the personal levels of citizen response and initiation. The "linkage function" of connecting policy formation with opinion formation lies close to the essence of political behavior.

Officers and reporters interact with countless other political participants in communicating governmental activities. No less important, however, is the recognition that they interact with one another. Their interrelationships constitute patterns of behavior quite distinguishable from their interactions with other political actors. This source-channel relation is a critical point of origin for messages of public political communication. Out of it arises a significant portion of the free flow of information back and forth between citizen and official. The different forms

---

[1] Gabriel A. Almond, "A Functional Approach to Comparative Politics," in *Politics of the Developing Areas*, ed. Gabriel A. Almond and James S. Coleman (Princeton, New Jersey: Princeton University Press, 1960), pp. 3–64.

of the relationship between news source and news channel have differential effects upon the functional communication process within the political system. Three general patterns emerge from the analysis of the role orientations of information officers and newsmen.

In spite of political and journalistic folklore that the relationship of reporters to government is inherently one of cold (if not hot) war, it is possible to identify one pattern in which both reporters and officers interact harmoniously. This pattern is referred to as one of cooperation. It is characterized in its extreme form by informal, but explicit, agreements between newsmen and officers directed at facilitating the flow of information from the bureaucracy. In this form, it is only rarely encountered. More commonly the cooperative mode is characterized by a high degree of informality between members of the press and information staffs. Communication between the two sets of actors is virtually continuous, obviating the necessity for formalities of interview appointments, specific release times, prearranged news conferences, and so on. It is not uncommon, for example, for correspondents to work out of offices conveniently located in the physical facilities of the particular department or agency being covered. Office doors between information officers and newsmen open virtually on one another. Newsmen become as well acquainted with the information operations as do the officers, and the two actors work harmoniously together. So harmonious was one relationship that, according to the officer, it was through the aid of newsmen that he was able to retain his job after a change of administration:

> In fact, I might relate that, when the election was over, I anticipated that I might be leaving the department. Fortunately I had friends among the news corps who prepared a statement to the secretary asking that if anyone stayed in the entire department, that it be me—that they were happy with the operation the way it is being run here, they are happy with the way I keep the store, and they would like to see me stay.

Differentiated from this type relationship is one characterized by less cooperation, but not to the point of antagonism between the two types of political communicators. This pattern has been identified as compatible. Relationships reflect greater tension, and communicators' acts do not necessarily reinforce one another. Contact between information officers and reporters is less regularized and more formalized. Scheduled activities in which the officer participates—interviews and press conferences —are the more common modes of interaction with the correspondent. Spontaneous inquiries are not ruled out but are less immediate and intimate than in the case of the cooperative pattern.

Finally, there are those relations between sources and channels which are avowedly not compatible and may fairly be labeled as competitive. Contact between officer and correspondent is far less frequent than in other patterns and often occurs in an atmosphere of mutual suspicion and distrust. Actors hang up the telephone or depart without satisfaction that they have accomplished their aims. In the extreme form, this pattern is characterized by communicators working at conflicting, cross purposes. Actors tend to "talk past" each other; information which the officer is attempting to convey as significant, the reporter looks upon as routine trivia. Likewise, the officer dismisses information the reporter feels he must have as idle speculation. Or he condescends to placate what he considers reportorial frustration.

Obviously the interaction of information officers and newsmen is not random. There are factors operating to which both sets of actors respond. The type of response to such variables depends in large measure on how they are perceived by officers and reporters. Similar perceptions and responses result in officers and newsmen performing similar tasks jointly; divergent views and reactions produce tension and open conflict.

FACTORS AFFECTING THE SOURCE-CHANNEL RELATIONSHIP

Several factors are likely to contribute to the development of any given pattern. An initial and convenient basis of comparison lies in the similarity of role orientations of actors to a broad range of influences. Political communicators' concepts of their functions and purposes significantly affect their behavior toward one another. In a cooperative environment, both role actors define their function as political communicators in the same terms. Both view themselves as scribes transmitting what the government is doing to the citizen. The method is factual reporting; both sets of political communicators accept the myth of reportorial objectivity, either in dispensing or gathering information. The activities of officers and newsmen within the bureaucracy overlap. Officer and reporter direct themselves to bureaus, sometimes together, to find out what is taking place. They share concepts of purpose which rule out either the publicizing or concealment of policy matters at the other's expense. The informer denies any overt effort to explain or promote policy; the recorder pleads innocence of any effort to interpret or recommend policy through reporting. Communicators revel in the belief that they are fulfilling the citizen's "need to know" the facts of official Washington.

Concepts of function and purpose of communicators in the compatible relationship are not shared as in the cooperative form. Access for reporters and officers to sources and channels respectively remains relatively unhampered. But interpretive material, whether sought by the newsman or by the officer, produces problems. Communicators whose purpose it is to transmit such material (educators and expositors) are open to more suspicion than those interested in purely factual transmissions. As the actors conceive such interpretation as their purpose, their concepts of function and goals tend to diverge. Depending upon the degree of such divergence, the relations of sources and channels move through compatibility toward competition. As the promoter releases information in direct proportion to its instrumental value in the selling of policy, the correspondent places less significance on the official news source in his newsgathering. Similarly, as prescribers misinterpret official policies or take deliberate stands contrary to official policies, information staffs begin to discount the use of such newsmen as useful channels of information-dispensing. It is in this relationship that the differing goal orientations of the two sets of actors are maximized and the harmonizing, promoting desires of the information

officer are incompatible with the controversial, scrutinizing tendencies of the newsman.

   Shared versus divergent concepts of function and purpose
are reinforced by, and in turn reinforce, orientations toward
other influences. Behavior of communicators takes place within
organizational environments. The degree to which perceived
service to that organization is valued above any common orientation toward service to a generalized public is a variable,
indicating the placement of a particular relationship on the
cooperation-competition continuum. In the extremely cooperative relationship, officers and newsmen see mutual interests as
prior to organization interests. Examples are the officer fighting
for release of information from the superiors and the reporter
putting "routine" material in news columns to the chagrin of
editors and publishers.

   Also relevant is the officer's or reporter's perception of the
other's status within his particular agency or news organization.
Information officers tend to yield access to special news stories
to those reporters of recognized status in their organizations,
particularly those "regulars" permitted by their editors to determine what information within an agency is especially significant for publication. Reporters, on the other hand, seek out
those information officers in whom agency officials place confidence. The extent to which officers are sought as news sources
depends upon their latitude in serving as agency spokesmen.
The information officer suffers in prestige in his relation with
the reporter to the extent that he does not speak for the agency;
the reporter suffers in prestige to the extent that his story is
subject to change by news media policy or superiors.

   Furthermore, the type of agency itself makes a difference.
In regulatory agencies, the information office is virtually the
only point of continuing access for the newsman. This stems
from (1) the closed nature of many agency procedures in
decision-making and (2) the technical aspects of the agency
work. In highly technical or secretive agencies, the information
officer becomes the sole source for public disclosure of compre-
hensible information. Furthermore, the extent to which the re-

porter seeks out the officer as a source of news depends upon the extent to which internal policy disagreements will be revealed by this source; it is precisely this disagreement which is newsworthy, but the type of information which the agency does not want revealed. It is with these agencies that the newsmen most often become disconcerted. In doing so, they direct their search for information from officers and agency officials to informal releases, off-the-record statements, tips, and so on. To the extent that the information personnel yield to the reporter's requests, cooperation with the reporter is promoted, but tensions rise with the organizational superior.

Cooperation in the source-channel relationship also is equated with the orientations of officers and reporters toward similar, if not the same, audiences. The degree of overlap of audiences each actor has in mind in considering a newsworthy event relates directly to the extent of cooperation of actors in releasing and gathering information. Cooperative relations are more likely when reporters communicate directly to audiences which are clienteles of the agency itself. The sharing of the definition of the newsworthy event itself is directly related to audience overlap. The sharing of common attitudes of what comprise elements of interest and importance promote cooperative ventures of the source and channel. As, however, officers and newsmen differ in the audiences to whom they wish to communicate, the elements of importance and interest in the news story will be viewed differently by each. The perception of differing audiences is in turn directly related to the interests served by the actors' organizations, the actors' assimilative and distributive goals, and the type of information each wants to transmit. Concepts of news and audiences are directly related to organizational influences; a large share of the behavior which occurs as source and channel actors interact must reflect conformity to the norms and expectations of the groups to which the actors belong and to which they give allegiance. These groups "constitute part of the real world of reference" as the actors see it.[2]

Information officers and newsmen are also audiences for

[2] Carter, "Newspaper 'Gatekeepers' . . . ," p. 136.

one another. They anticipate each other's reactions to news and information just as they do the reactions of superiors, colleagues, and competitors. The official news source may or may not measure up to the reporter's image of an ideal source of news; to the extent that he does, cooperation between the two actors is promoted. And, if he does not, the relationship may be characterized by competition. Similarly the correspondent may not be what the information officer requires in his ideal newsman, or he may be precisely that. Most detested of correspondents is the armchair speculator:

> It is possible to cover Washington without ever leaving your office—what you need is a ticker tape and a subscription to the leading newspapers. You can sit there with your ticker tape and newspapers and become an expert on anything that happens in Washington by reading. It is then possible to write articles and become a pundit, advising on what's the matter and what is going on in Washington. This is done quite often and primarily by the columnists because you see they are not interested in getting out into the vineyards and trampling up and down on the grapes to produce their wines; they are primarily interested in buying it already bottled.

Officers generally are more satisfied with reportorial performance than reporters are satisfied with information behavior. The degree of satisfaction relates directly to the degree of cooperation.

The image each has of the other's news values is also instrumental in promoting respect or disrespect among actors. A prime source of conflict is the newsman who feels he is being misled by his source or the official source who feels that the newsman is purposively using information in an inaccurate manner. The relative ranking of story values by actors contributes to the reputations built by information officers and newsmen among each other; each respects the other to the extent that he is able to regard his opposite as thinking "just as I do."

Friendships may also determine the degree of competition and cooperation in the source-channel relationship. Newsmen admit that personal friends may, and usually do, come from the "lower levels" of government—bureau chiefs, career officers, and so on.[3] To the degree that both information officers and newsmen participate in such friendships and share common attitudes toward that friendship, information-dispensing and newsgathering become cooperative. To the extent that they do not, their tasks are less complementary.

The use of particular techniques of information-dispensing and issues of government-press relations are perhaps as much a reflection of the type of relationship that prevails between source and channel as a result of it. It is not clear the extent to which particular institutional devices tend to pattern the relationships that may occur between the reporter and his source, particularly in the cases of those devices which have been in existence for a long time. Similarly, it may be that the presence of traditional problems between government and the press contribute to certain underlying attitudes of hostility and suspicion between political communicators. Certainly, such expressed attitudes as "press agents are always trying to put something over on you" or "reporters always want to make something sensational" are pervasive throughout the informational and press corps in Washington. Their presence may lead to misunderstandings among even the most cooperative of officers and reporters.

THE SIGNIFICANCE OF THE INSTITUTIONAL SETTING OF SOURCE-CHANNEL RELATIONSHIPS

Our resume has thus far emphasized the perceptual and attitudinal factors which underlie cooperation, compatibility, and competition in the source-channel relationship. In speaking of orientations toward such influences, what is being said essentially is that actors perceive numerous interests making claims upon their attention and performance. For both information officers and newsmen, these interests appear in the form of audiences to whom they must communicate. The reporter prepares his story not only for the buying public of which he claims to

[3] Alsop and Alsop, *The Reporter's Trade*, pp. 1–18.

be a representative; he has also within his audience framework his editor, his staff colleagues, his competing brethren, his friends, and his official and informal sources. The information officer, to no less extent, includes several audiences within his frame of reference. True, he has in mind a sense of the generalized public. But obtruding upon this image are the far more immediate audiences of his superiors, his agency colleagues— both information and operating personnel—the clientele served by agency activity, his friends, his competitors, members of legislative and judicial bodies, and his channels of communication. The manner in which he balances these interests competing for his attention will influence his goals and role concepts. These concepts feed back on a continuing basis to structure the interaction of the communicators. Cooperation, peaceful coexistence, or open conflict are differentiated results of that feedback.

   In addition, it is advisable to focus attention on the fact that information officers and newsmen work as members of separate and distinct bureaucratic environments, one being the official agency or governmental structure, the other the formal-informal organizational structure of the mass media. The institutional influences on the officer seldom overlap completely with those on the newsman; since each is responsible to differing organizational superiors, there is never a total identity of audiences. Occasionally, however, the gap is small and is adequately bridged so that reporter and officer are allied in the common cause of communication. This, however, is limited to those instances of close cooperation between informer and recorder. The norm is a divergence in orientations of officers and reporters. *Among* each set of actors there is a higher degree of consensus on functions, purposes, and roles than exists *between* the two sets of political communicators. The same is true with respect to audience orientations, organizational influences, friendships, story values, professional values, preferred techniques of news dispensing and gathering, problems of government and the press, and perceptions of one another. Furthermore, as tabular presentations of these dimensions have shown, the degree of consensus among information officers is often higher than that among reporters.

Such findings are to be expected if one is truly sampling two different institutions. Also to be expected is that within each institution there will be differentiated patterns of attitudes. Such patterns do exist, although the limited number of respondents made it very difficult to pursue the implications of such patterns as far as desired. *Within* either institutional complex, role types are based on goal orientations of officers and newsmen. As a result, informers, educators, and promoters have goal orientations *as information officers* similar to recorder, expositor, and prescriber orientations *as newsmen*. It must be emphasized that these role types occur within differing institutions; only in one of the patterns (between informer and recorder) are the goal orientations *between* political communicators so similar that separable institutional structures become perhaps less meaningful in determining the relationship of source and channel than the orientation toward the more generalized classification of political communicator per se.

The evidence indicates that bureaucratic and media structures overlap in the interaction of information officers and newsmen. That overlap is occasionally characterized by extreme cooperation, at others by extreme conflict. Rarely, however, does the minimum consensus on role concepts *defining* the institution become either identical between the two sets of actors or completely differentiated in every detail. The indication is that the normal relationship of information office to press is a compatible one, with the two structures being neither identical nor wholly antagonistic, neither integrated nor subject to disintegration. The greater probability of that compatible relation stems from the interrelations of the six role types described throughout this study. The type of source-channel relationship is directly dependent on interactions of source and channel role types. The norm of compatibility and the variations of cooperation and competition are illustrated in Table 32. Both consensus and conflict inhere in the source-channel relationship. It is this very compatibility which has extensive implications for the relationship of governmental publicity to the political role of the news media.

TABLE 32

ALTERNATIVES IN SOURCE-CHANNEL RELATIONSHIP
CONSIDERED AS A FUNCTION OF DIFFERING
ROLE INTERACTIONS

| | Source Typologies | | |
Channel Typologies	Informer	Educator	Promoter
Recorder	Cooperative	Compatible	Compatible
Expositor	Cooperative	Compatible	Competitive
Prescriber	Compatible	Compatible	Competitive

LEADERSHIP IN POLITICAL COMMUNICATION: TRENDS AND IMPLICATIONS

This section is avowedly devoted to speculation. Its thesis is simple: leadership is a requisite for the opinion processes of a democracy; neither the governmental information nor the non-governmental news establishments are prepared, willing, or capable at present to exercise that leadership.

If one accepts the value assumptions underlying the democratic approach to the organization and resolution of political conflict, he is led to emphasize those principles of popular control and consultation identified with the theory of democracy. The first principle implies a degree of popular participation in the selection of policy-makers; the second refers to the emphasis upon exchange of individual and group opinions which contributes to the effectiveness of the first. Assuming that political communication in the United States occurs within a system in which individuals are at least minimally committed to such an ethical framework, what are the consequences of source-channel behavior for putting these principles into effect?

The articulation of public opinion is not haphazard. The direction and intensity of political opinions are related directly to the issues around which individual and group opinion is distributed. Individuals are sensitized to issues and stands upon them through several communication channels: parties, interest groups, opinion leaders, direct contact with officials, and the news media. So significant a role has the press come to play in the articulation of issues that, as mentioned previously, it has been called the "opposition party," "the fourth estate," and more recently, the "fourth branch of government." One author has even called it the "dangerous estate."[4] Underlying such designations is an assumption encountered in the literature and reiterated in interviews with newsmen. Simply stated, the reporter is an agent of the governed. He is a representative, not unlike the popularly chosen congressman, performing the functions of issue articulation, scrutiny of official action, transmission of information, and opinion-making.

In essence, the function claimed for themselves by newsmen is one of political leadership. They regard themselves, as did one newsman, as the "eyes and ears of the reader" representing the citizen in official places. They view themselves as transmitting issues to the citizen for reflection, commentary, and action. Coupled with this purely reportorial role there is the implication that the newsman accepts responsibility for selecting issues around which public controversy is to take place. This selection is in itself a political act of leadership, one that divides individuals into conflicting publics. The conflict revolves about the issues articulated through the news media; opinion leadership is inherent when the newsman selects and articulates issues.

The potential for the news media to exercise such leadership responsibly depends upon both the desire to do so and consensus on those rules of the game which permit doing it. It is interesting, therefore, to recall the data in Table 27 which reflects the reluctance of newsmen to state that the reporter *should* engage in such leadership. Newsmen continue to look toward the official as the introducer of issues into the body politic and to approve of the official who employs the technique of conflict revelation to do so. But indications are that this approval does not stem from any desire to expose issues to public debate or to lead in opinion-making. Rather it stems from his reaction to a perceived norm of his trade—controversy makes news. He is not leading his readers; he is reacting to what he thinks they expect. It is suggested that the newsman is not will-

[4] Williams, *Dangerous Estate: The Anatomy of Newspapers.*

ing to accept the responsibility for leadership which inheres in
his definition of his role.

There is a trend toward an increase in the functions performed by the news media. Formerly the easily defined task of
policy explanation was accepted as the role of the press. The
recognition of policy-making functions was not apparent. Cur-
rently, however, the implicit policy-making functions of the
press are becoming as increasingly clear as the inherent opinion-
making ones. News selection, the publicity of policy, and the
revelation of policy negotiations are all part of a continuing
process of formulating public policy. As interviews indicated,
however, the newsman clings to definitions of a simpler age. A
fourth of newsman respondents denied political involvement
in their role; another group insisted that explanation and interpretation were sufficient terms to indicate the newsman's role
in society. There is a desire to retain the distinction of policy-
explanation and policy-making in preference to a clear-cut recognition that publicity is in itself a portion of the policy-making
process. As in the responsibility for leadership in opinion-
making, the newsman continues to defer to governmental officials
as sole decision-makers, while overlooking the political quality
of reportorial decisions in newsgathering.

Implicit here is another question too easily ignored. If
principles of popular control inhere in the democratic ethic,
then the newsman as a representative of the public in the policy-
making process must be responsive to such controls. On the
surface, it might be assumed that such controls are exerted by
the buying public. If the news media were solely for distribution
of information, then perhaps the citizens' votes in the market
place would be a control over the reporter's political behavior.
The media, however, as instruments of entertainment, make
appeals for consumer votes on a different basis, and success is
judged within the framework of broad distribution of entertainment and information. The newsman accepts this criterion
himself, perceives his audiences in the broadest possible terms,
and makes his appeals to that audience. This, in turn, reflects
the tendency to emphasize interest in the story rather than
utility. The implication is that, as representative of the citizen,

he relates to governmental publicity as a necessary source of leadership, then is critical of that leadership when issues of broad appeal are not forthcoming.

One other problem should be mentioned in assessing the potential of the news media as a "fourth branch of government." Consensus on the rules of the game which define the reportorial branch is imperceptible. Reporters wear their individuality as a badge of distinction. The structure to which the newsman assimilates new events is not the institutionalized rules and procedures of newsgathering, nor a broad framework of policy as in the case of the official, but his own reportorial experience. The event that does not "fit" that framework requires explanation. Such an explanation at first is highly dependent upon official interpretation, particularly in the rapidly changing environment of a crisis situation. It is precisely at this moment that the newsman's role as agent of the governed is most crucial, yet it is at this time when he is least likely to pass the test. One journalistic scholar pointed toward the tendency that arises for the press in a complex age; reporting tends to be superficial in its treatment of news, crusades direct their enthusiasms to negative sides of government, there is overdependence on outworn concepts, and an overdisplay of governmentally written news.[5] If such tendencies prevail, they will not be corrected by the recorder awaiting the latest press release or official statement. Nor will changes come from the prescriber waiting to write about the news or about existing issues, but not raising these issues himself. To the expositor falls much of the burden, but even he is less willing to accept it than to "interpret" what *is* for his readers without posing alternatives for public consultation. It is suggested that a lack of an internal leadership within the press corps, arising from an absence of commonly accepted rules of news coverage, contributes to the tendency of the press to be led, rather than to lead.

These problems of leadership within and of the press are introduced not as criticisms of the performance of the news media, but rather to indicate that the potential of the media to perform a role of agent of the governed in relations with the

[5] Merwin, *"The Reporting of Public Affairs,"* pp. 120–126.

government is limited. Such estimates are indicated by the generalizations based upon newsman role orientations. They have been suggested in other places as well. The Alsops, for example, pointed out that the difficulties of the newsman are twofold. The alliance of government and press works well when government indicates a strong and clear purpose, a purpose which the press can follow and report. Without that governmental leadership, difficulties are encountered. At the same time, however, the newsman must beware of being "taken in." These are problems of "truth-telling" with strong government and "truth-telling" despite weak government.[6]

The limits of the press corps' potential to play the role of popular representative were theoretically to be overcome by giving the reporter some aid in covering Washington. At least there was to be some alleviation of the newsman's problems by employing information staffs to direct correspondents to those items of importance around which public interest might form. Newsmen point out, however, that the presence of the public information office has had the opposite result. Rather than ease his way, it has forced him to seek out unpremeditated revelations of news; this is exactly what damages the source and accuracy of the news and may destroy the policy which is revealed prematurely. In short, the leadership potential of official news structures is also questioned.

Standards for news release, for distribution, and for determining the significant item undergo wider acceptance among information officers than among newsmen. Perhaps this is because of the formalized nature of limitations on publicity activities, perhaps it is due to the greater consensus on minimal rules of the game which define the bureaucracy to which officers belong. It would be expected that officers, visualizing their role as servants of the governed, would be ideally suited to the exercise of leadership in the articulation of public opinion. But although governmental publicity could serve to articulate issues, this is not the case. Rather governmental publicity aims at opposite purposes. Exposure of conflict, controversy, and disagreement are beyond the self-defined role of the information officer. Govern-

[6] Alsop and Alsop, *The Reporter's Trade,* pp. 16–18.

mental publicity is seldom seen as an inherently political means
of resolving conflict.

The informer defines legitimate publicity as information
about policies over which there is no longer any disagreement.
The educator insists that he explains policy to clear up misunderstanding and present a framework of truth. Even the promoter is directing his efforts at advertising the harmonious consequences of policy adoption. Governmental publicity does not
mean the conscious exposure of conflict as an instrument of communication, persuasion, and control. It is not the articulation of
issues, but the purposeful avoidance of them, which defines the
role of the information officer to himself, to his organization, and
to his audience.

The attitudes uncovered in the present study do not indicate
either a willingness or an ability on the part of either the information establishment or the news media to exert leadership in
the opinion process. Both the newsman and the officer defer to
the political official as the primary articulator of issues for public
debate. To information officers, conflict was inherently an evil
to be avoided in favor of agreement. To publicize agreement is
good; to publicize controversy is bad. The newsman views the
whole process differently. The publicizing of agreement, although
not bad, is also not news. To publicize controversy is the essence
of news. If the information officer values information, it is because he believes an informed public will be a supporting public;
if the newsman values news, it is on the assumption that the
interested public will be a satisfied public. Neither perceives it
as a primary role to articulate those issues which make all the
information necessary.

Yet it is to governmental publicity and news communication
that the citizen must look for the articulation of those issues that
intrude upon his personal experience. As the trend proceeds
toward a more complicated and technical set of issues around
which popular debate is organized, the information office increases its role as the interpreter to the newsman of the complexities of policy. And this role of the officer is reinforced by
another factor. Demands upon the political official's time make
him less available for long sessions at which he can explain the

subtleties of policy alternatives purely to satisfy the avid curiosity of reporters. Newsmen look back nostalgically to the time when he could do so. This is not to say that such sessions no longer take place. Certainly, the fashion of the Dulles backgrounder in the 1950's and the presidential backgrounders of the Kennedy Administration are ample evidence that officials do take time to be with reporters. But the question is *for what purpose?* Is it really to satisfy the informational needs of the reporter and his readers? At least the more sensational examples that come to mind indicate that there is more than this implied in the increasing popularity of background sessions. Rather, such sessions are to serve the official's purposes, and only secondarily to meet the reporter's desires. Those purposes, of course, may vary. In one instance the official may desire to court the favor of a prestigious press. Or he may wish to promote agency policy by revealing the degree of "harmony" that exists among public officials on the ends and means of policy. Or he may wish to expose conflict within a department or agency with the express intention of enlisting public support for the removal of a nonconforming colleague. And as often happens, he may wish to launch a trial balloon. But, whatever the desire, it is the official and not the reporter who takes the initiative. For the reporter, when faced with the fact of the official's growing isolation from the press, is only too willing to take advantage of those few opportunities when that official is available as a means of uncovering the "hard lead."

The politics of an open society imply that interest conflict will be carried on in an environment in which group leaders, political officials, and interested citizens will have the opportunity to voice opinions regarding a range of alternative policies designed to resolve such conflict. When such an environment exists, then political communication serves to operationalize the normative democratic principles of popular control and consultation. Underlying such communication is the implication that conflict will be revealed, that policy alternatives will be discussed, and that issues will be articulated for debate. But none of these occur haphazardly; the expression of issues around which opinions and publics form requires an element of leadership.

The simple question arises: from where is leadership in the opinion process to emerge?

The conclusion of our analysis must be that both the information establishment and the news media have foregone such leadership in an effort to protect given interest positions. That protection is most readily assured if the relationship between information officer and newsman is a compatible one. The information establishment cannot risk open conflict with the news media without raising the possibility of sacrificing access to the vital channels of communication. And, as the information officer himself becomes more crucial in the political promotion of public policy, the newsman cannot risk a breach of relations without threatening a loss of news sources. The question of which needs the other the most seems less relevant in the modern age than the realization on the part of both that they require each other. The controversy over official information policies in the Cuban affair of 1962 illustrates the reaction of newsmen to what they regarded as an overeager attempt on the part of the information establishment to provide leadership in matters of communication; and, the dissatisfaction of administration leaders with the press following the failure at the Bay of Pigs is an example of an equal dismay on the part of officials when the news media moves too anxiously in revealing matters of public concern. In both cases, leaders of each group quickly charged the other with a lack of "responsibility."

But perhaps it is not a problem of press and government acting in an irresponsible manner. Perhaps rather it is a matter of both press and government becoming too responsible. Perhaps each has gone too far in assuming that it can be responsible to the interests it represents only by shying away from the exercise of leadership in the opinion process. Indeed, perhaps reporter, officer, and official have redefined the meaning of leadership in opinion-making such that all are assuming "responsible leadership" to mean an agreement between government and press leaders that certain matters can be publicized as in the "national interest" while others must remain unrevealed, hidden, or even overlooked. We have discussed the nature of the compatible relationship that appears increasingly to be the norm among infor-

mation officers and newsmen. Has it become such a norm that
neither officer nor reporter, neither source nor channel, is willing
to risk the possibility of its disruption? In acceptance of that
compatibility, officers and newsmen abdicate opinion leadership
by backing away from the responsibility each assumes itself to
have in the opinion process—for newsmen, the exposure of
controversial issues for public debate and for officers, a public
explanation of what political officials are doing and why.

Alan Barth, editorial writer of *The Washington Post*, recently offered his opinion of the state of government-press relations in this nation:

> Nowhere in the United States has the press been muzzled
> by the government or had conformity forced upon it. It has
> simply, out of a sense of patriotism, of "responsibility,"
> silenced itself and supported the powers that be. I think
> that American newspapers are in little danger of having
> freedom of the press taken away from them. But many of
> them are in serious danger, I think, of losing their freedom
> through disuse, through atrophy.[7]

What Barth suggests is that an independent press in an open
society, as it performs its tasks, will inevitably find itself in conflict with the interests of governmental officials. We may add that
an information establishment performing a function of publicizing policy issues will just as inevitably find itself in conflict with
individual sectors of the press. Just as the first three Articles of
the Constitution build into the American political system an
inescapable tension between separate institutions sharing similar
powers, so does the First Amendment's guarantee of press freedom
structure a continuing tension between an operating, independent press and a functioning information establishment. Vigor on
the part of government and press leaders is less dangerous in its
implications for a free society than an all too ritualistic definition
of intelligence as being accepted for public exposure only when
in the national interest. For the determination of the national
interest in a democratic society is itself a subject for free inquiry
and not easily or permanently defined by citizen, official, or

[7] Alan Barth, "Freedom and the Press," *The Progressive*, XXVI (1962), 32.

reporter. Without such a permanent and absolute definition of
national interest, a block to free inquiry in the form of government-press consensus to suppress information not in that interest
is rather difficult to justify.

Acceptance of compatibility as the single defined relationship of sources and channels or of government and the independent press cannot be automatic, for conflicts of interest have been
formally tied into the system. If news sources and newsmen are
to accept responsibilities of leadership in policy-making and
opinion-making processes they must recognize (1) the inherently
political quality of their roles, (2) the inherently interdependent
quality of those roles, and (3) that policy and opinion-making
processes are themselves intertwined. Easy distinctions between
programs and policy, between explanation and formulation, between reporting and politics must be abandoned. This would
imply a continuing redefinition of source-channel relations with
realizations by political communicators that nothing is simply
informing *or* recording, educating *or* explaining, and promoting
or prescribing. Leadership requires an awareness by communicators that conflict and compromise are inevitable in politics and
that both government and press share not only a loyalty to "the"
national interest but share a responsibility in providing the environment of an open society within which that interest may be
defined. That implies an environment not only of consensus but
one in which conflict and controversy are an intrinsic feature.

One of the purposes of political knowledge is to dispel myths
regarding political behavior. For this reason, if for no other, the
findings outlined are relevant. The analysis of cooperation, compatibility, and competition between official news sources and
newsmen and of the role orientations which are the bases of these
patterns stands as an attempt to understand one point in the
process of political communication. The conclusions of that analysis, when related to the value system underlying such communication processes, raise problems connected with the viability
of an open opinion process in an age of increasing complexities
in political communication. Few processes are so crucial to effective democratic action as that of political communication. Citizen understanding, control, and acceptance of the legitimate

decision-making processes require not only information, explanation, and interpretation in communication. Popular control and consultation also imply the traditional requisite of democratic organization, the element of leadership. This analysis has outlined the source-channel relationship within which such opinion-making leadership may be expected from governmental publicity and the political activity of the press. Information and news contribute to public understanding only as long as leadership responsibilities are assumed by *both* government and the news media; if such responsibility is assumed by neither or by one alone, then news sources and news channels contribute to the survival of a free society more by chance than by design.

APPENDIX I
NATURE AND
METHOD OF
ANALYSIS

RESEARCH LITERATURE

Research and speculative effort has been devoted to exploring the role of governmental publicity and the role of the political journalist in the United States. Studies in bureaucratic publicity usually have been independent of those into political reporting. A few have dealt directly with governmental publicity as a problem within the larger framework of public administration. A leading example of this type of investigation is McCamy's *Government Publicity*, an effort to describe the publicity programs, techniques, personnel, and problems of federal departments and agencies. Subsequent efforts in this direction have been Pimlott's consideration of governmental publicity as a reflection of the general phenomenon of public relations in a democratic society, Fitzpatrick's experiments to obtain a useful measurement of federal publicity, Harding's descriptions of the growth of publicity in the Department of Agriculture and Willard's dissertation on public relations practices of the federal government. Each has examined the fact of administrative publicity by focusing on methods, organizational procedures, and techniques, with little attention devoted to exploring the relationships between publicity programs themselves and the channels through which such programs are made operational.[1]

Another line of research has considered the relation of mass communications and government. Noteworthy are Lippmann's ground-breaking efforts to explore problems of press responsibilities and capabilities in political communication. Other works have been concerned with the press and its relation to society, focusing on the constitutional position of the press and its moral and informational obligations in society. Additionally, there has been an abiding interest in the problems of administrative control over information.[2]

More relevant for the present study are materials comprising a body of research into the processes of communication, particularly studies centering around communicator analysis and depicting the work situations, social backgrounds, and political orientations of newsmen. A leading example is Rosten's *The Washington Correspondents,* which spawned such divergent and complementary efforts as Maxwell's investigation of United States correspondents abroad, the individual studies of Kruglak and Lambert on foreign correspondents in the United States, Fisher's account of columnists, Swanson's treatment of press agitators, and White's study of the "gate keeper." [3]

---

[1] Pimlott, *Public Relations and American Democracy;* Fitzpatrick, "Public Information Activities . . ."; *idem,* "Measuring Government Publicity . . ."; T. Swann Harding, "Informational Techniques of the Department of Agriculture," *The Public Opinion Quarterly,* I (1937), 83–96; Joseph Willard, "Public Relations Policies and Practices of Federal Departments and Agencies" (Ph.D. dissertation, University of Indiana, 1960).

[2] Walter Lippmann, *Liberty and the News* (New York: Harcourt, Brace & Howe, 1920); Commission on Freedom of the Press, *A Free and Responsible Press* (Chicago: University of Chicago Press, 1947); Rourke, *Secrecy and Publicity: Dilemmas of Democracy;* Wiggins, *Freedom or Secrecy;* Clark R. Mollenhoff, *Washington Cover-Up* (Garden City, New York: Doubleday & Co., Inc., 1962).

[3] J. William Maxwell, "U.S. Correspondents Abroad: A Study of Backgrounds," *Journalism Quarterly,* XXXIII (Summer 1956), 346–348; Theodore

Few works have been devoted to analysis of the interactions of newsmen and their news sources, particularly to treating the newsman as an actor involved in specific sets of political relationships with his Washington news sources. In recent years, attention has been restricted to the reporter's role in local political processes. As examples, there stand Carter's generalizations regarding relations between the members of the press and local governmental officials in North Carolina and Gieber's efforts to define the roles of sources and reporters making up a communications system.[4] During the development of this study, an analysis of the role expectations of news sources and news channels appeared; its conclusions parallel those in Chapter 3. A study into the city hall reporter and his sources, it was published as "The City Hall 'Beat': a Study of Reporter and Source Roles" by Walter Gieber and Walter Johnson. Because of the similarity of outlook and conclusions of Gieber and Johnson with those of this study, it is appropriate to outline the points of agreement. Using the same communications model as employed in the present study, Gieber and Johnson develop three models of the relationships between reporter and source based on the orientations of each to his social and bureaucratic system. Briefly, they are: (1) actors are members of disparate social systems, they remain independent of one another, and their perceptions of role and function are dissimilar; (2) actors are members of different structures, they cooperate to some extent, and they are partially agreed in perceptions of function; and (3) actors are members of convergent social structures and, as a result, share perceptions of function. The data from which such models were constructed was collected by investigating four areas of source-reporter relations: self-percep-

E. Kruglak, *The Foreign Correspondents* (Geneva, Switzerland: Librairie E. Droz, 1955); Donald A. Lambert, "Foreign Correspondents Covering the U. S.," *Journalism Quarterly*, XXXIII (Summer 1956), 349–356; Charles Fisher, *The Columnists* (New York: Howell, Soskin, 1944); G. E. Swanson, "Agitation Through the Press: A Study of the Personalities of Publicists," *The Public Opinion Quarterly*, XX (Summer 1956), 441–456; White, "The Gate Keeper.' . . ."

[4] Roy E. Carter, Jr., "Relations Between the Press and Local Government Officials in North Carolina," *Prod*, I (September 1957), 23–27; Gieber, "Two Communicators of the News. . . ."

tion of communications roles, perception of the role of the other, attitudes toward the press as a source of governmental information, and evaluation of the source-reporter relationship.[5]

On the federal level, only the absorbing work of Douglass Cater provides a fertile source of generalizations regarding the newsman's role in the political process. Two efforts have developed hypotheses regarding reportorial attitudes toward government publicity—Rivers' updating of Rosten's earlier work and Underwood's study restricted to the consideration of Washington military reportage. Methodologically, these studies have much in common with that of Fitzpatrick in seeking to assess the attitudes of correspondents toward administrative information services.[6]

Aside from these efforts at treating the specific relationships of government and the press, there have been works formulating many of the theoretical constructs utilized in this study. For example, the positing of a separable and distinct function identified as "political communication" in a systematic framework of other political functions is the recent conceptualization of Gabriel Almond. Briefly stated, the processes of communicating political intelligence are seen as essential to other political functions— political socialization, interest aggregation and articulation, rule-making, rule-application, and rule-adjudication.[7] The problem here is not to restate the Almond framework, but rather to cite the relevance of our treatment of information-dispensing and newsgathering processes to such a systematic formulation. For purposes of the present study, interpretation regarding political communication through governmental publicity and the news media should be made within the framework of an opinion "process" similar to that implied by Oliver Garceau in "Research

[5] Gieber and Johnson, "The City Hall 'Beat.' . . ."

[6] Cater, *The Fourth Branch of Government;* Rivers, "The Washington Correspondent: Significance for Government"; George V. Underwood, Jr., "The Washington Military Correspondents" (Master's thesis, University of Wisconsin, 1960); Richard S. Fitzpatrick, "A Survey of Opinions of Members of the Congressional Press, Periodical, and Radio Galleries on Information Services of Federal Administrative Agencies in Washington, D.C." (Master's thesis, American University, 1951).

[7] Almond, "A Functional Approach to Comparative Politics," 3–64.

in the Political Process," Avery Leiserson in *Parties and Politics,*
and V.O. Key in *Public Opinion and American Democracy.*[8]

A formulation of the opinion process which proved useful in
developing the problem of formation of personal opinions on
public issues is that of W. Phillips Davison in "The Public
Opinion Process." [9] A treatment of the overlapping opinion and
policy processes which attempts to specify the role of the mass
media within both is J.N. Rosenau's *Public Opinion and Foreign
Policy.* For technical treatments of the model of the communication process implicit in this study see the following: "A Conceptual Model for Communications Research" and "Research
on 'Fortuitous' Communication: A Review" by Bruce H. Westley
and Malcolm S. MacLean, Jr.; "An Approach to the Study of
Communicative Acts" by Theodore M. Newcomb; "The Communicative Act" and "Communicative Behavior" by Mapheus
Smith; "Toward a Psychological Theory of Human Communication" by Franklin Fearing.[10]

The development of the technique of data interpretation
through role analysis draws upon several sources: *Explorations
in Role Analysis: Studies of the School Superintendency Role*
by Neal Gross, Ward S. Mason, and Alexander W. McEachern;
The Legislative System: Explorations in Legislative Behavior
and "American State Legislators' Role Orientations Toward Pressure Groups" by John C. Wahlke, Heinz Eulau, William Bu-

[8] Oliver Garceau, "Research in the Political Process," *The American Political Science Review,* XXXXV (March 1951), 69–85; Avery Leiserson, *Parties
and Politics* (New York: Alfred A. Knopf, 1958), pp. 74–79; V.O. Key, Jr.,
Public Opinion and American Democracy (New York: Alfred A. Knopf,
1961), pp. 411–531.

[9] Davison, "The Public Opinion Process."

[10] Bruce H. Westley and Malcolm S. MacLean, Jr., "A Conceptual Model for
Communications Research," *Audio-Visual Communications Review,* III (Winter
1955), 3–12; *idem,* "Research on 'Fortuitous' Communication: A Review,"
Audio-Visual Communications Review, III (Spring 1955), 119–137; Theodore
M. Newcomb, "An Approach to the Study of Communicative Acts," *The Psychological Review,* LX (November 1953), 393–404; Mapheus Smith, "The Communicative Act," *The Journal of Social Psychology,* XXXI (May 1950), 271–281;
"Communicative Behavior," *The Psychological Review,* LII (September 1946),
294–301; Franklin Fearing, "Toward a Psychological Theory of Human Communication," *Journal of Personality,* XXII (September 1953), 71–88.

chanan, and Leroy C. Ferguson.[11] Useful systematic formula-
tions of the "theory" as distinct from techniques of role analysis
may be found in *Social Theory and Social Structure* by Robert K.
Merton; *The Social System* by Talcott Parsons; *Social Psychology*
by Theodore M. Newcomb; and *The Theory of Social Structure*
by S. F. Nadel.[12]

Despite this array of speculation and systematic investigation,
there has been little attention directed at exploring the consequences for political communication of the manner in which
official news sources and newsmen approach the task at hand and
each other. If there are instances, as there are, in which what
the citizen ultimately knows as news is the result of (1) what the
information officer has given the newsman and (2) what answers
the newsman has been able to obtain from the PIO, then the
attitudes of each of these actors toward each other, their respective functions, the techniques which they employ, and significant
problems in their relationship, are all of significance for a
broader understanding of how the citizen perceives government.
It is by a treatment of these elements in the relationship of
source and channel—PIO and newsman—that the present study
differs from previous studies in political communication.

THE EXPLORATORY STUDY

Knowledge in the form of tested and verified hypotheses
concerning the news source-newsman relationship is not extensive. Past studies have, at best, merely skirted the subject which
is the concern of this project. The dearth of tenable hypotheses
regarding the relationship under discussion makes it presump-

[11] Neal Gross, Ward S. Mason, and Alexander W. McEachern, *Explorations in Role Analysis: Studies of the School Superintendency Role* (New York: John Wiley & Sons, Inc., 1958), pp. 3–75; John C. Wahlke, Heinz Eulau, William Buchanan, and Leroy C. Ferguson, *The Legislative System: Explorations in Legislative Behavior* (New York: John Wiley & Sons, Inc., 1962); *idem*, "American State Legislators' Role Orientations Toward Pressure Groups," *The Journal of Politics*, XXII (May 1960), 203–227.

[12] Robert K. Merton, *Social Theory and Social Structure* (rev. ed.; Glencoe, Illinois: The Free Press, 1957), pp. 368–384; Talcott Parsons, *The Social System* (Glencoe, Illinois: The Free Press, 1951), pp. 36–45; Theodore M. Newcomb, *Social Psychology* (New York: Henry Holt & Co., Inc. 1950), pp. 298–334; S.F. Nadel, *The Theory of Social Structure* (Glencoe, Illinois: The Free Press 1957).

tuous to claim that research designed to formulate such hypotheses could, in itself, increase the body of *verified* knowledge about the processes involved or state prescriptive solutions for problems. What can be achieved is more modest but nevertheless useful for the understanding of political communication.

The research contemplated in the design of this study was unquestionably exploratory in nature; its purpose was "to gain familiarity with a phenomenon or to achieve new insights into it, often in order to formulate a more precise research problem or to develop hypotheses." [13] It rests on the suggestion by prior research or speculation that a particular problem is worthy of investigation. Yet it recognizes that the status of research is highly unsophisticated and that conclusions reached previously, although insightful, must be contingent upon exploration intended to develop hypotheses based upon observed evidence. Such hypotheses become statements of causal relationships, to be examined in projects designed for specific description, measurement, and testing. An exploratory study, then, is aimed explicitly at the systematic investigation of a research problem and the development of hypotheses which later will, if it appears profitable, be tested with precision.

The present research project was designed to make use of two methodological techniques common to exploratory studies. The first includes a thorough survey of the literature as a means of obtaining insights for guiding empirical research into the problem itself. Generalizations from this survey are later incorporated into the body of the study. On a few occasions, depending upon the nature of the problem, a survey of the literature alone proves sufficient as a source of hypotheses or leads to a more precise formulation of the problem. In this instance, previous research was too sparse to permit concluding with a survey of secondary sources alone. Investigations had to be conducted bearing directly on news source-newsman relationships. This meant talking with sources—public information officers—and newsmen —Washington correspondents. The result was what is termed in methodological parlance an "experience survey." [14]

[13] Claire Selltiz *et al., Research Methods in Social Relations* (rev. ed.; New York: Henry Holt & Co., Inc., 1959), p. 50.
[14] *Ibid.,* p. 55.

A researcher surveying individual expression on any topic bears a responsibility for making explicit the answers to a series of questions about the survey itself—who is surveyed, how the survey is conducted, for what purpose it is conducted, how the results are presented, and, finally, "So What?" The first two questions may now be discussed.

SAMPLE SELECTION AND DESCRIPTION

Survey techniques employed by political scientists have become increasingly sophisticated and elaborate. This is particularly true in research problems dealing with the opinion process. The type of survey technique employed must be governed by the nature of the problem under investigation and the purposes the survey is to serve; a reversal of this priority can lead to wasted effort and meaningless conclusions.

It was apparent early in the planning stages of the empirical investigations involved in this study that a particularly awkward problem would be encountered in selecting the sample of information officers and newsmen to be interviewed. The initial difficulty arose out of the nature of the survey itself. An exploratory study designed for purposes of defining a particular problem area and developing hypotheses about it would fail if the selection of the sample was an automatic one based solely on techniques of probability sampling and directed merely at meeting requirements of statistical representativeness. Given the nebulous state of each group and the total lack of an available listing which would permit a precise definition and resulting stratification of either population, it proved quite beyond the scope of the study to employ techniques of random sampling. Indeed, since one of the questions which the research was intended to answer was that of *who* are the official news sources of newsmen, it would prove an insurmountable obstacle to try to answer that question prior to the phase of data-gathering itself.

Techniques of random sampling and stratified sampling, therefore, were inappropriate to the problem at hand. A superior procedure of sampling respondents directly on the basis of experience in newsgathering and information-dispensing was followed, thus insuring a variety of significant ideas about the relationships of these processes—a variety not necessarily available from random sampling techniques. This implied a decision to direct attention away from a purely statistical description of either population group's standard characteristics of age, education, social-economic status, reading habits, or such. This also led to foregoing statistical accuracy and the traditional tools of statistical testing in favor of inferences based upon the responses of experienced information and journalistic personnel.

This directed technique for the selection of respondents formed a purposive sample. This type of sample proved more in keeping with the expressed purposes of the research: "The basic assumption behind purposive sampling is that with good judgment and an appropriate strategy, one can hand-pick the cases to be included in the sample and thus develop samples that are satisfactory in relation to one's needs." [15] The procedures for choosing respondents interviewed involved establishing relevant criteria on which to base the selection, searching for individuals that met those criteria, and determining of the availability of the chosen respondents.

Newsmen

In selecting newsmen, the following experience criteria were considered most important. First, the sample would consist primarily of "working" newsmen—those who regularly report information about government either from assignment to a particular area of governmental activity or specific story or because of their own selection of such an area or specific story. Furthermore, newsmen interviewed would be those contacting departments and agencies with information units, even though the units themselves might not be the prime sources of news. Although this group would make up the major portion of the sample, newsmen specializing in opinion commentary—editors, editorial writers, and columnists—would be included in order to have the benefit of this particular type of experience.

Second, the sample chosen would consist primarily of those

[15] *Ibid.*, pp. 520–521. See also William J. Goode and Paul K. Hatt, *Methods in Social Research* (New York: McGraw-Hill Book Co., Inc., 1952), pp. 218, 230–231.

newsmen who specialize in the reporting of activities of the executive departments and agencies rather than of Congress, the
Courts, or the Presidency. Third, the sample would contain,
within limits of feasible size, the representative experience of
newsmen with all types of news organizations focusing on newsworthy items not covered by the general news organizations and
transmitting to more restricted audiences—specialized news organizations. Fourth, the sample would contain newsmen with
varied lengths of experience in Washington reporting as well as
with varied types of experience.

Selection followed a study of various population listings of
Washington correspondents: the *Congressional Directory*,[16] the
established wire service assignment sheets, and lists of correspondents specifically accredited to the press rooms of each of
the departments and agencies. This provided, by type of news
organization, those newsmen who report on a regular basis from
each of the executive departments and agencies. The final sample
was based on these listings, suggestions of individuals who had
interviewed members of the Washington press corps, and records
of copy filed from departments and agencies.

The degree to which the selected newsmen measured up to
the criteria outlined is illustrated by a short description of the
sample. One goal in drawing the sample was to obtain respondents possessing wide experience in the coverage of executive departments and agencies—particularly those with information
units. Of interviews conducted with newsmen $(N = 35)$, the
breakdown upon the basis of coverage was as follows. Twenty-six
of the correspondents covered executive departments in their
reporting. At least one correspondent who covered an executive
department regularly was included in the sample. Seven of the
newsmen covered independent administrative agencies, and
eleven such agencies were covered by all of the individuals in
the sample. Each regulatory agency was also covered by one of
our respondents, and nine of the correspondents interviewed
made some regular attempt to cover these agencies. Because of
the multiple coverage in the routine runs of wire service corre-

---

[16] *Congressional Directory*, 86th Cong., 2d Sess., January, 1960. *Congressional
Directory*, 87th Cong., 1st Sess., April, 1961.

spondents, network correspondents, and those working for metropolitan dailies, the thirty-five newsmen obviously covered more than just an executive department, agency, or independent regulatory commission. In addition, sixteen of the respondents interviewed were on general assignment in Washington, covering such departments, agencies, and areas of interest as might suit their fancy.

An effort was also made to have represented in the sample individuals from as many types of news organizations as exist in Washington reporting. Nineteen of the respondents chosen were from that category described in Chapter 1 as general news organizations. Within that category, the distribution was as follows: correspondents with metropolitan dailies having multimember bureaus, seven; those from the major wire services, six; those working for news weeklies, three; those employed by radio and/or television networks, three. The other major category was that of individuals working in more specialized news organizations, of which the distribution was: news services and syndicates, four respondents; newspaper chains, one correspondent; opinion journals, two respondents; special interest and trade publications, two respondents; and metropolitan dailies with small (three-man) bureaus, seven correspondents.

Respondents' types of reporting appear in two major categories. One is based on method of assignment—coverage of a regular "run" on which the reporter handles news which he selects as newsworthy, coverage of a specific story assigned from the bureau, or coverage of a specific story on the basis of the newsman's own judgment. This categorization appears as follows: fourteen respondents engaged in "routine" reporting, twelve were given specific daily assignments, and nine were given the freedom to select their own areas of interest.

Another major classification is with respect to the manner in which the story is handled—written as "straight news" without inclusion of any other type of material, written with interpretive material placing the event in perspective, and written as news commentary. This classification is more subjective, based on the respondent's conception of his own role in the newsgathering process. Certainly the classes are not sufficiently rigid as to be mutually exclusive. However, the distribution is as follows: twelve engage in "straight" reporting, fourteen in "interpretive" reporting, and nine are columnists or news commentators mixing opinion with their reporting.

Information officers

The only listing of executive departments and agencies with information units was compiled from a questionnaire in 1955 by the House of Representatives Information Subcommittee, Committee on Government Operations.[17] Although it provided a handy base from which to determine what information units dealt most directly with the press, the passage of six years required that the listing be brought up to date. Once this was accomplished, the decision was made to draw individuals from information units presently located in Washington. Of existing units, thirty are co-ordinating units in departments and agencies which sampled newsmen cover on a regular basis. The newsmen, if they contact information officers, contact the following categories: (1) special assistants for public affairs, (2) directors of information, (3) directors of news services, (4) press officers, and (5) information specialists.

Utilizing the listing of information units, the task was to determine which officers in each unit the newsmen contact in seeking information—that individual officeholder designated in the 1955 study as the "responsible agency official" for press relations. Again in drawing the final sample, the cooperation of previous investigators proved helpful. A minimum of one respondent was chosen from each information unit. Success at obtaining personnel of co-ordinating units is demonstrated by the fact that eighteen officers worked in the executive departments and all departments are represented in the sample; eleven work in independent administrative agencies; and nine perform their information tasks within independent regulatory agencies.

Attention was directed in each information unit to choosing that individual who acted as spokesman to the press for the department or agency. In some instances, this was the director

---

[17] *Availability of Information*, H. R. Rep. No. 2947, 84th Cong., 2d Sess. (1956.)

of information or a special assistant for public affairs; in other cases, it was a director of the information unit's news services—where such units were elaborate enough to have such; and in others, it was a press officer of the organization. A deliberate effort was made, with success, to avoid information unit staff members whose duties were limited to clipping, mimeographing, and such duties. As the study progressed, it became apparent that, within certain units, the person most often contacted by newsmen had been omitted. This discrepancy was corrected as time permitted in order to obtain the views of those most experienced in each unit as spokesmen to the press. The breakdown of the sample along these lines is as follows. Twenty-three respondents were serving in the capacity of heads of information units—that is, in positions with responsibility for determining the information program and for serving as agency spokesman to the press. Of these two were special assistants for information, four were serving in the dual capacity of special assistant and director of information, thirteen were department or agency directors of information, and four were deputy directors. Six information officers were serving as heads of news service for a department or agency charged solely with the responsibility of agency press relations. Nine respondents held the designation of press officer and, hence, were not the responsible unit heads for information but did have primary responsibility for holding interviews and press briefings, writing releases, preparing speeches, and so on. This distribution comprised the total of the officer sample $(N = 38)$.

The personnel of information staffs is made up largely of career civil servants. In some cases, however, the director is a political appointee of the agency head, or a "special assistant" appointed by the agency head is inserted between the career director and the agency head. In two departments—State and Defense—the head information official is an assistant secretary, a presidential appointment. These political and career officers are distributed in the following manner: four were political appointees, two were Schedule "C" appointees, and the remainder —thirty-two—had risen to their positions through the procedures of career civil service.

Such descriptions are, of course, only preliminary profiles

based upon types of experience in information-dispensing and newsgathering. Obviously the accumulation of such data was not the primary purpose of the research project. Although it does illustrate *who* was in each sample, it does not illustrate the range of information that was sought from each respondent or the procedure used for gathering it. The data sought was attitudinal; the procedure used was the personal interview.

INTERVIEW PHASE

Interviewing was conducted in Washington between February 22 and May 19, 1961. Interviews were arranged by a standard procedure: writing a letter to the prospective respondent explaining the purpose and nature of the study being conducted, outlining the part to be played by the respondent, and requesting his cooperation. The follow-up was by telephone, arranging the time and place of the interview.

There was a marked difference in problems of arranging interviews between the two groups. The mobile nature of the newsman's job made the initial contact dependent on chance and the setting of a definite time for interviewing extremely difficult. However, most persons contacted made a sincere effort to arrange a meeting. In three cases, it was not possible to contact the person because he was out of town for the entire period; two refusals were encountered. Information officers presented far fewer difficulties in the arrangement of interviews.

The instrument used for gathering data was an interview composed of "open" or "unstructured" questions. Recording of responses was by portable tape recorder when both the respondent and the interview conditions permitted. Refusals to submit to the device were less than 5 per cent; difficult interview conditions—noise, failure of operation, interruptions, and so on—produced few problems. The use of the recorder made retrieving the maximum amount of data per interview a simple matter. Concern of the respondent over use of the recorder was obviously hard to measure, but it appeared to be negligible insofar as responses to the questions were involved. In those instances in which it was not possible to tape interviews, notes were taken, and the respondent's answers were paraphrased on tape immediately following the interview. Taped interviews were subsequently transcribed and used for coding and analysis. These are unquestionably more accurate than those recorded from notes after interview completion; yet, even in those instances in which the interview itself was not taped, the data retrieved was more substantial in quantity and quality than would have been the case if all interviews had been written in a form of amateur shorthand.

Seventy-three formal interviews were conducted; thirty-eight of these with information officers and thirty-five with newsmen. In addition, there were informal interviews conducted with individuals who had specialized investigative experience in the area under study. (These were not included in the sample as cases for analysis.) Interviews averaged seventy-five minutes in length—a mean of sixty-five minutes for newsmen and a mean of eighty minutes for information officers. On the average, seven interviews were conducted per week throughout the interview period. A better arrangement would have been the establishment of some pattern of interview scheduling, but this was not possible.

The purpose of interviewing was, of course, to sample the ideas and insights of persons who had experienced different vantage points through observation and participation in the processes of information-dispensing and newsgathering. This purpose governed the selection of survey techniques, and it governed the selection of the sample; accordingly, it governed the choice of the instrument to be used for data-gathering. A structured questionnaire of the "forced choice" variety was ruled out as an ineffective means of sampling respondent ideas; nor did a tightly constructed interview schedule seem appropriate for the task. It was extremely important to adopt an instrument and technique which would be sufficiently flexible to permit probing of the respondent on ideas brought up in the interview. It was determined, therefore, that an effort would be made to employ the techniques involved in a modified form of the nondirective interview.[18] Normally this technique is utilized to take advantage of the respondent's personal cognitive structure of the topics discussed and his own interpretation of the basic questions posed and to promote an atmosphere in which the respondent freely

[18] Selltiz, *Research Methods in Social Relations*, pp. 267–268.

develops and reveals his point of view. In order to prevent the interview from turning into a rambling, "stream of consciousness" situation, questions of an unstructured and general nature were framed in advance and used in all questioning. With basic questions in mind, a concerted effort was then made to encourage free expression of opinions by combining standard tactics of opportunistic probes, nods, and—in some cases—extreme patience. Reticence in talking was rare among both groups sampled; the greater problem was that of controlling the course of the discussion to permit completion of the interview in an alloted period of time. The ability to control was, for the most part, a function of the amount of experience gained in interviewing over the period, with a noticeable improvement as time elapsed. In the interview situation itself, the use of the recording device increased the effectiveness of the nondirective technique considerably.

At the conclusion of the field phase, interviews were transferred to Royal McBee Keysort cards on which all operations of coding, sorting, and counting were performed. The use of this particular tool allowed a combination quantitative and qualitative analysis with a minimum of duplicated effort.

A NOTE ON STATISTICAL TECHNIQUES

The hypotheses formulated from this research are based, partially, on inferences drawn from the analysis of patterns of attitude consensus and variation among information officers and newsmen. The research strategy spells out the theoretical framework of the study; its relevance to opinion and communication research; the focal point of the study itself, the data sought, and the manner of sample selection. Arising out of the procedure for sample selection is a tactical problem regarding the universe to which the hypotheses formulated in this study apply. The question is that of how encompassing the generalizations offered are —how much can they explain?

Discussion of patterns of consensus raises the problem of the measurement of that consensus. Such measurement is often statistical in nature and inferences drawn from a sample of a universe of activity or attitudes are deemed "significant" if supported by statistical tests. Such "tests of significance," however, could not be used for the selection of inferences applying to relationships, for example, between *all* information officers and newsmen, or between *all* information officers in federal executive agencies and Washington correspondents. The assumption underlying the use of statistical tests in a sample survey is that the sample itself has been chosen randomly from the total population under investigation.[19] The selection of random samples of information officers and newsmen was not deemed possible, practical, or desirable for an exploratory study; instead, a purposive sample was selected based on the criteria outlined. As a consequence, differences in patterns of consensus between or among the two samples of respondents apply validly only to the samples themselves, and inferences drawn cannot be extended to a larger population of information officers, newsmen, or one of interacting news sources and newsmen.

This should not be regarded as an indication of despair at the results of such research. Although inferences drawn from the survey data apply validly only to the samples involved, such inferences in the form of hypotheses can be extended to the broader universe of informational and newsgathering activity. Hence, the primary purpose of this exploratory study—the exploration of a field of inquiry and the formulation of tentative assertions as explanations—is accomplished in spite of the lack of "tests of significance" to prove that the patterns of consensus and variation of attitudes uncovered are typical of all official news sources and newsmen or are the "norms" of all explanatory and newsgathering behavior.

Furthermore, within the samples themselves, statistical tests of significance prove meaningless to demonstrate the validity of

[19] The position regarding the utility of statistical tests of significance taken in this study parallels that elaborated in the following: Hanan C. Selvin, *Statistical Significance and Sociological Theory* (Berkeley, California: University of California, 1960); *idem*, "A Critique of Tests of Significance in Survey Research," *American Sociological Review*, XXII (1957), 519–527; Leslie Kish, "Some Statistical Problems in Research Design," *American Sociological Review*, XXIV (1959), 328–338; James S. Coleman, "Statistical Problems," Appendix I–B in Seymour M. Lipset, Martin Trow, and James S. Coleman, *Union Democracy* (Glencoe, Illinois: The Free Press, 1956), pp. 427–432; Wahlke *et al., The Legislative System.*

the differences encountered. Any difference in consensus within either sample or between them is significant for the respondents involved by the very nature of the *existence* of such differences. The determination then made as to whether any obesrved difference can lead to an explanatory hypothesis is a function of its position in relation to other hypotheses being formulated from the study, its position in relation to other hypotheses from other research endeavors and speculation in the relevant literature, and the tests of logical inferences common to systematic inquiry. Hence, in this research report, statistical devices employed apply only to the description of the characteristics of the sample under discussion. The criteria of significance of the hypotheses formulated in this research must be social—how the assertions compare with other research—and logical—the consistency of such assertions with other findings.

APPENDIX II
PIO INTERVIEW
SCHEDULE

I. Background Data:

1. Sex: Male_____
   Female_____

2. Present Age:
   20–29_____
   30–39_____
   40–49_____
   50–59_____
   60–69_____
   Over 69_____

3. Organization by which respondent is employed:

   Executive department _____
   Executive agency _____
   Regulatory agency _____

4. Type of duty performed most often by respondent on job:

   Organize press conference _____
   Hold press conference _____
   Write news release _____

Edit or clear news release _____
Answer inquiries   _____
Write speeches   _____

5. Which of the following categories most adequately describes respondent's formal education?

College graduate   _____
Attended college but not graduate   _____
High school graduate   _____
Attended high school but not graduate _____
Did not attend high school   _____

6. Experience:

Number of years in journalism in any capacity: _____
Number of years as PIO in Washington: _____
What type of employment did respondent have just
    prior to entrance into service as a PIO: _____
Has respondent ever held any type of reporting job? _____
    (Specify) _____

II. Response Data:

1. Several departments and agencies have established information staffs which provide information considered by them to be worthy of public attention; what function does the PIO perform within the "governing process" in this country?

   (1.1) As a member/director of such a staff how would you describe your own job as to the purposes you have in providing information to the public and to the news media and the duties you perform?

   (1.2) Do you regard it your function to reveal matters of policy deliberations to newsmen if asked—policy disagreements, deliberations, etc.?

   (1.3) Generally, how extensively do you believe the public information officer should participate in the policy-making levels of the organization?

(1.4) Do you think that most information officers are permitted to exercise their own judgment about what and when to release information or are there restrictions on the information officer that you would cite?

(1.5) Do you regard it as a function of your office to promote, advocate, or otherwise influence policy?

2. Your office performs several types of services for members of the news media; would you list briefly what you consider to be the most important of these services?

(2.1) What function do you personally attribute to the news conference—for you and for the newsman?

(2.2) What function do you personally attribute to the background briefing—for you and for the newsman?

(2.3) What function do you personally attribute to the news release—for you and for the newsman?

(2.4) What function do you personally attribute to the interview—for you and for the newsman?

3. How would you describe the newsman's role as it relates to your own function of transmitting information to the public?

(3.1) Do you believe that your office normally causes any problems for the newsman in his job, even though unintentional, by exerting a degree of control over access to news?

(3.2) There are several types of reporters who are interested in obtaining news from departments and agencies—for example, the routine reporter assigned to a beat, the feature writer—would you draw any distinction between such types in the value to you in getting your organization's information before the public?

(3.3) Of such types as those mentioned, which do you believe most often contact your office of information?

(3.4) What kinds of information would you say are most often sought from you by newsmen?

4. Insofar as the provision of information of a newsworthy note to the media is one of the functions of your organization, your definition of news is of importance; how would you define news?

(4.1) Many newsmen insist that they have a duty to go beyond the reporting of news, that they must also interpret news for the reader; what consequences are implied for your work by the knowledge that a newsman is interested in more than the news which you might give him, that he also will be interested in interpretation?

(4.2) To the extent that it does prove difficult for some reporters to be objective in their work, what problems does this produce in putting the information which you deem that the public should have before them in as complete and objective manner as possible?

(4.3) In defining the relationship between news sources and newsmen, what is your general reaction about having personal friends among newsmen who write news about departments and agencies?

(4.4) In the performance of your job to make available to the public information, are there any particular types of people to whom you are providing information; e.g., to whom do you communicate this information—policy-makers, superiors, private groups, general public, attentive public, Congress, etc.?

5. If you were asked to list the characteristics of a "good" information officer in this organization—that is, one who could both inform the public adequately about activities and at the same time provide a source of hard news for the newsman—what attributes would you consider as the most important for him to possess?

(5.1) If you were asked to list the characteristics of a "good" newsman, what attributes would you consider as the most important for him to possess in order for him to adequately perform his function as you have defined it?

6. An information officer may have several requirements in mind about any story for which he gathers material and prepares to distribute to the public and the news media; that is, he may think that any story about his organization should possess certain characteristics—accuracy, comprehensiveness, prompt publication, interest to readers, usefulness to readers, publicizing of an event or person—what characteristics do you think a story written about your own organization by the news media should possess?

(6.1) Of the newsmen with whom your office normally deals, what would be your guess as to the characteristics they most highly regard in a story?

7. What do you believe to be the extent of the obligation for government officials to inform the public of their activities in carrying on the "public's business?"

(7.1) What are the sources of this obligation?

(7.2) What limitations do you feel can prevail which mitigate this obligation on the part of policy-makers—security, decision-making, etc.?

(7.3) In some quarters attention has been devoted to the problem of freedom of information—the right of the public and the news media to access to information about the activities of government. From your point of view, how serious do you believe this problem to be in keeping information flowing to the public?

8. What obligation is the policy-maker generally under to give consideration to public opinion in policy formulation?

(8.1) Upon what sources of public opinion can the policy-maker generally rely?

(8.2) Do you regard yourself as having any function of articulating public opinion for the policy-maker?

9. Some observers of government-press relations in the United States have argued that the relationship is one of inherent conflict, others that it is inherently harmonious. Do you think either is the case, and, in any event, how critical are government-press relations to the operation of democracy?

APPENDIX III
NEWSMAN
INTERVIEW
SCHEDULE

I. Background Data:
1. Sex: Male_____
   Female_____
2. Present Age:
   20–29 _____
   30–39 _____
   40–49 _____
   50–59 _____
   60–69 _____
   Over 69 _____

3. Organization by which respondent is employed:

Newspaper:

Dailies (small city, large city, those of national
   circulation)   _____
Special interest publications   _____
Wire or news service   _____

Periodical:

News weekly   _____
Periodical of opinion and comment   _____

Special interest periodical   _____
General interest periodical   _____

Radio-TV:

National network   _____
Affiliated with organization, but non-network
    (associates, film connected, newspaper
    connected, special programs, etc.)   _____
Independent station (local, etc.)   _____

4. Type of duty performed most often by respondent in job:

Write routine news	_____	Editor-in-chief	_____
Write specialized news	_____	Write editorials	_____
Write a column	_____	Bureau chief	_____
Edit news	_____	Wire editor	_____
Write magazine articles	_____	Other	_____
Newscaster	_____	(Specify)	
Managing editor	_____		

5. Does the respondent specialize in writing any specific type of news which is sent from Washington (e.g., news of agriculture, national defense, foreign affairs, the White House, etc.) or write dispatches covering several areas of news? If yes, specify _____

6. Which of the following categories most adequately describes respondent's formal education?

College graduate   _____
Attended college but not graduate   _____
High school graduate   _____
Attended high school but not graduate   _____
Did not attend high school   _____

7. Experience:

Number of years in journalism in any capacity: _____
Number of years as newsman in Washington: _____
What type of employment did respondent have just
    prior to entrance into service as a Washington
    newsman?   _____
Has respondent held any type of government office? _____

II. Response Data:

1. What do you believe to be the functions the newsman performs within what is referred to as the "governing process" in this country?

   (1.1) Within the framework that you have just mentioned, how would you describe your own job as to your purpose in reporting news and the type of stories with which you are concerned?

   (1.2) Normally, when you prepare your copy, what types of readers do you think will be reading it? To whom do you communicate in your reporting—policy-makers, superiors, private groups, general public, attentive public, Congress, fellow newsmen, etc.?

   (1.3) Would you say that most newsmen in your experience are allowed to report and interpret the news pretty much as they see it or are there restrictions operating on the newsmen that you would cite?

2. When you use the concept "news," what do you intend to indicate by it; what is your definition of the concept of "news"?

   (2.1) Some people distinguish between writing the news and interpreting it; do you see any such distinction, and if so, what do you think it to be?

   (2.2) Interpretation has at times introduced problems of objectivity; would you say that the newsman can generally perform his duties in an objective fashion?

   (2.3) Does the degree of freedom of the newsman generally aid him in obtaining information from news sources, especially in the executive agencies?

3. When you prepare a story about an event in the executive branch, to what types of sources do you normally turn first for ideas about what to write and about where to obtain information—newspaper files, PIO's, policy-makers' aides, fellow newsmen, line officials, friends, etc.?

(3.1) Is it generally true that you prefer to go as "high" as possible in obtaining access to the news of a department or agency? Explain.

(3.2) Do you believe that it is generally incumbent on the newsman to publish some new piece of information each day even though nothing new has actually happened either because he feels he must do it or his organization requires it?

(3.3) In defining the relationship between news sources and newsmen, what is your general reaction about newsmen having personal friends among officials of executive departments and agencies about which they write news?

4. Of the various means of gathering news—news conferences, background conferences, interviews, releases, leaks, etc.—which do you most often prefer as a means of getting reliable material for a story?

(4.1) What function do you personally attribute to the news conference—for you and for those interested in providing public information?

(4.2) What function do you personally attribute to the background conference—for you and for those interested in providing public information?

(4.3) What function do you personally attribute to the news release—for you and for those interested in providing public information?

(4.4) What function do you personally attribute to the interview—for you and for those interested in providing public information?

5. Several departments and agencies have established information staffs which provide information considered by them to be newsworthy; how would you describe the functions performed by such staffs in providing information to the news media?

(5.1) From your personal standpoint, do information staffs assist you in any way in your work and, if so, how and how often?

(5.2) Do you believe information staffs generally create problems for the newsmen by controlling access to news?

(5.3) Do you think that most information officers are permitted to exercise their own judgment about what and when to release information, or are there restrictions on the information officer that you would cite?

6. If you were asked to list the characteristics of a "good" newsman, what attributes would you consider as the most important for him to possess, particularly for the man writing political news?

(6.1) In general, what are the most important attributes a "good" news source should possess—one on whom you could rely from day-to-day as a source of hard news in your writing?

7. A newsman may have several requirements in mind when he gathers material and writes his story; that is, he may think that any story, to be a "good" news story, should have certain characteristics—accuracy, comprehensiveness, topicality, interest to readers, usefulness to readers, publicizing of an event or person. What do you believe to be the requirements of a "good" news story?

(7.1) Of the information officers that you have encountered, what would be your guess as to the characteristics they most highly regard in a story?

8. In some quarters, attention has been devoted to the problem of freedom of information—the right of the public and news media to access to information about the activities of government. Why do you think this problem receives attention periodically?

(8.1) In your job, do you find that the withholding of information is any problem?

(8.2) What do you believe to be the extent of the obligation for government officials to inform the public of of their activities in carrying on the "public's business"?

(8.3) In covering different political administrations in Washington, what differences, if any, have you encountered in the problems of obtaining news about what executive agencies and departments were doing?

(8.4) Do you believe that members of the news media tend to be less critical of some administrations than of others?

9. What obligation, in your opinion, is the policy-maker generally under to give consideration to public opinion in policy formulation?

(9.1) What are the sources of public opinion that policy-makers can generally rely upon?

(9.2) Do you regard yourself as having any function of either articulating public opinion or of shaping public opinion on an issue as well as informing the public?

(9.3) What obligation do the news media have to carry messages of publicity which are aimed not at public information as such, but are tactics in the passage or blocking of policy?

10. Some observers of government-press relations in the United States have argued that the relationship is one of inherent conflict, others that it is inherently harmonious. Do you think either is the case and, in any event, how critical are government-press relations to the operation of democracy?

BIBLIOGRAPHY

BOOKS

Albig, William, *Modern Public Opinion*. New York: McGraw-Hill Book Company, Inc., 1956.

Almond, Gabriel A., *The American People and Foreign Policy*. New York: Harcourt, Brace & Company, 1950.

———— "A Functional Approach to Comparative Politics," in *Politics of the Developing Areas*, ed. Gabriel A. Almond and James S. Coleman. Princeton, New Jersey: Princeton University Press, 1960.

Alsop, Joseph, and Stewart Alsop, *The Reporter's Trade*. New York: Reynal & Company, 1958.

Becker, Carl, *Freedom and Responsibility in the American Way of Life*. New York: Alfred A. Knopf, 1945.

Berelson, Bernard, *Content Analysis in Communication Research*. Glencoe, Illinois: The Free Press, 1952.

Bird, George L., and Frederic E. Merwin, eds., *The Press and Society*. New York: Prentice-Hall, Inc., 1951.

Boorstin, Daniel J., *The Image: Or What Happened to the American Dream*. New York: Atheneum, 1962.

Cater, Douglass, *The Fourth Branch of Government*. Boston: Houghton Mifflin Company, 1959.

Chafee, Zechariah, Jr., *Government and Mass Communications.* 2 vols. Chicago: The University of Chicago Press, 1947.

Coleman, James S., "Statistical Problems," Appendix I–B in *Union Democracy,* ed. Seymour M. Lipset, Martin Trow, and James S. Coleman. Glencoe, Illinois: The Free Press, 1956.

Commission on Freedom of the Press, *A Free and Responsible Press.* Chicago: The University of Chicago Press, 1947.

Cooley, Charles H., "The Significance of Communication," in *Reader in Public Opinion and Communication,* ed. Bernard Berelson and Morris Janowitz. Glencoe, Illinois: The Free Press, 1950.

Cross, Harold L., *The People's Right to Know.* New York: Columbia University Press, 1953.

DeFleur, Melvin L., and Otto N. Larsen, *The Flow of Information.* New York: Harper & Bros., 1958.

DeGrazia, Alfred, *Public and Republic.* New York: Alfred A. Knopf, 1951.

Dewey, John, *The Public and Its Problems.* New York: Henry Holt & Company, 1927.

Easton, David, *The Political System: An Inquiry into the State of Political Science.* New York: Alfred A. Knopf, 1953.

Fisher, Charles, *The Columnists.* New York: Howell, Soskin, 1944.

Goode, William J., and Paul K. Hatt, *Methods in Social Research.* New York: McGraw-Hill Book Company, Inc., 1952.

Gross, Neal, Ward S. Mason, and Alexander W. McEachern, *Explorations in Role Analysis: Studies of the School Superintendency Role.* New York: John Wiley & Sons, Inc., 1958.

Herring, Pendleton, *Public Administration and the Public Interest.* New York: McGraw-Hill Book Company, Inc., 1936.

—————— "Publicizing Administrative Activities," in *The Press and Society,* ed. George L. Bird and Frederic E. Merwin. New York: Prentice-Hall, Inc., 1951.

Hovland, Carl I., Irving L. Janis, and Harold H. Kelley, *Communication and Persuasion.* New Haven, Connecticut: Yale University Press, 1953.

Kelley, Stanley, Jr., *Professional Public Relations and Political Power.* Baltimore: The Johns Hopkins Press, 1956.

Key, V. O., Jr., *American State Politics: An Introduction.* New York: Alfred A. Knopf, 1956.

—————— *Public Opinion and American Democracy.* New York: Alfred A. Knopf, 1961.

Klapper, Joseph T., *The Effects of Mass Media*. New York: Columbia University Bureau of Applied Social Research, 1949.

Krock, Arthur, "The Gathering of the News," in *The Newspaper: Its Making and Its Meaning*. New York: Charles Scribner's Sons, 1945.

Kruglak, Theodore, *The Foreign Correspondents*. Geneva: Librairie E. Droz, 1955.

Lasswell, Harold D., "The Structure and Function of Communication in Society," in *The Communication of Ideas*, ed. Lyman Bryson. New York: Harper & Bros., 1948.

Lasswell, Harold D. and Abraham Kaplan, *Power and Society*. New Haven, Connecticut: Yale University Press, 1950.

Lasswell, Harold D. and Nathan Leites, *Language of Politics: Studies in Quantitative Semantics*. New York: G. W. Stewart, 1949.

Lee, Alfred M., *The Daily Newspaper in America*. New York: The Macmillan Company, 1937.

Lee, Ivy L., *Publicity*. New York: Industries Publishing Company, 1925.

Leiserson, Avery, *Parties and Politics*. New York: Alfred A. Knopf, 1958.

Lerner, Daniel, *The Passing of Traditional Society*. Glencoe, Illinois: The Free Press, 1958.

Lerner, Max, *America As a Civilization*. New York: Simon and Schuster, 1957.

Lippmann, Walter, *Essays in The Public Philosophy*. Boston: Little, Brown, & Company, 1955.

—— *Liberty and the News*. New York: Harcourt, Brace & Howe, 1920.

—— *Public Opinion*. New York: Harcourt, Brace & Company, 1922.

McCamy, James L., *Government Publicity*. Chicago: The University of Chicago Press, 1939.

MacIver, Robert M., *Academic Freedom in Our Time*. New York: Columbia University Press, 1955.

Matthews, Donald R., *U.S. Senators and Their World*. Chapel Hill, North Carolina: University of North Carolina Press, 1960.

Mayo, Henry B., *An Introduction to Democratic Theory*. New York: Oxford University Press, 1960.

Merton, Robert K., *Social Theory and Social Structure* (rev. ed.). Glencoe, Illinois: The Free Press, 1957.

Merwin, Frederic E., "Reporting of Government News," in *The Press and Society*, ed. George L. Bird and Frederic E. Merwin. New York: Prentice-Hall, Inc., 1951.

Mollenhoff, Clark R., *Washington Cover-Up*. Garden City, New York: Doubleday & Company, Inc., 1962.

Mott, Frank L., *American Journalism* (rev. ed.). New York: The Macmillan Company, 1950.

Nadel, S.F., *The Theory of Social Structure*. Glencoe, Illinois: The Free Press, 1957.

Newcomb, Theodore M., "Communicative Behavior," in *Approaches to the Study of Politics*, ed. Roland Young. Evanston, Illinois: Northwestern University Press, 1958.

———— *Social Psychology*. New York: Henry Holt & Co., Inc., 1950.

Park, Robert E., "Reflections on Communication and Culture," in *Reader in Public Opinion and Communication*, ed. Bernard Berelson and Morris Janowitz. Glencoe, Illinois: The Free Press, 1950.

Parsons, Talcott, *The Social System*. Glencoe, Illinois: The Free Press, 1951.

Pfiffner, John M., and R. Vance Presthus, *Public Administration* (3d ed.). New York: The Ronald Press Co., 1953.

Pimlott, J.A.R., *Public Relations and American Democracy*. Princeton, New Jersey: Princeton University Press, 1951.

Pollard, James E., *The Presidents and the Press*, New York: The Macmillan Co., 1947.

Reston, James B., "The Job of the Reporter," in *The Newspaper: Its Making and Its Meaning*. New York: Charles Scribner's Sons, 1945.

Rockefeller Brothers Fund Special Studies Project Report VI, *The Power of the Democratic Idea*. Garden City, New York: Doubleday & Company, Inc., 1960.

Rosenau, James N., *Public Opinion and Foreign Policy*. New York: Random House, 1961.

Rosten, Leo C., *The Washington Correspondents*. New York: Harcourt, Brace, & Company, 1937.

Rourke, Francis E., *Secrecy and Publicity: Dilemmas of Democracy*. Baltimore: The Johns Hopkins Press, 1961.

Schattschneider, E.E., *The Semisovereign People*. New York: Holt, Rinehart & Winston, 1960.

Schramm, Wilbur, "How Communication Works," in *The Process and Effects of Mass Communication*, ed. Wilbur Schramm. Urbana, Illinois: University of Illinois Press, 1954.

Selltiz, Claire, *et al.*, *Research Methods in Social Relations* (rev. ed.). New York: Henry Holt & Company, Inc., 1959.

Shannon, Claude, and Warren Weaver, *The Mathematical Theory of Communication*. Urbana, Illinois: University of Illinois Press, 1949.

Simon, Herbert A., Donald W. Smithburg, and Victor A. Thompson. *Public Administration*. New York: Alfred A. Knopf, 1950.

"Thomas Jefferson to the President of the United States, September 9, 1792," in *The Works of Thomas Jefferson*, ed. Paul Leicester Ford, Vol. VII. New York: G.P. Putnam's Sons, 1904–1905.

Tocqueville, Alexis de, *Democracy in America*, Vol. I. New York: Vintage Books, 1954.

Truman, David B., *The Governmental Process*. New York: Alfred A. Knopf, 1958.

Wahlke, John C., et al., *The Legislative System: Explorations in Legislative Behavior*. New York: John Wiley & Sons, Inc., 1962.

Wahlke, John C., and Heinz Eulau (eds.), *Legislative Behavior: A Reader in Theory and Research*. Glencoe, Illinois: The Free Press, 1959.

Wiggins, James Russell, *Freedom or Secrecy*. New York: Oxford University Press, 1956.

Williams, Francis, *Dangerous Estate: The Anatomy of Newspapers*. New York: The Macmillan Company, 1958.

———— *Press, Parliament, and People*. London: William Heinemann, Ltd., 1946.

PUBLIC DOCUMENTS

Commission on Organization of the Executive Branch of the Government ("Hoover Commission"), *Task Force Report on Departmental Management*. 1949.

Congressional Directory, 87th Cong., 1st Sess., 1961.

Congressional Directory, 86th Cong., 2d Sess., 1960.

Federal Power Commission, *Rules of Practice and Procedure (Including General Policy and Interpretations)*. 1958.

House Committee on Expenditures in the Executive Departments, Publicity and Propaganda Subcommittee, *Investigation of Part of Federal Officials of the War Department in Publicity and Propaganda As It Relates to UMT*, H. R. Rep. No. 1073, 80th Cong., 2d Sess. (1947).

House Committee on Government Operations, *Availability of Information from Federal Departments and Agencies*, H. R. Rep. No. 2084, 86th Cong., 2d Sess. (1960).

House Committee on Government Operations, *Availability of Information from Federal Departments and Agencies*, H. R. Rep. No. 2947, 84th Cong., 2d Sess. (1956).

House Committee on Government Operations, *Executive Branch Practices in Withholding Information from Congressional Committees*, H. R. Rep. No. 2207, 86th Cong., 2d Sess. (1960).

House Committee on Government Operations, Special Subcommittee on

Government Information, *Replies from Federal Agencies to Questionnaire Submitted by the Special Subcommittee on Government Information*, Committee Print, 84th Cong., 1st Sess. (1955).

PERIODICALS

Allport, Floyd H., "Toward a Science of Public Opinion," *The Public Opinion Quarterly*, I (January, 1937), 7–23.

Associated Press dispatch, *Lubbock Avalanche-Journal*, December 1, 1962, sec. 1, p. 1.

Associated Press dispatch, *Lubbock Avalanche-Journal*, November 1, 1962, sec. 3, p. 14.

Barth, Alan, "Freedom and the Press," *The Progressive*, XXVI (June, 1962), 29–32.

Berelson, Bernard, "Democratic Theory and Public Opinion," *The Public Opinion Quarterly*, XVI (Fall, 1952), 313–330.

——— "The State of Communication Research," *The Public Opinion Quarterly*, XXIII (Spring, 1959), 1–6.

Bingham, Worth, and Ward S. Just, "The President and the Press," *The Reporter*, XXVI (April 12, 1962), 18–23.

Brandt, Raymond P., "The Washington Correspondent," *Journalism Quarterly*, XIII (June, 1936), 173–176.

Breed, Warren, "Analyzing News: Some Questions for Research," *Journalism Quarterly*, XXXIII (Fall, 1956), 467–477.

——— "Social Control in the Newsroom: A Functional Analysis," *Social Forces*, XXXIII (May, 1955), 326–335.

Bush, Ted, "Defense News Policy Collision Course Set," *Navy Times*, April 29, 1961, p. 4.

Carter, Roy E., Jr., "Newspaper 'Gatekeepers' and the Sources of News," *The Public Opinion Quarterly*, XXII (Summer, 1958), 133–144.

——— "The Press and Public School Superintendents in California," *Journalism Quarterly*, XXXI (Spring, 1954), 175–185.

——— "Relations Between the Press and Local Government Officials in North Carolina," *Prod*, I (September, 1957), 23–27.

Childs, Marquis W., "The Interpretive Reporter's Role in a Troubled World," *Journalism Quarterly*, XXVII (Spring, 1950), 134–140.

Davison, W. Phillips, "The Public Opinion Process," *The Public Opinion Quarterly*, XXII (Summer, 1958), 91–106.

Donnahoe, Alan S., "Mass Communication Theory: A Macroscopic Approach," *Journalism Quarterly*, XXXIV (Fall, 1957), 443–451.

Fearing, Franklin, "Toward a Psychological Theory of Human Communication," *Journal of Personality*, XXII (September, 1953), 71–88.

Fellows, Erwin W., "Propaganda and Communication: A Study in Definitions," *Journalism Quarterly*, XXXIV (Fall, 1957), 431–442.

Fitzpatrick, Dick, "Measuring Government Publicity: Volume of Press Releases," *Journalism Quarterly*, XXVI (March, 1949), 45–50.

———— "Public Information Activities of Government Agencies," *The Public Opinion Quarterly*, XI (Winter, 1947–48), 530–539.

Garceau, Oliver, "Research in the Political Process," *The American Political Science Review*, XXXXV (March, 1951). 69–85.

Gieber, Walter, "Across the Desk: A Study of 16 Telegraph Editors," *Journalism Quarterly*, XXXIII (Fall, 1956), 423–432.

———— "Two Communicators of the News: A Study of the Roles of Sources and Reporters," *Social Forces*, XXXIX (October, 1960), 76–83.

Gieber, Walter, and Walter Johnson, "The City Hall 'Beat': a Study of Reporter and Source Roles," *Journalism Quarterly*, XXXVIII (Summer, 1961), 289–297.

Harding, T. Swann, "Genesis of One 'Government Propaganda Mill,' " *The Public Opinion Quarterly*, XI (Summer, 1947), 227–235.

———— "Informational Techniques of the Department of Agriculture," *ibid.*, I (January, 1937), 83–96.

Hyman, Herbert H., and Paul B. Sheatsley, "Some Reasons Why Information Campaigns Fail," *The Public Opinion Quarterly*, XI (Fall, 1947), 412–423.

Kish, Leslie, "Some Statistical Problems in Research Design," *American Sociological Review*, XXIV (June, 1959), 328–338.

Knebel, Fletcher, "Public Relations at the White House," *Public Relations Journal*, XII (September, 1956), 3–5, 19.

Koop, Theodore F., "Equality of Access for Radio in Covering Washington News," *Journalism Quarterly*, XXXIV (Summer, 1957), 338–340, 386.

Krock, Arthur, "National Security and the 'Flow' of Information," *The New York Times*, November 22, 1962, p. 28.

———— "Press vs. Government—A Warning," *The Public Opinion Quarterly*, I (April, 1937), 45–49.

Lambert, Donald A., "Foreign Correspondents Covering the U. S.," *Journalism Quarterly*, XXXIII (Summer, 1956), 349–356.

Lasswell, Harold D., "Research on the Distribution of Symbol Specialists," *Journalism Quarterly*, XII (June, 1935), 146–156.

——— "The Theory of Political Propaganda," *The American Political Science Review*, XXI (August, 1927), 627–631.

Leiserson, Avery, "Notes on the Theory of Political Opinion Formation," *The American Political Science Review*, XLVII (March, 1953), 171–177.

Lerner, Daniel, "Communication Systems and Social Systems. A Statistical Exploration in History and Policy," *Behavioral Science*, II (October, 1957), 266–275.

McCamy, James L., "Discussion: Measuring Federal Publicity," *The Public Opinion Quarterly*, III (July, 1939), 473–475.

MacLean, Malcolm S., Jr., and Bruce H. Westley, "Research on 'Fortuitous' Communication: A Review," *Audio-Visual Communications Review*, III (Spring, 1955), 119–137.

Mader, Joseph H., "Government Press Bureaus and Reporting of Public Affairs," *Journalism Quarterly*, XIX (June, 1942), 172–178.

Mahaffey, J. Q., "PR and the Press," *Public Relations Journal*, VI (June, 1953), 11–12, 15.

Maxwell, J. William, "U.S. Correspondents Abroad: A Study of Backgrounds," *Journalism Quarterly*, XXXIII (Summer, 1956), 346–348.

Merwin, Frederic E., "The Reporting of Public Affairs," *The Annals of the American Academy of Political and Social Science*, CCXIX (January, 1942), 120–126.

Miller, William Lee, "Can Government Be 'Merchandised'?" *The Reporter*, IX (October 27, 1953), 11–16.

Newcomb, Theodore M., "An Approach to the Study of Communicative Acts," *The Psychological Review*, LX (November, 1953), 393–404.

The New York Times, April 28, 1961, p. 14.

The New York Times, November 21, 1962, p. 10.

The New York Times, October 31, 1962, p. 34.

Patch, Buel W., "Access to Official Papers and Information," *Editorial Research Reports*, I (June 24, 1953), 417–433.

——— "Government and the Press," *ibid.*, I (May 6, 1953), 319–336.

Player, Cyril Arthur, "Review: The Washington Correspondents," *Journalism Quarterly*, XV (March, 1938), 58–60.

Pool, Ithiel de Sola, and Irwin Schulman, "Newsmen's Fantasies, Audiences, and Newswriting," *The Public Opinion Quarterly*, XXIII (Summer, 1959), 145–158.

Reston, James B., "Reporting on Foreign Affairs," *Nieman Reports*, III (July, 1949), 3–5.

"The Right to Know," *Army Times*, April 29, 1961, p. 12.

Rivers, William L., "The correspondents after 25 years," *Columbia Journalism Review*, I (Spring, 1962), 4–10.

Schramm, Wilbur, "Information Theory and Mass Communication," *Journalism Quarterly*, XXXII (Spring, 1955), 131–146.

———— "Twenty Years of Journalism Research," *The Public Opinion Quarterly*, XXI (Spring, 1957), 91–107.

Selvin, Hanan C., "A Critique of Tests of Significance in Survey Research," *American Sociological Review*, XXII (October, 1957), 519–527.

Sherman, Maurice S., "The Editor and the Columnist," *The Public Opinion Quarterly*, IX (Fall, 1945), 279–282.

Smith, Mapheus, "The Communicative Act," *The Journal of Social Psychology*, XXXI (May, 1950), 271–281.

———— "Communicative Behavior," *The Psychological Review*, LIII (September, 1946), 294–301.

Swanson, G. E., "Agitation Through the Press: A Study of the Personalities of Publicists," *The Public Opinion Quarterly*, XX (Summer, 1956), 441–456.

Wagner, Allen, "Government public relations," *Public Relations Journal*, IX (January, 1953), 19–20, 33.

Wahlke, John C., *et al.*, "American State Legislators' Role Orientations Toward Pressure Groups," *The Journal of Politics*, XXII (May, 1960), 203–227.

Westley, Bruce H., and Malcolm S. MacLean, Jr., "A Conceptual Model for Communications Research," *Audio-Visual Communications Review*, III (Winter, 1955), 3–12.

———— "A Conceptual Model for Communications Research," *Journalism Quarterly*, XXXIV (Winter, 1957), 31–38.

White, David Manning, "The 'Gate Keeper': A Case Study in the Selection of News," *Journalism Quarterly*, XXVII (Fall, 1950), 383–390.

Wiggins, James Russell, "The News Is the First Concern of the Press," *Journalism Quarterly*, XXIII (March, 1946), 20–29.

Wilson, Richard, "Reporting the Washington News," *The Annals of the American Academy of Political and Social Science*, CCXIX (January, 1942), 127–131.

UNPUBLISHED MATERIAL

Fitzpatrick, Richard S., "A Survey of Opinions of Members of the Congressional Press, Periodical, and Radio Galleries on Information Services of Federal Administrative Agencies in Washington, D.C." Unpublished Master's thesis, American University, 1951.

Rivers, William L., "The Washington Correspondent: Significance for Government." Unpublished Ph.D. dissertation, American University, 1960.

Selvin, Hanan C., "Statistical Significance and Sociological Theory." Berkeley, California: University of California, July, 1960.

Underwood, George V., Jr., "The Washington Military Correspondents." Unpublished Master's thesis, University of Wisconsin, 1960.

Willard, Joseph, "Public Relations Policies and Practices of Federal Departments and Agencies." Unpublished Ph.D. dissertation, University of Indiana, 1960.

INDEX